SMOKIN' RIGS

 AND  **REAL GOOD RECIPES**

 BY **DAN HUNTLEY AND LISA GRACE LEDNICER**

• • { **PHOTOGRAPHS BY LAYNE BAILEY** } • •

★ ★ ★ ★ ★ ★ ★ ★ ★ ★

D1377617

CHRONICLE BOOKS

SAN FRANCISCO

Page 9 constitutes a continuation of the
copyright page.

Library of Congress Cataloging-in-Publication
Data available.

ISBN-10: 0-8118-5318-7
ISBN-13: 978-0-8118-5318-7

Manufactured in China.

Designed by Fifth Letter

Distributed in Canada by Raincoast Books
9050 Shaughnessy Street
Vancouver, British Columbia V6P 6E5

10 9 8 7 6 5 4 3 2 1

Chronicle Books LLC
680 Second Street
San Francisco, California 94107

www.chroniclebooks.com

Dedication

To Susan, for allowing me to follow my food muse across several continents, and Lauren and Daniel, for eating my Boston butts before I learned to smoke 'em. —*Dan*

To Drew, for believing in me and believing it was possible. —*Lisa*

Table of Contents

Acknowledgments

Many people helped us during the writing of this book. It would be impossible to single everyone out, but here are a few who deserve special thanks:

First and foremost, our editor, Bill LeBlond, and our agent, Susan Ginsburg, for taking a chance on us;

Charles Eisendrath and the Knight-Wallace Fellowship program, for bringing us together and encouraging us to give voice to our wildest dreams;

Nicole and Layne Bailey, whose advice, enthusiasm, and hard work made this project better than it would have been otherwise;

And our families—especially our spouses—who endured broken commitments and endless debates about the finer points of brisket, chicken, and pork, and managed to remain cheerful and upbeat even when we weren't.

From Lisa...

Many thanks to Anne and David Lednicer, for dropping a great profile idea in my lap; Jim Monihan, Rick and Kate Naug, and Jim Minion, for introducing me to barbecue in the Pacific Northwest; Ed Roith and Carolyn Wells, for putting up with my endless questions about contest judging; Rabbi Larry Halpern, whose enthusiastic blessing for this project meant the world to me; Jenn Oberheuser and Amanda DeSilver, astonishingly gifted food enthusiasts; Rick Browne, for cheering me on; Luciana Lopez, for being a much-needed sounding board; and all the cooks and rig-builders in this book who made the writing of it such a grand adventure.

From Dan...

Thanks to the three guys who introduced me to barbecue — and helped me to see through the smoke: my dad, Baxter Huntley; my father-in-law, Carroll Robinson; and my former gym teacher, Ken Weaver, who loaned me his cooker to smoke my first whole hog in 1990; Kathi Purvis, who introduced me to Carolyn Wells, Jim Tabb and the Kansas City Barbecue Society, and John T. Edge and the Southern Foodways Alliance; Mike Gordon, for taking me to Birmingham to meet food maven George Sarris; also *Observer*ites Tommy Tomlinson, Jim Walser, Jack Betts, John McBride, Lolo Pendergrast, Diane Suchetka, and Ashley Barron (and her sisters); food book authors Marialisa Calta and Linda Eckhart, who both said "write this book"; Parisienne Brigitte Cox, who changed my life when she placed a dime-size slab of foie gras in my mouth; my many sous chefs at barbecues and oyster roasts at our weekend house on the Catawba River: Barb and Bob Leverone (who loaned me their camera and Mac knowledge), Mabel Huntley, Davis Allred, Carl Wharton, Walter Mull, Laddie Sartin, Steve Floyd, Ralph Coomer, Carrie Sturrock, Kris Klepinger, Seth Sutel, Andy Finkel, and Henry Gilbert; and my Napa Valley buddies who found me a genuine pig cooker in wine country when we needed one most: Andrea Immer and Sarah Jane Tribble.

Additional Photo Credits:

NO MAN IS AN ISLAND, John Donne said, and by our philosophy, no one truly cooks—or eats—alone. In all its forms and in any context, cooking is a connecting experience, and for many it is about passion: for life, for art, and for the people you care about. When you take the time to prepare a meal for those who give meaning to your life, they taste more than the food—they also taste the love and energy you've baked into your casserole or massaged into the brisket sitting in your oil-drum smoker.

For a certain class of hands-on backyard chefs with a quirkier side, that love and energy extends beyond the table to encompass the tools for preparing food—and not just using them, but creating them. Populating one extreme of the food-enthusiast spectrum, these are the contraption makers—the folks who'd rather spend hours shaping iron and metal into a humdinger of a rig than buy a sterile, slick-looking machine at an anonymous superstore.

Anybody can buy a gas grill at Sears and char some burgers in the backyard. But imagine the looks on your friends' faces when they see you grilling twenty whole chickens bathed in garlic on a rig that looks like a cast-iron satellite dish you found on the side of the road. Contraption cooking is more than the application of meat to fire. It is cooking on a rig so personal or outrageous that it allows a backyard chef to become a rock star. Maybe you have had the pleasure of eating such fabled fare; now we hope to give you a roadmap for finding your own culinary spotlight. As celebrated in the juicy pages of this book, contraption cooking generates great adventures, and great stories.

Clay Bush of Las Cruces, New Mexico, checks his smoked chicken on his custom smoker.

We've collected our favorite tales here, to entertain, inspire, and whet the appetite: how an ancient General Electric refrigerator–cum–smoker united two generations of a Midwestern clan spread halfway across the country; how a single father's beehive-shaped, wood-fired oven has become the center of his home; how a dead man's inventiveness lives on in the form of a massive iron rig named Lester.

The Roots

The obsession with building a better mousetrap seems to be coded into Americans' DNA, and the development of new and improved cooking machines has long been a particularly hot pursuit. From Ben Franklin's iron furnace stove to George Stephen's first Weber grill, we have a long, colorful history as a nation of culinary rig inventors. In a recent example of this combination of instinct and ingenuity, the bust of the Texas oil economy in the early 1980s led to a new career for some down-on-their-luck oilmen, who began making barbecue pits with the oil drums, pipes, and welding equipment left idle and abandoned in the refinery fields.

America is no longer known for its manufacturing prowess the way it once was, as more and more production is outsourced offshore. Health department regulations have largely shut down some of the older customs, such as selling food cooked underground. In an era of diminished outlets for invention and sanitized codes for cuisine, the rig builders in this book are keeping both industrial and folk traditions alive, a beautiful thing even if the results sometimes look bizarre. You may mock that rusted-out, banged-up barrel smoker, but all doubts go out the window when you taste a glistening piece of chicken, or your mouth waters as you watch morsels of pork butt fall off the bone. And therein lies one of the truisms of contraption cooking: a lot of the time, the crummier the rig is, the better the food tastes.

Contraption cookers can be as simple as a piece of string used to truss and roast a chicken in front of an open fire (see page 29), or as elaborate as a two-story mobile smoker with a winding staircase (see page 98). Building them often involves what is best described as "junkyard serendipity": stumbling across a heap of broken-down machine parts and having the vision to recognize them as something potentially wonderful. There must be a willingness to improvise—say, reclaiming a chrome bicycle wheel instead of getting a sheet metal guy to design the perfect cylindrical grate to hold your charcoal off the base of your cooker. Like great French chefs who never run to the grocery store if they're missing an ingredient or two, rig builders make do with what they have.

The Regions

Extreme barbecue can't be found in the Yellow Pages or at the mall; the world in which it exists lies well beyond the interstates. The people who build these rigs and cook this food are found at backyard cook-offs and barbecue contests, catering their buddies' weddings, or throwing graduation parties for their nieces and nephews. They practice their art with meat ranging from simple spareribs to a whole hog dressed up in Mardi Gras beads, sunglasses, and a straw hat.

One of the first things to learn about homemade barbecue cookers is that there is definitely no standard rig. Beyond the common denominators of metal, brick, or stone (or cardboard! see page 80) and fire, the rigs are as varied as the foods cooked in them—from an Italian pork roast braised in a wood-fire bread oven to oysters roasted in galvanized trash cans.

Likewise, there are no geographical rules. You can find practically any kind of contraption cooker in any part of the country—we saw a Southern-style pork rib smoker in the heart of Vermont and an underground hot rock *barbacoa* goat roaster in North Carolina.

That said, there are, naturally, certain cooking rigs you see more of in certain regions. The South abounds with whole-hog smokers, partly because the warm climate allows a longer outdoor cooking season and fosters ambitious rigs to match, and partly as a legacy of the nineteenth century, when pork, firewood, and time were all abundant. And we'd be surprised (well, actually, nothing surprises us anymore) to find Native Americans in North Dakota smoking fresh salmon over an alder vertical roaster in the style and spirit of their Pacific Northwest ancestors.

Americans move around a lot, and there's both a supply of and demand for tastes that have spread across the country's expanse. You've probably noticed that transplanting an American regional culinary style to another part of the country is a common technique in the restaurant business—for example, you might find a busy barbecue restaurant in Portland, Oregon, run by an

African American who brought his smoker with him from Mississippi. Whether they're labors of love centered around home or prized possessions displayed at contests, many extreme cooking contraptions are built to travel as needed. Since a lot of these rigs aren't hammered down, we had to travel more than thirty thousand miles—ranging from Seattle, Washington, to Shelby, North Carolina—to chronicle this tribe of traveling chowhounds.

If You Have a Sense of Adventure . . .

This book is more than just recipes; it's the stories of the people behind the smoke. It's for anyone who's ever had a Pavlovian response to the smell of burning hickory and the sound of meat sizzling over a hardwood fire. It's for folks who've made do with a rinky-dink charcoal grill on wobbly legs and wanted more. For anyone who likes their cuisine *con brio*, these contraptions let you go where most weekend chefs fear to tread.

Use this book as you would the blueprints for a basic starter house, but feel free to improvise. Install skylights. Or a fireman's pole. Or the kind of stuff you'd find in the Batmobile. Steal ideas verbatim from these pages, or use them for inspiration and go prowl scrap heaps, flea markets, and garage sales for equipment of your own devising. If you want more, get your camera and head for the meat-cooking meccas along the backroads of America, or hit some of the hundreds of barbecue competitions around the country. Bring the pictures back to your welder buddies with two cases of beer and the promise to cook brisket, pork butts, chicken, and anything else every Fourth of July if they'll build at your command. Your motto should be: "I need more funk in my life, and I'm starting with cooking contraptions."

This is your chance to drop your identity as a parent, spouse, sibling, and/or wage slave and be the P. T. Barnum of your neighborhood. It's a proven fact that anything cooked outdoors tastes better. And, take it from us, practically any food you cook on a homemade contraption will taste doubly better. Come out of the kitchen, drop the twenty-minute-meal mindset, and build a cooker so amazing that your friends will stay for hours after the sun goes down, kicking the tires on it and muttering, "Man, how'd you do it? Couldja build me one?" Just keep the rig, the smoke, and your beer-swilling buddies outside, and you'll be a hero in your household. ★

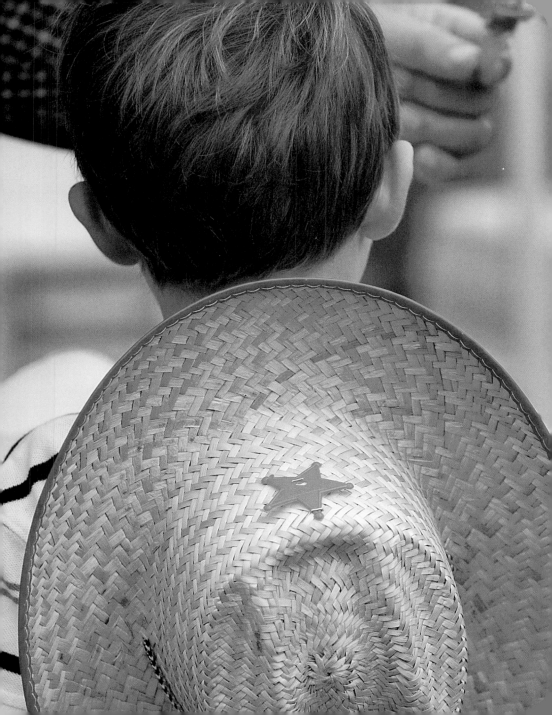

CHAPTER 1

HOMEMADE RIGS & RECIPES of the EAST

SOUTH

**IFFERENT REGIONS** of the United States claim different bragging rights for the origins of barbecue. One of our favorites comes from a guy who swears it originated in the mid-twentieth century at a Texas bar and pool hall named the Bar B Cue, and there are references from the mid-1700s to George Washington attending "barbeques" in Virginia.

Perhaps more objectively, historian Dr. Walter Edgar (as well as the *Oxford English Dictionary*) believes the term "barbecue" is derived from *babracot*, a Carib Indian word referring to a grid of green wood fashioned to hold meat over a fire. Pigs were first brought to North America by Spanish explorers in the mid-1500s, according to Edgar, who has researched and written extensively about barbecue. (As for eating it, he's partial to the mustard-based sauce served over pulled pork in the South Carolina midlands.) Caribbean pirates of the late seventeenth and early eighteenth centuries made forays along the southeastern coast, bringing with them the *babracot* style of cooking whole animals on a raised grid over coals, and, as Edgar writes, the tradition "drifted inland along the southeastern coast like wafts of hickory smoke."

As we explored the barbecue of the eastern United States, we found three compelling stories representing the more or less stereotypical image of a Southern white male cooking whole hogs in a smoker/grill made from an oil drum. But moving up the coast, the pot thickened to a stew rich with various historical and cultural influences.

In Charleston, South Carolina, Jimmy Hagood gave us a tour through his two-story smoker/grill with a spiral staircase. Steve Watts in Gastonia, North Carolina, cooks hobo-style on a campfire, using heated flat stones and a large tin can. T. R. McGrath of Newport, Rhode Island, is a third-generation master of the clambake, heaping fresh rockweed on a bed of hot stones to steam his seafood feast. In Niagara Falls, Canada, Reg Pelletier built a massive smoker whose air flow he can control with the simple twist of a lever. And we found Betsy Barstow's family in Adamant, Vermont, cooking a traditional New England "bean hole" bean supper—roasting huge pots of beans buried beneath a fire pit of simmering embers—in a style that dates back to Colonial America and earlier.

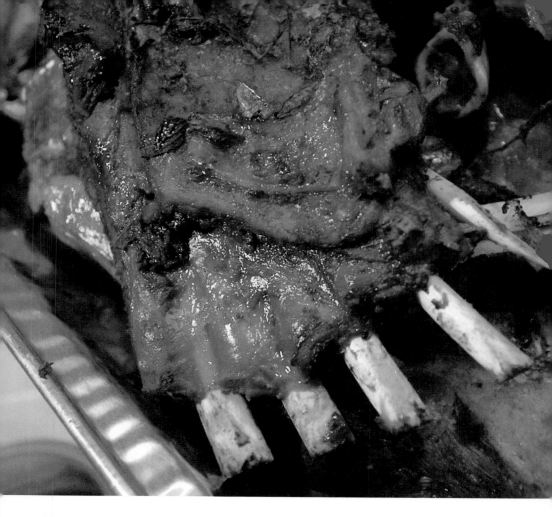

Goat ribs just beginning to draw back from the end of the bone, cooked to perfection by Maximino Rios in an underground Mexican-style *barbacoa*.

Read on for the stories and recipes of nineteen cooking rigs from east of the Appalachians, showcasing a diversity in fire-cooking techniques as extreme as the region's shifts in landscape. ★

Mike Shugart

How can you not love a cooking rig named for a dead man named Lester?

Would it help if it cooked Boston butts to beat the band?

We heard about Lester more than two years before we actually laid eyes on the sucker. A group of deer hunters in Chester County, South Carolina, first told us about this legendary cooker. Their tales got taller as we dug deeper—about an inventor/engineer who had built the cooking rig to beat all rigs, with a "Ferris wheel" contraption that rotated the meat; about how it had all these switches and valves and regulators; about how the instructions were written down in soapstone on the iron sides of the rig, but then a storm blew the roof off the hunt camp shed and washed the instructions away and the inventor died before he could get back to his meat machine . . . .

After more than two dozen dead-end phone calls, we finally thought we'd hit pay dirt. There was dirt, all right, when we made a boozy late-night trip down an endless unpaved road, through woods and pasture, to the Sweet Hope Hunt Club, only to hear, "Oh my God, someone has stolen Lester! Call the damn po-leece!" On another hot tip, we found our way to a dusty machine shop, but this time we got, "You're looking for Lester? You mean Lester Shugart? The fellah that made that cooking machine? Well, I'm sorry, son, but you're about nine years too late. Lester has done passed on."

Unable to confirm that it was anything more than a meat myth, we finally marked the Holy Grail of cookers off our list as unfindable. The very same week, Lester's nephew, Mike Shugart, called. "I hear you're looking for my cooking rig," he said.

Lester built his namesake at his machine shop in the early 1980s, customizing it for inside cooking by routing the smoke out through the shop's ventilation system. Eventually, Lester loaned it to some buddies and the cooker ended up at his hunt camp.

After Lester died in 1996, his widow, Genevieve Shugart, rounded up his nephews and cousins to go through his machine shop and see if there was anything they wanted before she sold it all. Mike ended up with the cooker, since he had helped build it and, later, helped Lester cook on it. With the help of a half-dozen friends, he moved the cooker from the hunt camp to his river house on Lake Monticello.

Mike Shugart turns meat in the Lester Rig.

Mike Shugart's dad died when he was eight. Lester took him under his wing at his machine shop, took him to job sites and down to his house on Lake Wateree for fish fries, hash suppers, and catfish stews. "Lester was a lot of things, a natural-born engineer who had a couple of patents and could build about any damn thing on earth, including a bridge," he says. "He had a limp because of a bad car wreck. He always had this smile and talked real sweet-like; he was a cool guy."

And so, when it came time, Mike got to help Lester build the famous cooker. One time Lester was trying to fine-tune an air-flow problem and needed someone small enough to get inside the cooking chamber with a cutting torch to open up some air holes. Mike climbed inside and did the deed.

"He told me he thought I'd be all right in there," he says with a laugh. "They used a sheet of cardboard to keep the fumes from getting to me." He survived to cook on the finished machine side by side with Lester.

On a sunny fall day, on a pristine lake in the South Carolina midlands, we beheld "the Lester" perched on a rise beside a stand of pines. "You can't imagine how solid and heavy this rig is," Mike said. "It took twelve men, a flat-bed trailer, and a small crane to move it out here." Shugart had recently spruced it up with a bucket of naval jelly and six coats of heat-resistant enamel; he was clearly attached to the Rube Goldberg–esque contraption. It looked like it was cut out of the engine room of a locomotive. It even had a small electric motor geared down to turn six revolutions per minute, to rotate trays of meat on a Ferris wheel–like device.

As we watched the rig gently spew forth thin wafts of hickory and oak smoke, we could hear the faint whine of the electric motor turning the internal meat wheel. Shugart proudly popped open the household oven door strapped to the iron behemoth and displayed a cornucopia of chicken, pork ribs, and butts. He identified the various rubs and marinades (a Cajun-rubbed butt had two toothpicks, a plain barbecue butt a single one). It's hard to imagine another cooker capable of accommodating the variety of cooking methods and types of meat we saw the Lester handle that afternoon. Lester himself used to fill the smoker up with eight to ten venison roasts at a time.

"You ain't never gonna find another cooker quite like this one," Mike said as he placed another stick of wood in the firebox. "It's sort of like Lester: one of a kind."

Lester made muscadine wine, invented a hush-puppy cooker, brewed beer, raised quail, made his own pecan nutcracker, and invented a bridge construction device called the Shugart Screed & Sluff Catcher. But mostly, he was a friend to many people. It's no wonder that the eight-year-old nephew he took under his wing more than forty years ago is still singing his praises.

And keeping the home fires burning in a rig named Lester.

Pork Butts and Chicken à la Lester

Serves
35

MIKE SHUGART LIVES in paradise, high above a pollution-free lake in the South Carolina midlands, with his own private beach and barbecue shack. On the weekends, he doesn't just cook for his wife and himself, he cooks for the whole neighborhood. Of course, you can scale down this recipe for your grilling gear and for a "normal" party crowd—but tell your guests to come hungry. For his rig, Mike uses 2 armloads of wood (about 12 pieces of split wood); he prefers hickory.

10 whole roasting chickens, 2 to 4 pounds each

10 bone-in Boston butts, 5 to 9 pounds each

2 cups all-purpose barbecue dry rub, purchased or homemade (page 54)

1 quart barbecue sauce of your choice (optional)

Build a fire in a smoker/grill for indirect heat. Maintain a temperature of about 300°F.

Season the meat with the barbecue rub. Load the meat in the smoker, on the side opposite the coals, placing the butts with the fat cap facing up to help keep the meat moist.

Get a water hose with a high-pressure nozzle—or load a shotgun—and be prepared to defend yourself from anyone downwind.

Turn the chickens once, after about 1 hour; do not turn the pork. The chickens will take about 1½ hours. Butts will take about 2 hours. The chicken is done when an instant-read thermometer inserted in the thickest part of a thigh registers 175° to 180°F, or when the juices run clear when a leg is cut at the joint. The pork is done when an instant-read thermometer inserted in the thickest part away from the bone registers 160° to 165°F.

When the meat is done, take it off the heat and let it rest for about 10 minutes. Cut, chop, pull, and/or mince. Apply the sauce or pass it in bowls alongside for dipping, if desired.

Grill-Smoked Salmon

Serves

★ 12–15 ★

SMOKING WHOLE FISH on the grill is deliciously rewarding, and if you haven't tried it before, you'll be surprised at how easy it is—and quick, compared to pork or chicken. There's no brining or curing here—essentially, the fish is "baked" in a tantalizing chamber of wood smoke. Hickory will flavor the fish strongly; you may prefer a milder wood such as oak (see the Wood Glossary, page 282). Feel free to substitute bass, flounder, catfish, bream, crappie, or whatever good-tasting fish you have available.

3 whole gutted salmon, each about 2 ½ pounds and 4 inches thick, head on or off

Build a fire in a smoker/grill for indirect heat. Maintain a temperature of about 300°F.

Put each fish in an aluminum foil roasting pan, bending the short ends if necessary to lay the fish flat. Place the fish "boats" in the cooker on the side opposite the coals.

Smoke the fish for about 35 minutes. (Smaller fish will take 8 to 10 minutes per inch of thickness.) The salmon is done when it is almost opaque throughout but still pink in the center. (If substituting white fish, cook until opaque throughout.)

Remove the salmon from the smoker. Transfer to a carving board and fillet or cut into steaks, or place on large platters and carve at the table.

Squash Casserole

Serves 6

THIS IS A SOUTHERN TWIST on the comfort-food classic macaroni and cheese, but using squash and crackers in place of the macaroni. It's from the kitchen of the Shugarts' friend Margaret Robinson. It's a good counterbalancing dish for a smoky meat barbecue.

6 tablespoons butter or margarine

2 cups peeled, seeded, and diced yellow squash

½ cup chopped onion

1 cup coarsely crushed Cheez-Its or other little cheese crackers

1 cup evaporated milk

2 eggs, beaten

Salt and freshly ground pepper

1 cup shredded cheddar cheese

Preheat the oven to 325°F.

In a flameproof casserole dish or Dutch oven over medium heat, melt the butter.

Add the squash and onion and sauté until tender, 12 to 15 minutes. Mash the squash smooth with a potato masher.

Add the crackers, evaporated milk, eggs, and salt and pepper to taste, and stir to mix well. Sprinkle the cheese over the top.

Bake until lightly browned and bubbly, about 40 minutes. Serve immediately.

Mike's Real Simple Barbecue Sauce

Makes About 1¾ Cups / Enough For 3 lbs. of Meat

MIKE'S SAUCE IS SIMPLE and sublime in its own right, but also a Holy Mother sauce of 'cue. Once you get the basics down, you can dose it into a sweeter, hotter, or more vinegary sauce—however you like it. And that is both a wonder and a blessing. Start with the basic red and then check out the variations, or put your own unique brand on it.

¾ cup ketchup

½ cup firmly packed brown sugar or molasses

2 teaspoons Worcestershire sauce

¼ cup apple cider vinegar or your favorite cola (or better yet, ⅛ cup each apple cider vinegar and cola)

1 teaspoon dry mustard

Salt and freshly ground pepper

In a bowl, stir together the ketchup, brown sugar, Worcestershire sauce, vinegar, and mustard and mix well. Season with salt and pepper to taste.

Variations

FOR HOT: Add 1½ tablespoons chili powder and dashes of hot-pepper sauce to taste (or until your hair catches fire).

FOR ZESTY: Add ¼ cup Italian dressing.

FOR HEARTY: Add 2 cups finely chopped onions or green bell peppers, or a combination (raw or sautéed).

FOR RICH: Add ¼ cup olive oil.

Shug's Potato Salad

YOU CAN'T REALLY APPRECIATE the down-home goodness of this version of classic spud salad until you play it off the richness of smoky pork or chicken grilled to the color of a mahogany burl. It's just the antidote to cut the heat of some red-hot 'cue. You can peel the potatoes if you prefer, but Shug wouldn't.

20 medium potatoes, scrubbed but unpeeled

2 large Vidalia or other sweet onions (or any kind, but sweet onions make it sing), finely chopped

1½ tablespoons sweet pickle relish

2 tablespoons minced fresh dill or 2 teaspoons dried dill (but fresh is best)

1 cup mayonnaise or ranch dressing

Salt and freshly ground pepper

In a large pot three-quarters full of lightly salted boiling water, cook the whole potatoes until tender but still firm (a sharp knife should pierce them fairly easily but with a little resistance), 15 to 20 minutes.

Drain the potatoes thoroughly and let cool. Cut into ½-inch cubes.

Put the potatoes in a large bowl and add the onions, pickle relish, dill, mayonnaise, and salt and pepper to taste.

Refrigerate for at least 1 hour or up to overnight to allow the flavors to blend. Serve at room temperature.

Shug's Black-Eyed Pea Salad

Serves

★ **6-8** ★

ALTHOUGH EASY AS PIE to put together because it uses canned peas, this tasty side dish of Mike's is summer fresh when made with a ripe garden or farmers'-market tomato. He says you can also make it in any season, but use a couple of drained canned Italian (plum) tomatoes in place of the cardboard crop tomatoes in the grocery stores during winter.

2 cans (12 ounces each) black-eyed peas, rinsed and drained

1 small Vidalia or other sweet onion, finely chopped

1 small ripe tomato, finely chopped

1½ tablespoons mayonnaise, or to taste (better to use too little than too much)

Salt and freshly ground pepper

In a large bowl, combine the black-eyed peas, onion, tomato, mayonnaise and salt and pepper to taste. Refrigerate for at least 1 hour or up to overnight to allow the flavors to blend. Serve chilled as an appetizer with tortilla chips, or as a side dish.

HOECAKES

Hoecakes, a product of one of the most basic early-American cooking contraptions, were born of both necessity and heartache.

African American slaves, and some poor whites as well, learned to use the back of their three-by-six-inch iron hoe as a makeshift skillet.

"If a slave wanted something hot in the working field during a lunch break, it was hoecakes or nothing," says Kitty Wilson-Evans, a slave re-enactor at Historic Brattonsville, a restored 775-acre nineteenth-century working farm in York County, South Carolina.

One fall morning, Wilson-Evans built a simple wood fire outside of a cook's log cabin. After the fire burned out, she cleaned the back of a hoe and heated it over the coals. She placed several pieces of salted fatback pork on the hoe and fried it gently. From a pouch, she took a handful of cornmeal and added some water to make a thick mush. She put a biscuit-size pile of the cornmeal mush on the hoe and fried it in the pork fat. To flip it, she removed the hoe from the fire and just turned it over with her hand.

"It was an incredibly simple yet amazingly efficient solution to the hard life in the fields," says Wilson-Evans, a retired schoolteacher who once studied opera at Heidelberg University. "Your cooking utensil was your work tool and the dried fatback had enough grease and salt to flavor the cornmeal."

Wilson-Evans also made what she called "poor folks' fast food"—several sweet potatoes in the ashes of the fire. Then she went into the cabin and demonstrated an equally simple method of cooking in front of the indoor fireplace: roasting a whole chicken on a piece of string.

She trussed the bird with the string and then hung it from the mantel about a foot off the floor and two feet from the fire. She placed a pan under the chicken to catch the drippings, which she later used to baste the meat. "You just gently spin the chicken about every four or five minutes," she said. "It tastes wonderful—fresh poultry, fire-roasted with a little salt, pepper, and sage. It's one of the few nineteenth-century meals that is almost impossible to make taste better today"

T. R. McGrath

A genuine New England clambake requires one of America's original contraption cooking rigs: heated rocks and seaweed. The technique comes from Native Americans, who taught it to the early colonists in the 1600s. Building and using a clambake oven is easily the most labor-intensive cooking process around, considering you have to harvest barrels of fresh seaweed off the beach and procure granite bowling balls from the quarry. Oh, and don't forget to pick up a dozen hardwood pallets to build the fire.

"It's pretty much a full day's work to put on an authentic clambake," says T. R. McGrath, a third-generation bakemaster from Newport, Rhode Island.

A Virginia Tech grad, T. R. bought the family business, McGrath Clambakes, from his dad in 1999. His grandfather first started doing the clambakes on the Rhode Island shore in the 1930s. McGrath caters to customers throughout New England, coming to their home or a nearby beach and setting up a clambake for weddings and shorefront soirees, and he's traveled as far away as Florida to work his seafood magic.

T. R. acknowledges that his business is now also an enterprise of preserving tradition; clambakes are a dying art, with most people opting for indoor steamer-pot "bakes" on the kitchen stove. "There's no two ways about it, it's a good bit of work, even if you have all the tools like we do," McGrath says.

No two clambakes are alike, T. R. explains—some people even bring chicken and hot dogs to the rocks. He goes with the traditional ingredients: lobsters, mussels, clams, fish, *chouriço* (a spicy Portuguese sausage), onions, ears of sweet corn, and Red Bliss potatoes. Dessert is the perfect summer fruit: slices of chilled watermelon.

On a crisp October morning at the historic Mount Hope Farm in Bristol, Rhode Island, T. R. and assistant Philip Quarry backed up the truck and began the three-hour cooking process. This was after three hours of prep work—gathering two trash barrels of fresh rockweed, the granite, and the pallets and preparing the seafood.

On a grassy point overlooking the blue chop of Narragansett Bay and a rocky beach, they started by clearing off a section of the white shell drive to get down to the dirt. They stacked a few pallets—they prefer the hardwood pallets over firewood because it burns faster and falls into place—followed by

T. R. McGrath (right) and his assistant, Philip Quarry, prepare for a New England clambake near the beach at Mount Hope Farm.

the rocks and then more pallets, and ignited the pyre with crumpled newspaper at the base.

After the flames had turned the wood to embers, McGrath and Quarry went into action. First they spread the rockweed thickly and carefully to prevent any hot spots. Then they put stainless-steel racks on the hissing rockweed, arranged the food in the racks, and layered wet sheets of canvas on top. (If you're doing this yourself, you can just put the food in cheesecloth sacks directly on the rockweed, instead of on a professional caterer's stainless-steel racks.) Then, as if tucking someone into bed, they carefully tamped down the edges of the canvas with leftover rock and shells.

Once the clambake was sealed over by the canvas, we could hear the tiny bubbles of seaweed burst into steam. "There's just no need for spices." McGrath said. "You're basically steaming seafood and vegetables with salt water. We certainly have butter for your corn and lobster, but it's not needed."

With the clambake underway, the cooks went off to prepare "stuffies," baked clam cakes served in the shell, as appetizers. After about two hours, when McGrath determined the clambake was ready, the guests were summoned by a dinner bell. There was a chorus of "ohhhs" and "ahhhhs" when the canvas was pulled back and a cloud of steam rose, revealing a colorful cornucopia: fiery orange lobsters, yellow corn on the cob, rosy potatoes, and clams and mussels opened like tiny dark flowers.

And T. R. McGrath was right: no butter was necessary.

Old-Fashioned Clambake

Serves
20

DON'T EVEN THINK about throwing a clambake if you don't have at least two quasi-sober helpers and about 6 hours of prep time to devote to it. Don't forget about a truck and a trip to the quarry or rock supplier for the stones (we're not kidding), and go out of your way for the wood called for below; cordwood will burn too slowly. In the absence of canvas tarps, additional seaweed can be put over the food, then covered with several layers of burlap and topped with still more seaweed to cover and weigh down the burlap.

But your reward for all that schlepping is an incredible spread that marries local products—seafood and produce—with a strong sense of place (a New England beach) like perhaps no other American culinary tradition. And, actually, it's not that much more trouble than cooking a whole hog.

The principles of a clambake oven are fairly simple—it's essentially a huge pressure steamer. Rather than cooking over the coals, the coals heat the rocks and the hot rocks cook the food. When you cover the rocks with seaweed, nestle the food on top, and seal the whole thing with piles of wet canvas, you cut off virtually all the oxygen and the fire goes out. That produces a miraculous combination of steaming, baking, roasting, and smoking.

Note: Always check with local fire officials to obtain necessary burn permits.

Materials

Shovel

Gravel rake

6 old shipping pallets (old oak pallets work best; be sure the pallets are completely clean of any paint, varnishes, etc.) or comparable amount of driftwood from a beach

About two dozen 8-to-10-inch-diameter rocks (granite field stone works best)

Newspaper for kindling

Garden hose and water supply

Pitchfork

Lots of cheesecloth (about 10 square yards)

20 small brown paper lunch bags

Kitchen string

5 bushels of seaweed (in New England, fresh rockweed with air bubbles)

6 to 8 heavy-gauge canvas tarps, clean and untreated with any type of water-repellent chemicals, thoroughly soaked with water

Ingredients

5 pounds cod fillets, cut into 4-ounce portions

20 small live lobsters, about 1¼ pounds each

10 pounds steamer clams, scrubbed

10 pounds mussels, scrubbed and debearded

20 ears yellow sweet corn, thick outer layers of husk removed only (leave on a layer or two to help keep in the juices), stalk and silk ends trimmed

40 red potatoes (about 3 inches in diameter, 7 to 8 pounds total weight) preferably Red Bliss, scrubbed but unpeeled

20 small yellow onions, peeled but left whole

5 pounds spicy sausages, preferably Portuguese chouriço, cut into 1-inch slices

5 pounds butter, melted (optional)

Continued . . .

On a bed of seaweed, ready to eat, lay steamed trays of lobsters, corn, sausage, potatoes, onions, and clams, prepared by McGrath Clambakes.

Using the shovel and/or gravel rake, clear and level a 20-by-20-foot area. If your clambake is on a beach, clear loose sand until you reach a firm base; it is not necessary to dig a deep hole. On dirt or on a green, moist grass surface, again, it is not necessary to dig a hole; however, the base area should be flattened. Note that even green grass will get scorched.

Stack 4 of the pallets in the prepared spot. Cover the top pallet with the rocks. Stack the remaining 2 pallets on top of the rocks.

Crumple the newspaper at the base of the pallets, and light it. The fire will burn very hot and very fast for the first 30 minutes or so; for safety purposes never leave the fire unattended, and have the garden hose ready nearby if needed to control the fire. Use the pitchfork to tend the fire. Meanwhile, bag the food: Cut double layers of cheesecloth into 20 pieces about 24 inches square. Wrap each portion of cod in a small brown paper lunch bag (this helps hold the delicate fish together during steaming). Divide the wrapped fish and all the remaining ingredients among the cheesecloth squares, stacking the food in the centers with vegetables on the bottom and shellfish arranged on top. Draw the corners of the cheesecloth pieces together to make bags and tie the tops securely with kitchen string.

When the fire has settled down to a bed of coals (about 1 hour), any remaining pieces of wood should be raked out of the fire in preparation for putting the clambake on. Be ready to work quickly but carefully, to capture as much heat and steam as possible. Rewet the tarps, if necessary, so the canvas is completely soaked.

Spread seaweed over the hot rock base, layering it thickly in the center but also making sure there are no exposed rocks on the sides of the clambake. Arrange the bags of food in a single layer on the seaweed, starting in the center. Cover the food bags with the wet tarps, stacking one on top of the other.

Cook for 1 hour, dampening the canvas with the garden hose approximately every 10 to 15 minutes. Continue cooking for about 1 hour longer; during the second hour of cooking, the canvas will probably only need to be dampened every 20 to 30 minutes.

The food will be ready about 2 hours after you sealed the clambake oven off with the canvas. Gather your guests around the clambake and peel away the layers of canvas like a seductive lover—slowly, to maximize the effect. Soon, a billowing cloud of steam will rise and reveal a bed of fire-steamed edibles.

Serve immediately, accompanied with the melted butter, if you like.

Rhode Island Clear-Broth Quahog Chowder

Serves

★ 25–30 ★

Who needs cream or tomato sauce for their clam chowder? This is the real deal—a rich, hearty quintessence of New England shellfish chowder. The McGrath family has been serving this side dish at their clambakes for more than a half century. Quahog is a Native American name for the East Coast hard-shell clam, the largest of the hard-shell clams traditionally chopped and used in chowders. Quahog juice is preferred here, but any clam juice can be substituted.

7 to 8 pounds red potatoes, preferably Red Bliss, scrubbed but unpeeled, cut into ½-inch dice

1 heaping tablespoon salt

1 heaping tablespoon ground white pepper

1 heaping tablespoon dried thyme

1½ pounds ground salt pork

1½ pounds yellow or Spanish onions, chopped

1 quart shucked quahogs, chopped

1 quart quahog juice

In an extra-large stockpot, combine the potatoes with water to cover by 1 inch. Add the salt, pepper, and thyme. Bring to a boil, then reduce the heat and simmer until the potatoes are tender, 10 to 12 minutes.

Meanwhile, in a large skillet over medium heat, cook the salt pork until the fat is rendered, about 10 minutes. Add the onions and sauté until translucent.

Add the quahogs, quahog juice, and salt pork mixture to the stockpot. Return to a gentle boil, then reduce the heat to a simmer and cook for 30 minutes. Taste and adjust the seasonings, and serve hot.

Clam Cakes

Makes
4-5 Dozen / **Serves** 20

THESE GOLDEN FRITTERS dazzle as an appetizer, or as a main dish served with salad and crusty bread. The white pepper and beer are what make this recipe a standout. McGrath says this is one of his most-asked-for recipes. Quahogs are the largest hard-shell clams and can be chewy if not thoroughly chopped. Quahog juice can be bought in most New England and other seafood stores; if it's unavailable, any clam juice can be substituted.

6 cups all-purpose flour

½ cup baking powder

½ tablespoon ground white pepper

½ teaspoon salt

2 extra-large eggs

1½ pints shucked quahogs, chopped

1½ pints quahog juice

12 ounces beer

Canola oil for frying

Tartar sauce for serving

Mix together the dry ingredients in an extra-large bowl. Add the eggs, quahogs, quahog juice, and beer and mix until well blended.

In a deep fryer or deep saucepan, heat the oil to 350°F. Working in batches, scoop the batter in about 2-tablespoon portions into the hot oil using a large spoon or a #30 ice-cream scoop. Do not crowd the pan. Deep-fry until golden brown on the first side, about 2 to 3 minutes. Turn with tongs and fry until golden on the second side, about a minute longer. Using a slotted spoon or skimmer, transfer to paper towels to drain. Repeat to cook the remaining clam cakes.

Serve warm, with the tartar sauce.

Maximino Rios

What we found in Maximino Rios's backyard, behind a white fence in a suburban neighborhood near Charlotte, North Carolina, was not your everyday barbecue rig.

Yes, he was cooking meat for his family and friends, but not on a charcoal- or wood-fired grill, or a gas one. Rios wasn't cooking twenty-first-century American; he was cooking fifteenth-century Mayan. He was using *barbacoa*, the ancient method of heating stones and then steam-roasting meat underground in a covered pit.

"This is the way we cook meat for a celebration in my Mexican homeland in Oaxaca," he said. "It is much trouble here, but at home, this is what we do to celebrate a birthday, a wedding, a family gathering. It reminds us of where we have come from."

Rios and several friends constructed his *barbacoa* pit mostly from discarded building materials he found on his construction jobs—broken or leftover bricks, pieces of plywood, and wood scraps for kindling. They dug a hole about four feet long, three feet wide, and three feet deep, and lined the bottom and sides with stacked bricks to make an earthen oven.

Family friend Hector Guasco explains that the secret of this style of cooking is a long, simmering steam-roast with a minimum of smoke. "Here in America, barbecued meat is almost always smoky. In Mexico, the *barbacoa* is not smoky at all. What smoke you might get is from the chipotles [smoked jalapeño chiles]," he says.

To prepare the *barbacoa*, Rios and his wife, Ernestina, had to start the night before. They began by soaking chunks of goat in a tomato-based marinade with chipotles, as it is served in his native state of Oaxaca.

The next day, Rios built a hardwood fire about two hours before putting on the meat. Once he had a thick bed of glowing coals—but still with some flames—he dropped about a dozen large rocks into the fire pit. (In Oaxaca, Rios points out, one would use volcanic rocks; he uses rocks he finds when landscaping.) The rocks help collapse the remaining burning wood.

After the rocks had heated for about half an hour and there was almost no smoke, Ernestina brought Rios a pot of chicken broth loaded with chipotles. He carefully lowered the pot onto a flattened area in the *barbacoa* and sprinkled *hoja de aguacate* (avocado leaves) over the stones. The leaves, which can be found in most Mexican markets, look like large bay leaves, and impart an anise flavor to the dishes.

Maximino Rios pulls cooked goat from his backyard *barbacoa*.

Rios then wrapped the goat meat tightly in sheets of heavy-duty aluminum foil to seal in the juices. (In Mexico, the wrap might be banana or cactus leaves.) He then placed the packets on the hot rocks.

After the meat was placed in the pit, Rios used a broom to sweep away the dirt around the pit's edges. He placed a piece of clean plywood, slightly larger than the hole, over the pit and hosed it down so it wouldn't catch fire. Finally, he shoveled dirt on top of the wet plywood to completely seal the oven. Now no smoke could escape, and any remaining fire was extinguished because of the lack of oxygen.

The marinated goat is wrapped in foil over heated rocks and buried underground.

Then Rios simply left the pit. Because it was so thickly insulated, the pit would maintain a temperature of about 350°F for several hours. Traditionally, the family gathers to talk, dance, and make music while the meat roasts. When the time is up, usually the oldest male at the gathering will uncover the meat—Rios's father, Encino, would do it for their family in Oaxaca.

On this afternoon, Maximino Rios uncovered the pit. He loaded the goat on platters and carried it and the soup to the house, where it was served with tortillas, frijoles, salsa, and mole sauce.

"*Barbacoa* is celebration time," Rios said, as his family and the members of his folk music band gathered around the table. He tasted the meat and pronounced his verdict: "It is not Oaxaca, but it is our home and it is good."

Chicken Thighs with Mole Sauce

Serves
6

ERNESTINA RIOS got this recipe from her mother-in-law, Paulina Ibarra Santiago. It's common to Oaxaca, Mexico, the state the Rios family left to come to North Carolina. What makes it special is that it's easy to cook and has a wonderfully rich flavor. Her son, Maximino Jr., says the dish reminds him of their Mexican homeland. Guajillo chiles have tough skins and therefore must be cooked longer than most dried chiles.

⅓ cup corn oil, plus 1 teaspoon

2½ pounds chicken thighs, bone-in, skin-on

12 guajillo chile peppers

4 medium tomatoes

1 cup sesame seeds

¼ cup raisins

¼ cup sliced almonds

1 teaspoon dried oregano

1 teaspoon dried thyme

4 cups water

Salt

In a large saucepan, heat the ⅓ cup oil over medium-high heat until almost smoking. Add the chicken and cook until golden brown and opaque throughout, about 5 to 6 minutes per side. Transfer the chicken to a plate. Pour off all but 2 tablespoons of the oil and set the pan aside with the drippings and reserved oil.

Place several ice cubes in a medium bowl of water.

Place a large saucepan, half-full of water, over high heat and bring to a boil. Add the chiles and tomatoes and cook for 1 minute. Remove the tomatoes with a slotted spoon and plunge into the bowl of ice water. Continue cooking the chiles for 10 minutes longer. Meanwhile, when the tomatoes are cool enough to handle, peel them

Continued . . .

Maximino Rios tends the fire in his backyard *barbacoa* pit. He is waiting for the fire to burn down to coals before placing rocks in the pit to heat the foil-wrapped goat.

and transfer to a blender. Remove the chiles with the slotted spoon and add to the blender with the tomatoes.

Heat the 1 teaspoon oil in a small saucepan over medium heat. Add the sesame seeds, raisins, and almonds and cook until the raisins are plumped and soft and the sesame seeds are golden, about 5 minutes.

Transfer the sesame seed mixture to the blender with the tomatoes and chiles. Add the oregano, thyme, and 2 cups of the water. Blend until the chiles are thoroughly mixed, about 1 minute.

Reheat the reserved oil in the large saucepan over low heat. Pour the sesame seed mixture through a coarse-mesh strainer into the saucepan and bring to a simmer. Scrape the solids in the strainer back into the blender, add 1 cup water, blend for 1 minute, and strain again into the large pan. Repeat the process a third time, using the remaining 1 cup water. Discard any solids remaining in the strainer.

Raise the heat to medium-high, and cook until the mole sauce bubbles and steam rises from the surface, at least 15 minutes. Season with salt to taste.

Transfer the chicken to a shallow serving bowl or platter, pour the sauce over, and serve at once.

Betsy Barstow

On a rainy autumn morning in Adamant, Vermont, with the clouds draped over the trees like long skeins of cotton, Betsy Barstow dashed among three stoves that held nine pots of beans. She stirred one pot, dipped into another, frowned that this batch was too chewy, that batch too firm. Finally, in a mute plea for help, she thrust a spoon into a visitor's hand. "It's stressful," said the slender, dark-haired woman, with a nervous laugh. "You really want them to be wonderful, but you don't know."

Barstow was parboiling twenty-five pounds of Great Northern beans for a traditional New England bean-hole bean supper. It would take a truckload of wood and two burly volunteer firefighters to generate enough charcoal to cook the beans for twenty-four hours. The beans would sit five feet under the ground in a brick-lined pit, with the fire-warmed soil above cooking them to a rich caramel.

"This is slow-mo," joked Greg Pelchuck, one of the firefighters. In a couple of hours he'd don his thick yellow jacket and a fire hat to ward off the heat and the sparks as he carried the pots from the stove and sank them into the pit. Right now, though, he stood in his rain poncho, tamping down the gigantic flames that had been going since dawn. "It's like the race between the rabbit and the turtle, okay? We're the turtle."

Bean-hole bean cooking originated with Native Americans and was adopted by the Pilgrims, who would prepare enough beans on Saturday so that they wouldn't have to cook on the Sabbath. Later, in the twentieth century, bean-hole bean suppers became popular among loggers in Maine and other New England states. Camp cooks served beans at every meal, using the same method Barstow uses: digging a pit, lining the bottom and sides with stones, building a fire to form a bed of coals, then lowering a covered pot filled with beans into the pit and blanketing everything with dirt and charcoal left over from previous suppers. The next day, the beans were ready to eat.

Today, the tradition lives on in New England church suppers, Grange meetings, and gatherings at local firehouses. For the past twelve years, Barstow—guided by lifelong Adamant resident Lois Toby—has organized an annual bean-hole bean supper to raise money for the Adamant Community Club, which is headquartered in a converted one-room schoolhouse at the end

Greg Pelchuck (left) helps Rick Barstow use logging chains to hoist a simmering pot of beans out of an ember-laden fire pit, where the legumes have been cooked for twenty-four hours.

of a dirt road in this hamlet just outside of Montpelier, the state capital. The schoolhouse was built in 1894 and still has its original chalkboard and wood floors. At least two villagers remember tramping through the snow to get to classes in the 1930s, and one woman claims she rode the family cow to school.

Barstow flavors the beans with her own homemade maple syrup, and recruits volunteers to cut mountains of cabbage for the coleslaw that always accompanies them—she says using a food processor makes the shredded cabbage too mushy. Buying the ingredients, cooking on the club's 1960s-era stoves, and feeding the two hundred fifty people who attend the supper is an enormous job, which is why the fundraiser is held only once a year. The money goes toward insurance and repairs on the white clapboard building, where residents gather for Maypole dances, potlucks, Halloween parties, Easter egg hunts, and a Christmas tea party and cookie swap.

About a decade ago, the community club almost folded. People had stopped coming to the potlucks, and only six residents, including Barstow, kept things going. But the group fanned out to Adamant's sixty residents and persuaded them that losing the schoolhouse would mean the disappearance of an important gathering place in a town where many residents are self-employed. Now, Barstow says, folks are streaming back to the suppers.

But with the widening appeal of turning period schoolhouses into private homes, Barstow and others worry that Adamant's community center might disappear someday, too, if no one is around to keep the bean-hole suppers alive.

"Every year we look at each other and think, 'God, should we keep doing this?'" says Rose Pelchuck, Barstow's friend and Greg's wife. "But this is such a rich tradition, how can we stop?"

Bean-Hole Beans

Serves
★ 160 ★

THIS RECIPE IS NOT for the faint of heart. Betsy Barstow begins prep at 7 a.m. the day before, and the only way she's able to get everything done is to enlist the help of her husband, Rick, and their two kids. Friends Greg and Rose Pelchuck pitch in, too. As Greg, a volunteer firefighter, doused the flames before Betsy put on the beans, he recalled the time the fire got so big that it singed the power line above, disabling the electric water pump and forcing Rick to borrow a fire truck to douse the flames. This time, everything went according to plan and the beans emerged in a state of perfection from the hot

Continued ...

pit. They were rich and—not surprisingly—earthy, with a smoky sweetness gained from slow cooking and melding of flavors. The classic comfort-food dish had the additional magic of down-home hearth food.

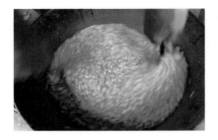

Materials

1½ tons ½-inch granite pieces

Long-handled shovel

About 200 firebricks

Newspaper, matches, and kindling

80 to 100 old shipping pallets (hardwood works best; it's okay to mix it with slower-burning cordwood)

Garden hose and water supply

Heavy-duty leather gloves

Rake for the coals

Two 25-gallon stainless-steel stockpots

Two ¼-inch chains, each 8 to 10 feet long, with hooks on each end

4 or 5 pieces of sheet metal, about 8 or 10 feet long, for covering the pit

Ingredients

25 pounds dried Great Northern beans, preferably organic

7 pounds onion, sliced

5 pounds salt pork, sliced

1 gallon grade B Vermont maple syrup

2 pounds firmly packed dark brown sugar

1 pound granulated white sugar

½ cup dry mustard

½ cup salt

5 tablespoons freshly ground pepper

3 tablespoons garlic powder

Dig a hole measuring 8 feet by 5 feet and 5 feet deep. Line the bottom with the crushed granite to a depth of about 1 to 1½ feet. Line the bottom and sides with the firebricks, setting the bricks as level as possible on the granite and using the granite to fill the chinks between the bricks.

Pick over the beans and rinse them. Place them in several large bowls with water to cover and let soak for at least 4 hours, or up to overnight.

About 5 hours before you're ready to lower the beans into the hole, build a fire inside the bean hole with the newspapers, kindling, and a few pallets. Every 30 minutes, throw 8 to 10 more pallets on top, hosing down the fire as needed so it doesn't get out of control. When the

Caramel-colored beans are the perfect comfort food on a cool autumn day.

pallets are all burned and the coals are ready, while wearing the gloves and using the shovel, remove—but keep nearby—enough coals to leave a 6- to 8-inch-thick layer on the bottom of the hole before the beans go in. Rake the coals smooth.

Meanwhile, drain the beans, divide them among large saucepans or stockpots, and add fresh water to cover by several inches. Cook on the stovetop over medium-high heat until almost tender, or until the amount of liquid is even with the amount of beans in the pots, about 45 minutes to 1 hour. Divide the beans and their cooking liquid between the 25-gallon stockpots that will be lowered into the pit. Divide the sliced onions and salt pork between the stockpots.

In a large bowl, combine the maple syrup, brown sugar, granulated sugar, dry mustard, salt, pepper, and garlic powder. Divide the mixture evenly between the stockpots and mix thoroughly.

Cover with tight-fitting lids and wrap the pots in aluminum foil. Hook the chains to the handles and carefully lower the pots into the bean hole, making sure they're resting level. Remove the chains.

Put most of the coals that you scooped out of the hole back in, placing them on top and around the sides of the pots. Layer the pieces of sheet metal on top to cover the hole, then mix the remaining coals with dirt and rake the mixture smoothly over the top of the pit. Let the beans cook for 24 hours.

When ready to serve, again wearing gloves, uncover the hole, hook the chains to the stockpots, and lift the pots out of the ground. If the coals are still hot after the supper, douse them with water and cover the hole with the sheet metal.

Bean-Hole Bean Supper Coleslaw

Serves
30

THE SPICES in this recipe give it an extra kick, Barstow says. And take another page from Betsy's (and her crew's) book—don't cut corners with store-bought pre-cut cabbage or by using a food processor to slice the cabbage; the slaw just won't come out well. Don't assemble the coleslaw more than 1 hour before you're ready to serve, so the cabbage stays firm.

Betsy Barstow savors the fruits of her labors.

4 large green cabbages, about 8 pounds total weight, cored and thinly sliced by hand

2½ pounds carrots, peeled and shredded

1 quart mayonnaise

½ cup apple cider vinegar

1 tablespoon celery seed

2 tablespoons Jane's Krazy Mixed-Up Salt

Combine the cabbage and carrots in an extra-large bowl.

In a large bowl, stir together the mayonnaise, vinegar, celery seed, and seasoned salt. Add to the cabbage mixture and toss to mix well. Refrigerate until ready to serve.

A WAREHOUSE OF RIGS

Think that folks in the twenty-first century have a patent on funky-looking contraptions? For a truly entertaining look at the rigs people used to cook with, take a spin through the Culinary Archives & Museum at Johnson & Wales University in Providence, Rhode Island. Inside a former warehouse are display cabinets stuffed with the tools, stoves, gadgets, and inventions that, over the centuries, turned food preparation from a dreaded chore into a show-stopping exhibition.

There's a portable cookstove designed by Alexis Soyer, a nineteenth-century French chef and philanthropist whose advice to the British during the Crimean War was responsible for dietary improvements for the malnourished and badly supplied troops. The stove he built was easily broken down during maneuvers and required less fuel for cooking than an open fire.

There's also the Manson Campbell Company's all-aluminum "fireless cooker," a 1909 version of the Crock-Pot. The cook heated up a thick disk of metal or soapstone in the morning, dropped it to the bottom of an insulated cylinder, then put the food in an aluminum pot with a lid and placed it on top of the heated disk. The container would then be sealed with a tight-fitting metal lid. The food, snug in its well-insulated chamber, would cook for 4 to 8 hours undisturbed.

And there's an assortment of the stuff we all remember from our grandmas' kitchens: Florence stoves, Hamilton Beach triple mixers, and the clunky refrigerators that once stored glass bottles of milk and home-churned butter. It evokes an era even the Slow Food movement can't quite recapture.

Jimmy Kennedy

From Elvis's birthplace to Plainfield, Vermont, Jimmy Kennedy came a long way to his River Run restaurant, which lies hard by the Winooski River in rural New England.

Jimmy grew up in Brewer, Mississippi, next to Tupelo. His uncles raised goats, which they frequently barbecued for family gatherings. He also helped out at their catfish fries, and later worked as a sales rep for the catfish industry. But he says he had no idea, growing up, that he'd ever be a chef.

After working on Capitol Hill as a legislative assistant, Kennedy went to New York City, where he met his wife-to-be, Maya. Soon after, they married and moved to Maya's hometown of Plainfield.

Jimmy was looking for work, and observed that Plainfield needed a good, down-home restaurant. They converted the town's former post office into a restaurant in 1991, and it wasn't long before customers like Pulitzer Prize–winning playwright David Mamet were singing the River Run's praises, calling it "the best place on Earth." *New Yorker* illustrator Ed Koren is also a regular. With Goddard College nearby, the restaurant's clientele is a mix of academics in running shoes and hippies in various stages of bloom, as well as farmers, truck drivers, and blue-collar Joes.

Before long, Jimmy, longing for a bit of the Delta in New England, installed a meat smoker. Inspired by the results he was getting, he decided to upgrade, drawing on the southern tradition of turning anything metal with three walls and a door into a meat smoker. A second, larger smoker replaced the original in 2003 after the restaurant moved next door. Then Jimmy's crew converted an unused fridge into a hulking smoker. His wife christened it the "Jimmy Rig." He had a new smoker, but also a new problem: how to move the monolith.

"I had no idea it would be so heavy. I had four loggers come in and they couldn't even budge it off the ground," he says.

With some furniture moving equipment, they were able to get it to a deck next door behind his old restaurant. A woodstove was converted into the firebox, and Jimmy anointed Doug Metcalf as River Run's new smoke-meister.

"Because it's so big—it has ten racks—it takes a while to heat up, but then it holds the heat well," says Metcalf, who has attempted to smoke practically

Jimmy Kennedy (left) with his master meat man and smoker, Doug Metcalf, and the Jimmy Rig cooker.

every food substance. Just dare him. "I smoked some water once," he says. "It was okay, but I don't think I'd pay to drink it."

Jimmy adds, "We have a lot of vegetarians, and we smoke lots of vegetables for our omelets. We've smoked tofu, cheese—heck, we even smoked butter, but I wasn't sure what to do with it. Like with any smoke-meister, when the Budweiser gets to flowing, Doug gets pretty creative with the smoker. He has mastered his machine."

They smoke mostly with maple wood, and some apple; they've found that fruitwoods pair well with their hugely popular bone-in Boston butts, which they smoke at 200° to 250°F for eight to ten hours.

Smoked pork, a Southern staple, has done well in its travels northward: on a

recent Saturday afternoon at River Run, the last twelve orders of the lunch rush were all pulled pork. "When you grow up down South, you think that real barbecue is everywhere—but it's not," Jimmy says. "I've found that once people try it, they generally like it. We couldn't do it without our smoker, though."

Another house specialty is catfish, mostly fried but sometimes smoked; the restaurant serves more than 120 pounds of it a week. They buy farm-raised, clear-water catfish, but their supply is sometimes supplemented: a championship sport fisherman, Jimmy recently returned from Lake Ontario with seventy-five pounds of cleaned fish. They've experimented with brines, usually using a mix of salt and granulated garlic, and they make an exceptional smoked trout pâté with just a hint of sweet smoke. It's excellent on crusty bread.

Jimmy, who looks like a younger, leaner Sam Shepard, says the smoker is a win-win situation—it reminds him of home and it's good for business.

"The customers can't get enough of it," he says with a grin. "It's just barbecue down home, but up here, it's meat candy."

Note: The following recipes are from **The River Run Cookbook: Southern Comfort From Vermont**, *by Marialisa Calta, Jimmy Kennedy, and Maya Kennedy, New York: HarperCollins, 2001. Reprinted with permission.*

Country-Style Spare Ribs

Serves
4

JIMMY SAYS COUNTRY-STYLE spare ribs are one of their big sellers at River Run. Despite the name, these are not really ribs, but are cut from either the loin or the butt of the pig. They just *look* like ribs. From the loin, they are completely boneless, and from the butt they are mostly boneless. Talk to your butcher to make your pick. Do not baste the meat with the barbecue sauce while cooking; use it as a dipping sauce after the meat is cooked.

2 to 3 pounds country-style spare ribs

½ cup Jimmy's All-Purpose Barbecue Dry Rub (page 54)

1 to 2 cups Jimmy's All-Purpose Barbecue Sauce (page 55)

Build a fire in a smoker/grill for indirect heat. Maintain a temperature of about 225°F. For an extra dose of smoke, add a handful of wet chips to the hot coals.

Season the meat with the rub. Load the meat in the smoker on the side opposite the coals.

Smoke the ribs until they are brown and the meat pulls apart easily, or until an instant-read thermometer inserted into the center registers 160°F, about 2 hours.

Near the end of the smoking time, build a fire in a charcoal grill, or preheat a gas grill or the broiler.

When the ribs are done, remove them from the smoker and grill or broil them until you are happy with the color and charring of the exterior, 3 to 5 minutes per side. Transfer to a carving board and let rest for about 5 minutes, then cut into serving pieces.

Heat the sauce in a saucepan. Spoon or brush some sauce on each portion and serve the ribs, passing more warm sauce at the table.

Note: To make the ribs in the oven, line a baking sheet with heavy-duty aluminum foil. Arrange the ribs on the foil and sprinkle with the rub. Cover with more foil and seal the edges. Bake at 350°F until very tender, about 1½ hours.

Jimmy's All-Purpose Barbecue Dry Rub

Makes About / Enough For
2 Cups / 12-15 lbs. of Meat

JIMMY CREDITS former River Run cook Josh Grinkler with developing this rub, which works well with pork, chicken, fish, beef, even tofu. Jimmy uses it in all of his barbecue dishes. And it's handy to have on your kitchen shelf to spice up practically any dish—try it on meatloaf or to season soup. Despite the name, don't rub it in, just sprinkle.

Behind the River Run restaurant, smoke-meister Doug Metcalf splits wood to feed the Jimmy Rig.

6 tablespoons granulated sugar

2 tablespoons light or dark brown sugar

¼ cup salt

¼ cup ground cumin

¼ cup coarsely ground black pepper

¼ cup chili powder

½ cup paprika

1 teaspoon cayenne pepper

In a bowl, mix all the ingredients well. Store in an airtight container in a cool, dry place and it will last a long time.

Jimmy's All-Purpose Barbecue Sauce

Makes About 1 Quart / Enough For 8-10 lbs. of Meat

JIMMY KENNEDY is from Mississippi, where they take barbecue seriously. In his family, goat was usually on the barbecue menu because his uncles raised them, but he swears this sauce is right for just about any critter you want to smoke. He even uses this versatile sauce on spaghetti.

3 cups ketchup

1 cup cider vinegar

¼ cup Worcestershire sauce

1 tablespoon dry mustard

1½ teaspoons freshly ground black pepper

½ teaspoon cayenne pepper

½ teaspoon chili powder

4 cloves garlic, peeled and minced

¼ cup chopped onion

¾ cup water

¾ cup firmly packed brown sugar

Combine the ingredients in a heavy-bottomed pot and stir until well mixed.

Cook over medium heat for 10 minutes, stirring occasionally to avoid burning the bottom of the pot.

Reduce the heat to low and simmer, uncovered, for 1½ hours, stirring occasionally.

Use immediately, or refrigerate, covered, for up to 1 week.

Joe & Steve Whitener

There's a reason that food gatherings become *annual* food gatherings—it's more than just good food prepared every year at the same time.

It's good times.

Like most food traditions, the Whitener brothers' annual oyster roast in Blacksburg, South Carolina, started off simple: a pile of oysters roasting on the top of a 55-gallon barrel, and a couple of six-packs. "That was it," says Joe. "My brother Steve had moved down to Charleston, and when he came back up here for Christmas, he brought a half-bushel of oysters."

More than twenty-five years later, things have grown a bit.

It was a cold but sunny December Saturday when we arrived for the most recent incarnation of the Whitener Brothers Oyster Roast. We huddled with more than 250 people around a small airplane hangar off Interstate 85. A big-chested Santa in combat boots landed his plane, unloaded a bag of toys, and accepted a plastic cup of chug-a-lug.

On the tarmac, the Whitener boys had lined up an unlikely armada of oyster cookers—five gleaming, galvanized trashcans atop propane burners with blue flames licking out from underneath—in front of a hungry crowd. It looked like a high school rocket launching. When we looked more closely, we saw whiffs of steam rising from the lids of the cans.

"What can I say? The party got bigger and we needed bigger pots to roast the oysters," says Steve. He was at an oyster roast at Lady's Island in Beaufort County when he first saw the trashcan cookers. "My first reaction was, 'Oh my God, what could they be cooking in there?' Then I tasted them and became a convert. It's a fast and delicious way to roast a lot of oysters."

Like the best contraption cookers, the trashcans are more than a novelty: they work like a steam-powered freight train.

Before the cooking, however, a little about oyster prep from the Whiteners:

❧ Get the freshest oysters you can and keep them cool, covered, and moist until ready to cook.

❧ Even if the oysters have been cleaned, wash them yourself with a scrub brush and pressure hose. You don't want your guests handling mud or

Joe Whitener (left) hoists a burlap bag full of oysters from his trashcan steamer, while his brother Steve (right) waits in anticipation.

getting grit in their mouths. The Whiteners have a friendly volunteer fire department that allows them to use their high-pressure hose to clean the oysters fast.

☙ Toss out any oyster whose shell is beginning to open and doesn't close when you tap it.

☙ You need an oyster-shucking table; an easy and ideal solution is a sheet of ¾-inch marine plywood supported by two sawhorses.

🦪 Provide oyster knives, towels, and gloves for your oyster shucking friends. The knives are specially designed to make a somewhat tricky task easier, and gloves are crucial for protecting hands from sharp shell edges.

🦪 Don't even think about attempting to have an oyster roast indoors. A garage, maybe, but never inside your house. You don't want to wake up to the smell of oyster juice on your kitchen floor. Your family will thank you.

🦪 After the party, boil out the trashcans to remove the salt; this will prevent the cans from rusting out.

Trashcan Oyster Roast

Serves Or About

8-10 / 5 Serious Oyster Fiends

Materials

1 large, heavy-duty galvanized trashcan with lid, new or thoroughly washed out (it's a good idea to boil out any can before using it)

1 propane burner with stand (the kind used to fry fish)

½ concrete block or a few bricks

1 burlap bag (you can usually get them for free from the place where you're getting the oysters)

Oyster knives, gloves, and kitchen towels for the shuckers

1 wheelbarrow (optional; the perfect place to throw empty shells)

Ingredients

½ bushel fresh oysters in the shell (about 5 dozen)

Joe's Trashcan Oyster Roast Sauce (page 60) for serving

Soda crackers, quartered lemons, cocktail sauce, and melted butter for serving

1 tub of ice-cold beer

Gleaming trash cans full of fresh oysters are being steamed to perfection at the Whitener brothers' annual galvanized-trashcan oysterfest.

Place the trashcan on top of the propane burner. Put the concrete block or bricks in the trashcan to keep the oysters off the bottom. Pour about 2 inches of water in the can and fire up the propane. Put the oysters in the burlap bag. When the water is boiling, place the bag in the trashcan. Cover and steam until the oysters begin to pop open, about 20 minutes (depending on the weather). After about 15 minutes, start checking to see if the oysters are beginning to open. Remove them when all the shells have opened, including those in the center of the bag, which may cook more slowly. Discard any oysters that fail to open.

Dump the oysters on the table and start shucking—and jiving. Pop off and discard the top shells and eat the oysters out of the bottom shells, with the sauce and/or any of the other accompaniments and frosty beer.

Note: Replenish the water in the trashcan before steaming more oysters.

Joe's Trashcan Oyster Roast Sauce

Makes About 2 Quarts / Enough For 3 Bushels of Oysters

JOE WHITENER INVENTED this sauce—with the help of a few beers—one night at his annual oyster roast, when he ran out of store-bought cocktail sauce. "Our oyster roasts were getting so big, it was becoming cost-prohibitive to buy those little bitty bottles of cocktail sauce," says Joe. "Now our guests prefer this over the store stuff. Heck, I get requests from strangers who want to buy my sauce for their oyster roast."

This is also good on boiled shrimp, fried fish, and chicken wings.

2 quarts ketchup, preferably Hunt's

1¼ cups prepared horseradish

⅓ cup fresh lemon juice

2 tablespoons coarsely ground black pepper

2 tablespoons red pepper flakes

¼ cup Worcestershire sauce

½ cup dried parsley

2 tablespoons (about 10 shakes) Tabasco or other hot-pepper sauce

1 teaspoon cayenne pepper

In a bowl, mix all the ingredients well. Refrigerate for at least 2 hours before serving to allow the flavors to blend.

The sauce will keep, covered and refrigerated, for up to 1 week.

Doris Whitener's Hot Barbecue Slaw

Serves
5

THIS RECIPE COMES from Steve and Joe Whitener's mama, who passed away in 1989. It's a great accompaniment to pulled pork barbecue, but it has also made a lasting impression with the Whitener family as a condiment on cheeseburgers with sliced onion. "At Christmas, birthdays, and family gatherings, that's what we cook, and Mama's hot slaw is what makes the meal special," says Joe.

1 large green cabbage, about
2 pounds, cored and shredded

1 cup mayonnaise

1 cup ketchup

*¼ cup **Worcestershire** sauce*

2 tablespoons Tabasco or other
hot-pepper sauce

Red pepper flakes
to taste

Salt to taste

Coarsely ground black pepper to taste

In a large bowl, mix all the ingredients well. Refrigerate for at least 1 hour before serving to allow the flavors to blend.

Steve Whitener (left) and his brother Joe (with a mouthful of crackers and oysters).

Fuzzy Monnes

The Monnes homestead, south of Charlottesville, Virginia, is made of stone but held together with love—of family and food. It consists of James "Fuzzy" Monnes and his teenage, blonde sprite daughters, Sally Rose and Mary Pearl.

Fuzzy, a stonemason, built the house on a wooded hillside, with help from buddies who are carpenters. The handworked craftsmanship is on display throughout the house's three levels, but what catches your eye is that there's a kitchen on every level—and a fourth kitchen on the ground floor, if you count the wood-fired oven by the stone-and-brick courtyard.

On a fall afternoon, the girls were in town and Fuzzy had been up since before dawn, firing the oven and preparing an Italian extravaganza—a delicate, smoke-tinged, made-from-scratch pizza and an entrée of roasted pork glazed with apples, garlic, and rosemary.

"Cooking began in ovens like this," he said as he slid the pizza off a wooden paddle into the radiance of the oven. In less than three minutes, the light dough began to bubble in the 800°F cavern; a pan of roasted garlic and homegrown tomatoes hovered nearby. "Yes, it takes time to cook like this, but the flavors make it worthwhile."

Fuzzy has been laying stone for three decades, but when it came to making a bread oven, he had to travel to the motherland—Forna Allegna, in southern Italy.

"They've never stopped cooking in these ovens there," he says. "Many small towns even have a communal oven where families will bring their own bread to cook. They may be poor, but they have incredible artisan breads."

Maybe it was the masonry angel seated by the licks of fire escaping from the chimney, the wooden-stump chopping block supported by a granite post, the bust of the leering Zig-Zag man by the stove door, or the rose pink mortared dome, but—we had to say it—this cooker was dangerously close to being a work of art.

Fuzzy laughed it off. "Hey man, I'll build you one just like it, anywhere, anytime, for five thousand bucks."

He's built them in West Virginia, Montana, and the Shenandoah Valley. He recently completed a massive stonework job for Carter Beauford, the drummer in the Dave Matthews Band.

James "Fuzzy" Monnes, master stonemason and gourmand, stands by the wood-fired oven he built on his mountain homestead.

Fuzzy was born in Portland, Oregon, and grew up as a military brat—five grammar schools. He says the travel made him a bit of a class clown. He inherited his love of cooking from his grandmother, Lillian Scott. "My ancestors were Norwegian, and she lived in Wisconsin where she cooked for a road gang working across the state," he says. "She baked bread for all three meals, and the best apple pies, too, on a wood stove. Nobody messed with the cooks; they ran things. And the road-gang camp was rough and nasty, but she ruled that kitchen, and I kind of liked that—about food and order."

But enough about cooking. Fuzzy wants to talk about his daughters, whom he has raised and fed on weekdays for the last twelve years (they live with their mom on weekends). They're vegetarians who gravitate to the oven for meatless pizza, veggie burgers, vinaigrette salads, and their favorite—sautéed tofu with mushrooms smothered in Thai peanut sauce.

Fuzzy has tried to teach them that cooking is a tactile art. "I taught them they have 'brains in their finger tips,'" he says. "And they could learn a lot about their food by simply working it with their hands."

He says they've all learned in the kitchen.

"They're sweet girls who have made my life complete," he says. "But no one tells you that one of the hardest things about being a single parent is coming home after working all day and feeding the kids, every night. It was weird, it was hard work, but it brought us together."

Here's what the girls say about their dad:

- "What makes my dad feel good is cooking; it's almost as if it's a type of meditation for him . . . I love to watch my dad cook, because I love to see him happy . . . He always tries to get my older sister and I involved in what he's making . . . Not often will you catch my Pap cooking without a smile on his face."—*Sally Rose Monnes, age fourteen.*

- "When my dad became a single parent, a sort of emptiness was left around us. To make his children full, my dad learned how to cook. When he began, it was just a means to fix the brokenness, but it became this amazing passion in him. He worked to create something good to put in us. I have always had the greatest appreciation for my dad's dedication to that. Every night he makes a beautiful meal, a symbol of his constant love and presence. For my family, food has become the giving and thankfulness we have for each other. It is something that I hope to learn to give as sincerely as my dad does."—*Mary Pearl Monnes, age seventeen.*

Puerto Appleito

Serves
★ **6-8** ★

AFTER A TRIP to Italy, Fuzzy was inspired to come up with an Italian twist on a roasted pork shoulder. He developed this recipe for his wood-fired oven, but you can also cook it in your oven or smoker. This makes an excellent centerpiece for a dinner party.

1 boneless pork shoulder, about 8 pounds (do not remove fat cap)

½ cup firmly packed brown sugar

½ teaspoon kosher salt

½ teaspoon freshly ground pepper

5 sprigs rosemary

5 cloves garlic, crushed

2 tablespoons olive oil

6 thick strips bacon

1 Red Delicious apple cut into thin slices with the peel still attached

1 cup apple cider

Build a medium fire in a wood-fired stone oven or preheat a conventional oven to 325°F.

Ask your butcher to butterfly the shoulder, or do it yourself with a sharp knife: Carefully cut into the shoulder, about 1 inch deep, down the length of the pork. Slowly unroll the meat as you continue to cut it in half evenly, stopping

Continued ...

A pan of fire-roasted tomatoes and garlic in olive oil will be the topping on Fuzzy's Pizza Italiano.

1 inch from the opposite end. Open it like a book and lay it flat. The result is a rough rectangle of meat about an inch thick.

In a bowl, stir together the brown sugar, salt, and pepper. Reserve 1 tablespoon of the mixture and sprinkle the rest over the meat, along with the leaves from 3 of the rosemary sprigs and the garlic. Roll up the meat and tie the roll every few inches with butcher's twine. Sprinkle the outside of the meat with the remaining brown sugar mixture.

Heat the olive oil in a cast-iron skillet and brown the meat on all sides, about 2 to 3 minutes per side. Turn the meat fat cap up, lay the remaining 2 sprigs rosemary across it, and drape the bacon slices over all. Arrange the apple slices on top of the bacon. Place in the oven and bake, basting with the apple cider about every 30 minutes, until an instant-read thermometer inserted in the center registers 160°F, about 90 minutes.

Remove from the oven and let stand for 10 to 15 minutes. Slice and serve.

Fuzzy's Pizza Italiano

Serves
★ **2-3** ★

THIS DISH WAS also inspired by Fuzzy's trip to Italy. The trick is making your own dough and baking it at a high temperature so that it cooks quickly. It's far removed from the doughy Americanized pizza smothered with goopy tomato sauce—this pizza has no sauce at all, just fresh, simmered, and roasted tomatoes. It's surprisingly light, with a hint of wood smoke.

3½ cups all-purpose flour

1 cup warm water

1 envelope (1½ teaspoons) active dry yeast

Pinch of sugar

1 tablespoon extra-virgin olive oil

3 tomatoes, peeled and sliced

3 cloves garlic, minced

2 tablespoons finely grated Parmigiano-Reggiano cheese

1 tablespoon finely grated Asiago cheese

1 tablespoon fresh oregano leaves

Salt and freshly ground pepper

Build a hot fire in a wood-fired stone oven or place a pizza stone in a conventional oven and preheat to 425°F.

In a large bowl, combine 1¾ cups of the flour, the water, yeast, and sugar to make a slurry. Let stand until the yeast is foamy, about 5 minutes. Stir with a fork and let stand for 1½ hours. Stir in the remaining 1¾ cups flour and let stand for 30 minutes longer.

In a skillet, heat ½ tablespoon of the olive oil over medium heat. Add the tomatoes and garlic and simmer for about 15 minutes. Remove from the heat and set aside.

Cut the dough in half and knead until smooth and elastic. Roll out each dough half into a 10-inch circle. Drizzle with the remaining ½ tablespoon olive oil, spreading it with the back of a spoon. Place a dough round in the bread oven or on the pizza stone. Bake until it begins to bubble up, 2 to 3 minutes. Remove from the oven and spread half of the tomato mixture on top. Sprinkle with half the cheeses and the oregano, and salt and pepper to taste. Return to the oven and bake until the cheeses are melted. Remove from oven and repeat with the remaining dough round. Cut and serve.

NOT YOUR AVERAGE BARREL SMOKER

Back in 1978, during the early days of the Memphis in May barbecue competition, John Willingham's rig was the talk of the contest. Surrounded by clumps of 55-gallon drums, his cooker—the one with a glass door and hanging meat rack that twirled above the heat—was, well, different.

"There were people that saw us and thought it was a popcorn machine," Willingham says, chuckling. "It was absolutely the reddest thing you ever saw; we'd painted it with red paint. People couldn't figure out what the heck it was."

The idea for the unusual rig came to Willingham while he was living in Washington, D.C., and working for the Department of Housing and Urban Development. "Every time my Weber and I would go out to cook, the grease drippings would go on the bottom and it'd stink to high heaven," he says. "You'd have the taste of lighter fluid on the meat and belch it later.

"So I woke up in the middle of the night and drew on a sketch pad beside my bed, and I built the first cooker."

He's been a grand champion twice at Memphis in May and twice at the American Royal—the barbecue equivalent of winning four Grand Slam tennis tournaments. He sells a line of sauces and equipment, and somehow manages to serve as a Shelby County Commissioner in Memphis, Tennessee.

As for that first cooker? More than twenty-five years later, it's still going strong.

Doc Hill

Doc Hill has more than a hundred cooking rigs at his riverside camp in rural South Carolina, but his pièce de résistance is his Hot Rod Rig.

The contraption could be an exhibit in a Ripley's Believe It or Not Museum; it features the chrome handles from a casket, an anchor, a barroom spittoon, a stove door from a nineteenth-century plantation house, and the serpentine headers from a 327-cubic-inch Chevy engine. Its core is a 250-gallon heating oil tank mounted on a sailboat trailer salvaged from Topsail Beach, North Carolina—we can only assume he found it *above* the high tide line. "Nothing was too good for this cooker," he says. "I spent close to thirteen dollars."

It's a rig, all right, and Doc is a master showman when he demonstrates its bells and whistles. When he cooked for us, he slid out the grilling trays to turn the steaming meat with a flourish. "The finest custom grills don't have this kind of access," he said. "Do you see how easy it is to check out your meat and turn it, away from the heat?" He beamed at it lovingly, despite its dings from a recent highway crash.

(Note: Part of the Contraption Cooker's Credo is, "Avoid loaning a cooker that requires interstate travel, particularly if said cooker is barely able to support its own weight in your backyard." But that's another story.)

At first Doc wanted to paint the rig before we photographed it, but he finally relented. "That grill is so pretty it would make a monkey make love to a bulldog," he said.

Doc variously describes himself as a kindly pyromaniac, five times retired, and a confirmed tinkerer. He is a former motorcycle racer who has replaced or retrofitted his knees and ankles at least five times (must be his lucky number). He's an inventor and promotions man who has worked in NASCAR and textiles.

But to sum it up: "Just say I'm a half-assed Texan from North Carolina."

Besides grilling, one of Doc's hobbies is recycling abandoned store-bought cookers. "I just can't pass up an old gas grill on the side of the road waiting for the trash dump," he says.

Hill has rescued hundreds of Charbroils, Brinkmans, and Sunbeams. He has 118 grills in various states of rehabilitation. On some rigs, the grates had rusted out, on others the gas lines had clogged—on his favorite fixer-upper, a $2.95 ignition switch had gone bad on an otherwise perfectly fine $300 twin-burner grill. Down there by the riverside, they were lined up in ruler-straight lines like steel soldiers awaiting orders to be returned to the fire.

"Most backyard grillers have more money than sense, and they toss 'em. It's ridiculous, but that's the American throw-away culture," Doc says.

On some, he simply makes the repairs and gives the rigs to friends and family. But the bulk are too far gone and require radical surgery—for example, he may rip the guts out of a gas grill and convert it to charcoal. "It's easy," Doc said as he picked up a pair of bolt cutters.

He's got a bountiful supply of wire shelves from old refrigerators. He simply uses the bolt cutters to snip the shelf to fit the size of the gas grill box. He props the shelf off the bottom of the gas grill with a couple of firebricks, then lights the charcoal, and in twenty minutes, the reconfigured grill is ready to go to work on a couple of wrist-thick ribeyes.

The weird thing is, from the outside, when you close the lid, most of Doc's contraptions look like they just came off a display rack at Lowe's.

Doc is like a lovably deranged EMT with a set of jumper cables waiting on the roadside: "These are perfectly fine cooking rigs," he says. "They just need a jump-start to bring them back to life."

Pork Chop and Steak Sauce

Makes About / Enough For
2 Cups / About 5 lbs. of Meat

DOC HAS MORE GRILLS than anybody in this book, but had surprisingly few recipes. "I do the important stuff—I get the fire and grill ready, and the beer on ice," he says. He generally allows others to prepare the side dishes before he becomes the maestro who applies the meat to the heat. On his custom rig he uses a variety of techniques to cook chicken, ribs, and pork: indirect heat, light hickory smoke, and light basting. He stresses the need for a covered dome smoker/grill that can capture the Holy Trinity: heat, smoke, and moisture.

Doc Hill tends to his chicken on his Hot Rod Rig (note the casket handles) as the sun sets by his camp on the banks of the Catawba River.

"It's just a matter of knowing when it's done. And if you're cooking several different types of meat and one gets finished first, just wrap it in foil and hold it. Make sure you have a good folding chair and some cold beers. Grilling is really not that hard. Just know your meat and your heat."

Here are two sauce recipes that are variations on a vinegar/mustard theme, one created by Doc and one by his wife, Anne.

¼ cup granulated sugar

1 cup ketchup

½ cup firmly packed brown sugar

2 tablespoons Worcestershire sauce

1 tablespoon apple cider vinegar

1 tablespoon prepared yellow mustard

⅛ teaspoon freshly ground black pepper

⅛ teaspoon chili powder

Pinch of red pepper flakes

Mix all the ingredients together in a large saucepan. Bring to a boil, then reduce the heat to very low and simmer for 1 to 2 hours, or until nice and thick. Use immediately, or cover and refrigerate for up to a month.

Anne's Grilled Chicken Sauce

Makes About / **Enough For**
2 Cups / 2 Whole Chickens

ANNE IS DOC'S SCHOOLTEACHER WIFE, and the one who keeps him in line. This is a piquant sauce to perk up backyard grilled chicken. The tartness comes from the vinegar and a double dose of mustard, wet and dry. Chicken treated with this sauce goes well with a crisp salad or creamy coleslaw.

Doc Hill quaffs a cool one in the shade as his meat smokes into nirvana-ville.

1½ cups distilled white vinegar

1 tablespoon salt

½ teaspoon red pepper flakes

3 tablespoons dry mustard

1 teaspoon dried thyme

Tabasco or other hot-pepper sauce to taste

3 tablespoons prepared yellow mustard

5 tablespoons Worcestershire sauce

Mix all the ingredients together in a saucepan. Bring to a boil, then reduce the heat to very low and simmer for 1 to 2 hours, or until slightly thickened. Use immediately, or cover and refrigerate for up to a month.

Carroll Robinson

Culinary legend Jean-Anthelme Brillat-Savarin (1755–1826) opined, "A man can become a cook, but has to be born a *rotisseur.*"

Brillat-Savarin would enjoy a visit to the red brick garage/grill laboratory in which Carroll Robinson builds large, whole-animal rotisseries and smoker/grills.

Robinson was raised on a South Carolina farm. He served in the Navy during World War II, worked in textile and steel mills, painted houses, and upholstered cars. He has slowed down in the past decade—he no longer cruises his 1976 Harley-Davidson Super Glide out on the interstate, but sticks to the backroads of his hometown of York, South Carolina. In his spare time, Carroll is also a shade-tree car mechanic, welder, plumber, brick mason, roofer, electrician—and a cooker of catfish stews, chowders, and whole-hog barbecues.

And, oh yeah, he was a NASCAR fan way before it became cool. He attended his first Daytona race in 1953—drove all night to see it after getting off work at the mill. He's only missed three races since, and those were mostly due to the births of his three daughters.

In his garage in York, all his skills come together. When we met him one evening, he was wearing a pair of grease-monkey overalls and had an unlit cigar in his mouth. The bluish glow of his welding torch illuminated his face and welder's glasses. He looked like a silver-haired, twenty-first-century Michelangelo.

With a ball-peen hammer, drill press, grinder, and welding torch, Robinson can make practically any cooking contraption known to man. And he has, including an oyster steamer made from junkyard iron, a gas burner from an old water heater, a championship pig cooker from a 220-gallon home-heating oil tank, and a charcoal starter that can bring a bag of Kingsford to glowing embers in twelve minutes flat. But his signature piece of scrap-heap art is a six-foot-long rotisserie of angle iron married to an electric motor, upon which he cooks whole lambs, goats, and pigs.

"Well, I saw a picture of one of those rotisserie spits and figured I could make one just as well, if not better," he said, while taking a break from building his newest cooker—a stainless-steel pig cooker heated by propane gas, mounted on a trailer. "The hardest part was setting up the chain drive and the gear reduction for the motor, so that it would turn slowly enough."

Carroll Robinson sits on a welder that he used to build his seven-foot rotisserie driven with his grandchild's bicycle chain. He's roasting a whole lamb basted in a garlic-ginger-rosemary infusion over an oak ember fire.

The results of that effort were beautiful to see: a rectangular iron rig with a two-and-a-half-by-six-foot firebox made from a sheet of 11-gauge steel. It has two angle irons that can be adjusted to hold the rotisserie spear from eighteen to thirty inches above the coals. He used a bicycle chain to turn the sprocket. "Different meats require different cooking heights," Robinson explains. "Lambs are mostly thin, and they'll burn to a crisp—because of their fat and any oil-based marinade you might use—if you place them too close to the fire." He spent about twenty hours putting his rotisserie together and puts a value of about $1,000 on the rig.

Robinson prefers cooking on rotisseries for two principal reasons:

First, time savings. The beauty of a good rotisserie is that the meat bastes itself; by slowly rotating, it catches its own drippings, and the juices are naturally spread over the meat. And you don't have to constantly watch the meat, either, because it doesn't have to be turned and rarely flames up if the cooking height is set correctly.

Second, the Pavlovian response from your guests. Carroll attests that there is nothing more appetizing than watching a browned side of meat slowly turning over a bed of glowing coals, occasionally dripping juice to create a fragrance of angelic smoke. And, he says, if you want to send a guest into paroxysms of ecstasy, stop the rotisserie for a taste test. Slice off a slightly charred, crisp outer piece of meat and offer it to them off the end of a wood-handled fork—or better yet, off your fingertips.

Some rotisserie-meisters use balancing weights on the spit rod to counteract the heavier side of the meat because they feel it can lead to an uneven "spin of the spit." Robinson scoffs at this. On his rig, weights are not necessary because the 7-rpm motor is strong enough to compensate; for added assurance, he binds the meat close to the spit rod.

Robinson's advice for a successful rotisserie of whole animals: Get the spit rod as close as possible to the backbone, and then use baling wire and pliers to cinch the meat as tightly as possible to the rod. Also bind the legs and/or head to the rod so the body does not flop.

"If there is a perfect way to grill meat over an open fire, surely it's the rotisserie," says Carroll. "The meat practically cooks itself, it tastes great, and your guests get to see a great show before the meal is served."

Carroll's Spit-Roasted Lamb

Serves
12

THIS IS FOR PEOPLE who get the big picture when it comes to lamb—and for those who don't. Carroll says people are funny about lamb; sometimes they've had bad experiences with it and just don't want to try it again. Europeans excel at grilling it—usually with a liberal basting of olive oil mixed

with garlic and rosemary—and serve it medium-rare so it resembles fork-tender prime rib. To get past skeptical dinner guests, Carroll sometimes serves a mixed grill of similar-cut cubes of beef, chicken, and lamb. "You'd be surprised at the people who rave over the beef, when what they're really eating is properly grilled lamb," he says.

You can also use this perfect marinade (reduce the amounts accordingly) for a leg of lamb prepared either on a rotisserie or a grill or in the oven.

Carroll's good, but even he relies on an instant-read thermometer—if you don't have one, he says, "invest in one. Your lamb—and your guests—will thank you." A 5-pound leg of lamb cooked at 275°F will be ready in about an hour. A whole lamb will take 2 to 2½ hours. Be sure to start checking the meat with your thermometer early to avoid overcooking. Carroll recommends pulling the meat off the heat at about 115° to 120°F and letting it rest for about 15 minutes to allow the juices to redistribute. The meat temperature will continue to rise another 8 to 10 degrees. Some authorities recommend an internal temperature of at least 160°F to destroy harmful organisms, but at that temperature Carroll says you're likely to end up with "gray, overcooked lamb." You decide.

1 whole lamb, 30 to 35 pounds

10 cloves garlic, cut lengthwise into thirds

About 4 inches thumb-sized fresh ginger, cut into 30 slices ⅛-inch thick

1 quart Allegro marinade or 2 cups olive oil mixed with 2 cups soy sauce

1 large onion, coarsely chopped

Juice of 1 lemon, juiced halves reserved

¼ cup firmly packed brown sugar

6 sprigs rosemary, plus more for garnish

1 tablespoon salt

1 tablespoon freshly ground pepper

Prepare the lamb by making 24 cuts about 1 inch deep and ¾ inch long, spaced evenly across the body, plus 3 cuts in each leg. Insert 1 piece of garlic and 1 piece of ginger in each slit.

In a ceramic bowl or other non-reactive container, combine the marinade, onion, lemon juice and reserved halves, brown sugar, and rosemary sprigs. Place the lamb in a large trash bag and pour the marinade over the lamb, turning to make sure all the meat surfaces are coated with the marinade. Unless you have access to a commercial-size refrigerator, place the trash bag of lamb in a large cooler with a large bag of ice and marinate for at least 4 hours or up to overnight.

Build a fire in a smoker/grill with a rotisserie. Maintain a temperature of about 275°F.

Remove the lamb from the cooler and reserve the marinade. Rub the meat with the salt and pepper. Place the lamb on the rotisserie in the smoker and start the spit. (If you're not using a rotisserie, place in the smoker on the side opposite the coals, and then cook for 2 to 2½ hours.) Transfer the marinade to a saucepan, bring to a boil, and simmer for at least 20 minutes. Use the reduced marinade to baste the meat about every 30 minutes.

Continued . . .

After about 90 minutes, begin checking the temperature of the lamb using an instant-read thermometer inserted in the thickest part. It's important not to overcook lamb; it's best served rare or medium rare. A whole lamb usually takes about 2 to 2½ hours. Remove the lamb from the heat when the thermometer registers about 120°F, tent with aluminum foil, and let rest for about 15 minutes (the temperature will continue to rise; 125°F is rare).

Serve on a large platter, garnished with big sprigs of rosemary.

Carroll's Smoked Wing Dang Doodle

Serves
12

IF YOU LIKE Buffalo wings, you gotta try these wang thangs—they'll make you sit up, bark, beg, and roll over. But be prepared: they're so labor-intensive that when a small Carolina restaurant put these on the menu, their customers got hooked, and the place eventually went out of business because the wings took so much prep time. That won't be a problem for you, because you're just cooking for your buddies. Serve with ample supply of ice-cold brewskies.

50 chicken wings, preferably fresh, cut in half and wing tips removed

2 quarts buttermilk

2 tablespoons Tabasco or other hot-pepper sauce

Peanut oil for frying

2 pints Hooters Wing Sauce or other purchased wing sauce of your choice

Rinse and pat the wings dry. In a large ceramic or other nonreactive bowl, soak the wings in the buttermilk and Tabasco and store in a cooler or refrigerator for at least 4 hours; overnight is preferred.

Build a fire in a smoker/grill for indirect heat. Maintain a temperature of about 250°F. (Carroll likes to soak a couple chunks of hickory in water and toss them onto the hot coals just before putting the wings on the smoker/grill.)

Pour oil into a large, cast-iron skillet to a depth of about ½ inch and heat over medium-high heat until almost smoking. Carefully place the chicken in the skillet using tongs—not a fork—taking care to not crowd the skillet; fry in batches, or use multiple skillets. Cook until golden brown, about 10 to 12 minutes, turning once.

Repeat until all the wings are fried. Drain on paper towels or brown paper bags, then place in a large bowl. Pour the wing sauce over the wings and toss gently to coat.

Place the wings in the cooker on the side opposite the coals for 45 minutes. Serve immediately.

Molly, Maggie & Krista Serpi

Leave it to the Girl Scouts, whose motto is "Be Prepared," to design an outdoor contraption that's so cunningly simple, it leaves the rest of us wondering why we bother dragging our Coleman stoves along on camping trips.

Maggie and Molly Serpi, both preteens, built a portable box stove to earn their Girl Scout proficiency badges in cooking. It works like this: You take a sturdy box—Maggie got hers from a liquor store—and fold back the flaps. Take a metal rack from a toaster oven or grill and place it inside the box atop four empty cans to make a shelf. Line the box with aluminum foil. Just before cooking, place hot charcoal in a pan and put it at the bottom of the stove. The food cooks on the rack above.

The whole thing took about an hour to assemble, Maggie says, but that's only because all fifteen girls in the troop helped build it during a weekly Girl Scout meeting.

"It was very cool, being in fourth grade and cooking our food," she says. "It just made things taste better because we did it ourselves."

Maggie has used the oven to bake brownies and cupcakes. She insists it would work equally well for breads, biscuits, and birthday cakes. The bigger the box you make—hers is eighteen inches square—the more food you can cook.

Maggie's mom, Krista, who is also her troop leader, remembers making her own box oven thirty years ago. Whenever she teaches the girls how to make it, she says, they start out skeptical.

"At first they look at you and say, 'This is never gonna work.' But once you open the oven and see those golden biscuits staring you in the face, they just can't believe they were able to do it."

Cooking in the wilderness has changed her daughters' view of food, Krista says. "At home, if they see a piece of toast that's burned, they won't touch it. At camp, because they made it themselves in a box, they'll eat something that looks like charcoal."

Although it's small and homely, you still need to be careful when using a box oven. It should always be placed in a fire ring with rocks around it, Maggie says, not on top of a picnic table where someone can knock it over. Keep the smaller kids away from it. And wear oven mitts when handling the pans, since the temperature of the charcoal can reach 350°F, just like a regular oven.

Who needs iron? Sisters Maggie and Molly Serpi show how to cook in a foil-lined cardboard contraption cooker.

Even if you're not a Scout, a box oven is a handy thing to have around the house in case of an emergency. When everyone in town was fretting over Y2K, Krista says, the girls in her troop were confident that the oven would see them through.

Of course, these ovens don't last forever. They can get crushed when camping gear goes in and out of the car, and cardboard won't stand up to the heat indefinitely. But they give you a good run: Maggie's oven is going on five years now, and Krista figures it's nearing the end of its natural life span. Long after it gets trashed, though, Krista's kids will still remember what it taught them.

"It's about taking care of yourself and being self-sufficient," she says. "If that can stick with them twenty years from now when they get in a bind, that's a good thing."

Box Oven Blueberry Muffins

Makes 12 Muffins

GIRL SCOUT RECIPES are rarely exact, since preteens and teens who find themselves in the wilderness tend to use what they can scrounge up and hope it works. The Girl Scout troop that Krista Serpi leads in Waynesboro, Pennsylvania, is very budget-conscious and tends to buy its ingredients at discount grocery chains. This recipe for blueberry muffins is one Krista picked up while training to become a troop leader more than a decade ago.

2 cups all-purpose flour

1 cup sugar, plus 1 tablespoon

1 tablespoon baking powder

1 teaspoon salt

½ teaspoon ground nutmeg

2 eggs, beaten

½ cup milk

½ cup (1 stick) butter, melted

¾ cup blueberries, fresh or dried

¼ cup sliced almonds

1 tablespoon sugar

Place 10 charcoal briquettes in a metal pan and light until they glow. Slide them into the box oven. Or, preheat a conventional oven to 400°F.

Mix the flour, 1 cup sugar, baking powder, salt, and nutmeg in a small bowl. Scoop out 1 tablespoon of the mixture and set aside.

In a separate bowl, combine the eggs, milk, and melted butter. Add to the dry ingredients and stir until well moistened.

In another bowl, toss the blueberries with the 1 tablespoon reserved flour mixture. Stir into the batter. Spoon the batter into a 12-cup muffin tin lined with paper liners. Sprinkle with the almonds and the 1 tablespoon sugar.

Bake for 15 minutes, or until a toothpick inserted in the center of a muffin comes out clean. Serve warm.

Brown Bears in the Orchard

Serves **20**

THIS WHIMSICALLY NAMED DISH is really a version of an upside-down cake. Members of Krista Serpi's Girl Scout troop had been trying to earn their proficiency badge in outdoor cooking for two years, but couldn't because the area was under drought restrictions and open fires were banned. Over the weekend the restrictions were lifted, it rained—but the girls made the cake anyway. "The girls said it was the best cake they'd ever tasted in their lives, because they were so cold," Serpi laughs. "Gingerbread feels so homey, it makes you feel like you're warm inside."

Two 12-ounce jars applesauce

1 box (14½ ounces) gingerbread cake mix

1 egg

1¼ cups water

Place 8 or 9 charcoal briquettes in a metal pan and light until they glow. Slide into the box oven. Or, preheat a conventional oven to 350°F.

Pour the applesauce into a 9-by-13-inch baking dish (if the box oven isn't big enough to hold it, use smaller dishes and divide the mixture accordingly).

Prepare the gingerbread mix with the egg and water as directed on the package, then pour on top of the applesauce and smooth the top. Do not stir.

Cover the dish with aluminum foil and bake for about 30 minutes, or until a toothpick inserted in the center comes out clean. Let cool slightly, then invert and serve.

Steve Watts

Steve Watts is an outdoor kitchen magician.

Parachute him into the wilderness and he'll be cooking by the end of the day, without a pot, pan, or matches. While almost all modern cooking contraptions are made of metal, remember: primitive man had nothing but stone, bone, and wood. And like primitive man, Watts uses the forest as his kitchen hardware store.

For the movie *Cast Away* with Tom Hanks, Watts was the guy who came up with the idea for the coconut canteen, the ice-skate ax, the videotape rope, and even Wilson, the volleyball with a face.

"I guess it was my twenty seconds of fame," says Watts, who was a technical consultant on the movie. "It was a matter of survival, and what it comes down to is a reliance on primitive technologies."

Watts has a master's degree in divinity from Duke University; he is the author of *Practicing Primitive: A Handbook of Aboriginal Skills* and has been director of Aboriginal Studies at the Schiele Museum of Natural History in Gastonia, North Carolina, since 1984. Clearly, he has delved deeply into how primitive man lived, survived, and even ate. He credits his early interest in the primitive to his days with Boy Scout Troop 5 in Cherryville, North Carolina, which was led by his dad, Olin S. Watts.

"He made it interesting. In the woods, he thought like a kid," Watts said with a laugh one winter morning, while we watched him tending a hobo fire. "In the woods, you can get a kid's attention with food. Tarzan steaks cooked on hot rocks—what kid would not love that?"

He also has an interest in what is known as woodcraft and the golden age of camping in America, 1890–1920. The founding fathers of this movement were men like Daniel Carter Beard and Ernest Thompson Seton, who helped organize the Boy Scouts of America. The art was also practiced and perfected on a daily basis by the hobos of the Depression era, who camped practically every night in the woods. They cooked and ate using what they could find—tin cans and pocketknife forks.

Watts has written about these primitive contraption cookers: "[Hobos] knew the smell of wood smoke and the taste of honest grub cooked over the flames and embers of mankind's oldest friend—the campfire. They possessed the skill to fashion cooking tools and gizmos from the woods and the tin-can castoffs

Steve Watts cooks a hobo breakfast of eggs and bacon on top of a No. 10 can, fueled by a handful of twigs.

of early-twentieth-century America. Their focus was on skill and the cooking and eating pleasures of traditional camp life—not some freeze-dried concoction boiled up on a $200 five-ounce stove."

Watts acknowledges that this style of camping "left lots of footprints" in the woods, but he argues that these woodsmen experienced a direct relationship with the natural resources that were available to them. And they did so, he writes, without the "highly efficient technological wonders of the twenty-first century" (much of which are made from nonrenewable resources).

Next to the crackling oak fire, Watts sat on his haunches and turned a split-bamboo spit of salmon to the color of a fire-broiled orange. When it was done, he broke off a moist, charred chunk and handed it to us piping hot.

No fork needed.

Fillet of Salmon on a Split Stick

Serves
1

THIS RECIPE REPRESENTS the essence of what Watts has leaned about how primitive humans cooked. He developed it by studying the tools that were available at the time, then improvised until he landed on a workable primitive cooking rig. "They were ingenious because they had to be, in order to survive," he told us as he fashioned a miniature grill of bent limbs to support a fillet of fish. This recipe's secret is that there is nothing to get in the way of the flavor of the grilled fish. Besides a slab of salmon, everything he needed, from tools to heat, he found in the woods.

Watts laughed when asked about the meat's smoky flavor. "Primitive man wasn't concerned about inserting gourmet wood smoke onto his meat; the smoke was just a by-product of cooking over an open fire."

The smoke on this fish may have been unintentional, but it still resonated through every morsel.

1 salmon fillet, about 6 inches long, pin bones removed, skin intact

Salt and pepper

1 lime, halved

Build a hardwood fire and let the flames die down to a good bed of coals.

Find a straight 5-foot-long limb of nonresinous wood such as bamboo or oak, about 1½ inches in diameter. Using a sharp knife, skin the bark off of about 1 foot of one end. Using the knife and a mallet or fist-sized stone, carefully split the limb into quarters for about 15 inches, starting at the skinned end.

From thin branches of nonresinous wood, cut 3 or 4 skewers about 6 inches long. Run the skewers in and out the width of the fish. Slide the fillet lengthwise into the split in the limb. Tie the loose ends of the split stick together gently with string to hold the fish secure, soaking the string first so it won't catch on fire. (Watts is a stickler for authenticity; he used thin, green vines gathered from the woods, but he says it's acceptable to substitute kitchen string.)

Find a sturdy forked stick and drive it into the ground next to the fire so that the crook of the fork is 8 to 10 inches above the coals. Place the tied-off end of the cooking stick in the V of the fork. Hold the spit so the fish is horizontal over the hot coals. Cook, rotating a few turns, until the fish is crisp, nicely charred, and nearly opaque throughout, about 4 to 5 minutes per side.

Season with salt and pepper and squeeze lime juice over it. Untie the fish and eat it right off the stick.

Hobo Jungle Breakfast

Serves
1

WHAT A FUN WAY to turn a kid on to cooking outdoors—preparing a yummy breakfast using a can and a forked stick. Watts said this was a standard on his Boy Scout campouts. You'll need a clean No. 10 can (the large cafeteria size, about 6 inches in diameter). To cut the can, use a regular can opener to remove the top of the can, an old-style can opener with a triangular cutting edge to make vent holes, and a pair of sheet metal shears to cut a door for the fire.

1 No. 10 can, contents removed

2 eggs

2 strips bacon

Using a can opener, remove one end of the can. At the open edge, cut a 3-by-4-inch hole in the side with metal shears to make a door for the fire. With an old-style can opener, cut several holes for ventilation on the can's side, opposite of the fire hole.

Place the can, hole side down, on a flat stable surface. Gather some dry twigs and small kindling, place inside the can, and light.

Find a small forked branch to turn the bacon.

Place the bacon on top of the can and begin frying. Turn the bacon as needed. When the bacon begins to crisp, loosely drape it around the edges of the can to form a "fence." Crack the eggs in the center of the can and fry until done. Wearing gloves, lift the can off the fire. Breakfast is ready!

Tarzan Steak

Serves
1

STEVE WATTS'S DAD developed this dish while he was leader of a Boy Scout troop. It's a lot of fun for kids making their first foray into the woods for an overnight camping trip. What could be better than cooking on hot rocks?

Note: A pair of heavy leather gloves should be used to pick up the hot rocks.

1 round steak, about ½ pound and about ½ inch thick

Salt and pepper

Build a hardwood fire and let the flames die down to a good bed of coals.

Find 2 smooth, flat rocks about the size of your palm (don't use porous rocks because they may split when heated). Place the rocks on the coals and heat for about 10 minutes.

Wearing gloves, remove the rocks from the fire (be careful, they're very hot). Brush the ashes off with the back of a glove.

Place the steak on one rock and put the other rock on top of it. Let it sit; it should be cooked to medium-rare in 5 to 6 minutes. Season it with the salt and pepper and eat it like Tarzan would—with your hands.

RIG IN A SACK

The global barbecue circuit has more than its share of full-blown eccentrics, but the king of them all could well be Jaan Habicht, a Ph.D. in molecular biology from Estonia. Arriving at the 2004 Jack Daniel's Invitational in Lynchburg, Tennessee, Habicht climbed out of a cab carrying a rather large round container wrapped in a cotton sheet and secured with duct tape.

"Theese is my pig cooker. All I need is meat and a match," he said as he unveiled a lime green 55-gallon barrel. He paused and then snapped his fingers: "Wait a second, no photos until I put my chef's suit on." Then he stripped to his underwear, near thousands of people, and put on a black jumpsuit. "Now let us cook, my American friends."

This guy had just flown eighteen hours from the former Soviet Union with a barrel in which he said he was going to cook a pig. How he got past airport security on two continents with what looked like a drum of enriched nuclear plutonium was a mystery.

The only way to describe the rig that Habicht assembled on a grass field near a group of hairy bikers grilling hot dogs is to call it the Swiss Army knife of pig cookers.

He carefully dismantled the barrel and reassembled it into a two-level cooker, with a firebox on the bottom connected by two stovepipes to the smoker barrel on top. It was an amazing feat (and if you don't think so, try hauling your smoker to Moscow).

"It is engineered to the most exacting standards; I've applied for a patent," he said. "It will revolutionize barbecue on a global scale. You will be able to travel anywhere in the world with your pig cooker."

And he managed to cook some incredibly tasty pork, basting it with papaya, which, he explained, you must "get at molecular level to tenderize the tissue of the pork." He also had some kind of blackberry-currant-cherry dipping sauce that was out of this world.

There's actually an organization called the SSBS (Secret Soviet Barbecue Society), he told us, and proceeded to list his international barbecue credentials from "Sweden, Ireland, Jamaica—it is a barbecue world." Then he was swept up by a contingent of festival-goers drinking paper cups of whiskey (in this decidedly dry county with a distillery) and disappeared.

Reg Pelletier

From far away, Reg Pelletier's smoker looks like a miniature barn with a tiny silo on top. Just like barns are repositories for everything on a farm from tractors to potato sacks, Reg's rig can smoke everything from olives to ribs.

Although born and raised in Canada and now residing on the Canadian side of Niagara Falls, Reg has become an expert in cooking Southern-style barbecue and an ambassador of the cuisine to his countrymen and -women, who, he says, still don't understand the difference between grilling and barbecuing. "To them, it's all the same," he says. "They don't get the low and slow part. They just don't."

When we met Reg, it was hard to believe that a guy who tends to pepper every sentence with "eh?" instead of "y'all" and lives in the frozen tundra of the North instead of the languid heat of the South could master the finer points of American barbecue—until he revealed how he did it: by scouring the Internet for all the recipes he could find and teaching himself how to prepare them.

A caterer by trade after years in the construction business, Pelletier says he needed an impressive contraption to show folks he knew his 'cue: "You are what you cook on. If you show up with a classy machine, people expect the best out of you." And so he built one.

Pelletier spent years working out the diagram for his dream rig in his head, then enlisted the help of a welder buddy to put his plans to work. The finished product is seven feet wide from fender to fender and, he says, extremely easy to work on. Both a cold and a hot smoker, it's been featured in a barbecue magazine, and at least one fellow chef has copied the design. Pelletier says he's gotten offers as high as $5,000 for it, but won't ever sell. "It's too valuable to me," he says. "It just brings interest from everywhere."

He's won a slew of barbecue contests cooking on the rig, including the Home Cooking from the Homeland category of the Jack Daniel's World Championship Invitational Barbecue contest in Lynchburg, Tennessee. For that competition, he made a memorable pork loin roast with barbecued acorn squash and beat out teams from England, Germany, and Switzerland. In addition to his guest appearances on television food shows, he's also lectured at the Niagara Culinary Institute at Niagara College, where professors invited him to provide barbecue tips for their "pork symposium."

Janice Pelletier with her husband Reg's cooker at the Jack Daniel's World Championship Invitational.

One of those 'cue-centric chef professors, Peter Blakeman, describes Pelletier's smoker as "quite unique," a virtual buffet of steel and smoke. With the twist of a handle, Pelletier can control the air flow into his smoker. He uses a lever to open and close his firebox, which allows him to maintain a consistent temperature—crucial for cooking unforgettable meat. That's a lot different from the ceramic egg-shaped grills that many Canadians are used to, which work by trapping heat more like a tandoori oven than a finely tuned instrument.

Pelletier's rig isn't particularly polished or attractive, but Reg is a wizard with it. "He hasn't jazzed it up with fancy chimneys," Blakeman says. "You've got some crazy rigs out there—some of them could be rolling trailers for NASCAR. But when you look at a champion, does he want all those fancy bells and whistles?"

The college has a commercial smoker, but Blakeman hopes to persuade Pelletier to build them something of higher quality—something like his own. "It's kind of like the difference between commercial food and homemade," Blakeman says. "Industrial smokers work great, but they don't quite have the touch of his homemade smoker. For me, it's a better way to cook."

Award-Winning Pork Loin

Serves
8

REG PELLETIER BLAMES the low-fat craze for making pork so lean that it's virtually tasteless. He's lucky—for years, he ate the hogs his father-in-law raised, so he knows what good pork should taste like. For folks who can't head to Canada for a taste, he suggests using the finishing glaze in this recipe, since it makes the hog really flavorful.

1 bone-in pork loin, about 8 pounds

1 batch Basic Brine (page 94)

Reg's Rub

2 tablespoons onion powder

2 tablespoons garlic powder

2 tablespoons paprika

2 tablespoons ground white pepper

2 tablespoons ground black pepper

2 tablespoons chili powder

Finishing Glaze

½ cup port wine jelly (or grape jelly, in a pinch)

½ cup purchased barbecue sauce of your choice

2 tablespoons cider vinegar

Juice of ½ lemon

Continued . . .

Brine the loin for 24 hours in a refrigerator or large cooler.

Build a fire in a smoker/grill for indirect heat. Maintain a temperature of about 275°F.

To make the rub, combine the ingredients in a small bowl. Remove the pork from the brine and pat dry. Season the loin all over with the rub. Place the loin in the smoker on the side opposite the coals and smoke until a thermometer inserted in the center registers 150° to 155°F, about 2½ hours.

Meanwhile, make the glaze: in a small saucepan over low heat, whisk together the jelly, barbecue sauce, vinegar, and lemon juice and cook, whisking, for 3 to 4 minutes, until warmed and smooth.

About 10 minutes before the loin is finished, open the cooker and brush with 3 or 4 separate coats of the glaze.

When the pork loin is done, transfer to a carving board and tent with aluminum foil. Let rest for 10 minutes, then carve and serve.

Basic Brine

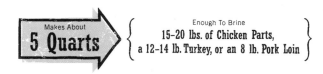

Makes About **5 Quarts**

Enough To Brine
15-20 lbs. of Chicken Parts,
a 12-14 lb. Turkey, or an 8 lb. Pork Loin

REG PELLETIER has won a slew of barbecue awards on both sides of the U.S.-Canadian border, so he knows what he's talking about when he says this brine is essential to making top-quality chicken, turkey, or pork loin. It helped him pick up a trophy at the 2004 Jack Daniel's World Championship Invitational Barbecue Contest in Lynchburg, Tennessee.

5 quarts water

1 cup coarse salt such as kosher

1 cup firmly packed brown sugar

1 large onion, cut into quarters

2 stalks celery, cut into chunks

3 bay leaves

4 cloves garlic

1 tablespoon peppercorns

Combine the ingredients in a large pot and bring to a rolling boil. Cook for 10 minutes, or until the onion is soft. Pour through a strainer and discard the solids.

If brining a turkey, place the bird in a 2-gallon plastic pail or other large nonreactive container, pour the brine over it, and refrigerate for 12 to 16 hours. If using chicken parts, pour brine over the parts in a bowl and refrigerate for 4 to 6 hours. For pork loin, brine and refrigerate for 24 hours.

Smoked Turkey on a Throne

Serves
16

THIS IS A VARIATION of "beer can chicken," using a turkey instead. The steam from the throne provides an extra source of heat, which combines with the smoker to make the turkey extra-moist inside. This method makes a lot of sense, Reg says, when you're trying to satisfy family members who want white meat and dark meat, which finish cooking at different temperatures. He's used it since the early 1990s.

1 turkey, 12 to 14 pounds

1 batch Basic Brine (facing page)

1 batch Reg's Rub (page 93)

Canola oil for brushing

Throne

1 cup chicken stock

1 small onion, cut into quarters

3 cloves garlic

1 bay leaf

5 fresh sage leaves

Continued . . .

Brine the turkey for 12 to 16 hours in a refrigerator or large cooler. Remove and pat dry. Place the bird back in the refrigerator for 3 to 4 hours to dry out the skin.

Build a fire in a smoker/grill for indirect heat. Maintain a temperature of about 275°F.

To make the throne, in an empty 14- to 19-ounce galvanized steel can, combine the chicken stock, onion, garlic, bay leaf, and sage leaves. Fit the cavity of the turkey over the can, legs down, so the bird appears to be dancing.

Brush a thick coat of oil over the bird and season liberally with the rub.

Place the turkey on its throne in the smoker and smoke until an instant-read thermometer inserted in the center of the breast registers 155°F degrees, or 175° to 180°F in a thigh away from the bone, about 5 hours.

Remove from the throne, transfer to a platter, and tent with aluminum foil. Let rest for 10 minutes, then carve and serve.

HOSANNAS FOR A HOMEMADE RIG

Mark Hyman is a great example of someone who doesn't need a fancy rig to win a major barbecue contest. He won the prestigious American Royal Invitational in 2005 with a rig built from a trash barrel—the same one that folks once made fun of.

"I can't say enough good things about it," he gushes. "It's taken me from the bottom to where I am now."

As Hyman says, the cooker is so simple, it's stupid. You dump a bunch of briquettes in the bottom of the barrel, light them with charcoal starter, add some fruitwood like oak or apple, wait for about forty-five minutes until the barrel hits 325°F, throw your meat on a grill, and you're good to go. It's all direct heat. No sitting up tending meat for hours the night before, nursing your way through a hangover and wondering why you're out there in the rain or wind or whatever, next to guys with $20,000 smokers and tricked-out trailers and corporate sponsors.

"Barbecue's about going with the bare essentials and using what you have," Hyman says. "I don't have a lot of money and I definitely don't have a lot of time. I keep it as simple as I can."

Hyman's modesty masks a ferocious commitment to the craft of 'cue. Every time he cooks, he notes down the date, temperature, and climate conditions. His journals go back more than a decade. He mentors other cooks and works a second job helping a friend sell barbecue out of a concession stand. Even though Hyman's a champion, he still talks wistfully about learning his friend's tricks of the trade to someday make a go of opening his own barbecue business.

Hyman can tell you highly technical information about the air-to-fuel ratio needed to cook great chicken, and will even share the recipe that won him $12,000 and a shiny Kingfisher grill—exactly the type of smoker his rivals cooked on to try to beat him in the Royal. Hyman plans to use it, but don't expect him to junk his prize-winning trash barrel.

"That's my baby," he says happily. "I've never had any problems with it, whether it be cold or windy or rainy. I can fire it up and I know how it's gonna react every time."

HYMAN'S WINNING CHICKEN

Serves 8 to 10

❧ *2 cups Italian dressing*
❧ *3 pounds chicken thighs*

RUB

❧ *3 tablespoons coarsely ground pepper*
❧ *3 tablespoons onion powder*
❧ *3 tablespoons garlic powder*
❧ *1$^{1}/_{2}$ tablespoons paprika*
❧ *3 tablespoons Lawry's seasoned salt*

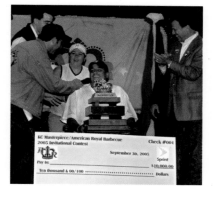

Pour the dressing into a large zippered plastic bag. Add the chicken and seal. Refrigerate for at least 24 hours.

Preheat a smoker to 325°F.

In a bowl, stir together all the rub ingredients. Take the chicken out of the bag and sprinkle the rub on all sides.

Cook for 1 hour, turning every 15 minutes. Remove from the smoker and serve. Accept extravagant compliments graciously.

Jimmy Hagood

It's called the Big Red Rig and you can spot it in traffic ten blocks away. It's the ultimate way to stand out in a stadium parking lot of tailgaters: a bright red, two-level, thirty-foot trailer with two massive cookers and a spiral staircase.

Did we mention the 500-watt stereo system and poles that hoist state flags forty feet off the ground?

"It definitely gets people's attention," says Jimmy Hagood, a caterer and championship barbecuer from Charleston, South Carolina. He traces his family's roots to David Maybank, who arrived in Charleston in 1670.

The one-of-a-kind rig was built by barbecue impresario Frank Collins as a marketing tool and ultimate portable catering kitchen; Hagood bought it from Collins in the spring of 2005.

The heart of Hagood's rig is his two cookers. The first is a Jedmaster rotisserie with five rotating shelves that can hold up to 5 pork shoulders or 125 pieces of chicken. It has an ingenious "ring of fire," which can keep the heat at a constant 230°F for up to ten hours without tending. The narrow ring of charcoal that surrounds the rotisserie gradually spreads its heat from coal to coal like a long fuse. "I like the convenience of gas, but I don't want to cook on it because I miss the charcoal taste. And I don't have time to be reloading hot charcoal onto a cooker every hour or so . . . This is the perfect solution for me."

On the rear of the rig is a traditional 200-gallon converted-fuel-drum cooker with an offset firebox in the rear. "In my business," Hagood says, "you have to have a rig large enough to cook a whole hog, and this cooker gives me the versatility I need as a caterer." He prefers cooking over wood when possible; he smokes with pecan, peach, hickory, mesquite, and apple.

Like many barbecuers, Hagood's first experience with smoked meat was tinged with alcohol. "It was your typical frat boy thing: dig a hole in the ground, build a fire, try not to burn the pig, and drink as much beer as you can," he says with a laugh.

Well into his thirties, barbecuing and cooking was no more than a weekend dalliance for Hagood. Then he met cooking mentor Nick Zervos, with whom he worked in the insurance business.

"We'd be out on the road and we wouldn't talk insurance, we'd talk cooking," Hagood says. "Nick could do it all—barbecues, Brunswick stews, and pork

Jimmy Hagood climbs the spiral staircase of his two-story Big Red Rig with a smoked pork shoulder.

hashes. He was a silent partner in a couple of restaurants. He's food-crazy." Their bond over food was a catalyst for the two men. They mounted a couple of cookers onto trailers and began to hit the weekend barbecue circuit.

Things really began to percolate in 1995, when Hagood won second place in the Whole Hog category at the Southeastern Wildlife Exposition. In 2001, he was a lottery pick to compete at the Memphis in May barbecue contest, where he placed eighth in the pork shoulder category.

And then in 2002, he came to a personal and culinary crossroads—in the space of forty-five days, he got married (he has three children from a prior marriage), won the Wildlife Exposition's Grand Championship in barbecue, quit his insurance job, and became a full-time caterer.

He likens the transition to navigating a boat into port. "I didn't just jump into it. It was like I was following the signs, the green and red navigational lights that lead you into Charleston Harbor. Pretty soon, I could see the church steeples and I knew this was the route I needed to take in my life," he says.

It sure seems like he was right. He's launched his own line of barbecue sauces and dry rubs, and his company, Tidewater Foods and Catering, is booked practically every weekend year-round for oyster roasts, barbecues, and shrimp boils. In the fall, he stays busy during football weekends at the University of South Carolina, Clemson, and the Citadel, and Carolina Panthers football games.

And it keeps getting better: At the time of this writing, Hagood, at age fifty, and his wife, Anne Marie, were expecting their first child.

Brown Paper Bag Baby Back Ribs

Serves

★ **6-8** ★

JIMMY COMPILED THIS RECIPE from a half-dozen rib recipes he's picked up from barbecue competitions across the South. When asked to explain the significance of the brown paper bag, he shrugs his shoulders. "I can't. I just know it works. It must be something about holding the heat in while allowing the meat to breathe, or maybe it's just the magic of Kraft brown paper bags."

Most barbecuers on the competition circuit remove the white membrane from the insides of pork ribs before smoking. Hagood has experimented with a variety of tools, including slot-head screwdrivers, fork handles, and butter knives. But he believes the best tool is a pair of flattened needle-nose pliers, which can be found in most hardware stores. Another worthwhile tool for rib smokers is a rib rack, available at kitchen and grillware stores. It helps produce perfect ribs by allowing the chef to stack several racks of ribs sideways, which exposes the ribs more fully to smoke on all surfaces, and it also conserves the limited grill space on most cookers. But if you do not want to invest in one, put the ribs directly on the grate.

Hagood recommends his BlackJack brand of rubs and sauces to finish these ribs (see Sources, page 284).

4 racks baby back pork ribs, about 1 pound each

¼ cup barbecue dry rub, purchased or homemade

½ cup vinegar-based barbecue sauce

½ cup tomato-based barbecue sauce

Prepare the ribs by pulling off the thin, silvery membrane on their underside, using needle-nose pliers or a flat-head screwdriver.

Wash the ribs in cold water, pat dry, and lay them in a pan. Sprinkle dry rub on each side (for extra spicy ribs, rub in the spices on the edges). Let stand at room temperature for at least 30 minutes or up to 1 hour.

Soak 2 cups of wood chips (preferably hickory or mesquite) in a bucket of water. Remove the upper grill grate of your smoker/grill and set aside.

Fill a charcoal chimney, light, and let burn until the coals are covered in a light ash. Place a 10-by-12-inch aluminum foil pan filled halfway with water in the center of the lower grate and distribute the charcoal evenly on two sides of the pan. Drain the wood chips and drop a handful on the coals.

Replace the upper grill grate. Position the ribs on rib racks or directly on the grate in the center of the grill above the aluminum pan; the meat should not be directly over any coals.

Cover the grill and open the top vents two-thirds of the way. Initially, the heat inside the grill will probably hover around 350°F. Over the 2-hour cooking period, it will drop to about 250°F. If the temperature falls below 230°F, add another pound of charcoal.

Cook until the meat begins to pull back from the ends of the rib bones, about 2 hours. Remove the ribs from the grill and mop with the vinegar sauce, then wrap them tightly and completely covered in aluminum foil. Put the foil-wrapped ribs in a heavy-duty brown paper bag and fold the bag over the ribs. Let rest at room temperature for 1 hour.

Remove the ribs from the foil and cut into 2-bone sections. Mop with the tomato-based barbecue sauce and serve.

Grilled Bacon-Wrapped Quail

{ As An Appetizer } / { As A Main Course }

Serves 4 / Serves 2

QUAIL, OR BOBWHITE, are plentiful in the South, and Hagood pays regional homage to the minuscule game birds in this dish. Commercially raised quail are available in some grocery stores, and in a pinch you could substitute Cornish hens. You may also want to check with a gourmet specialty store or butcher shop to see if they can be special-ordered. This dish was developed for a backyard kettle-type grill, which Hagood also carries on his Big Rig trailer.

4 quail, about ⅓ pound each

2 cups marinade of your choice, preferably BlackJack Marinade sauce

1 teaspoon chopped fresh thyme

1 teaspoon chopped fresh rosemary

1 teaspoon chopped fresh basil

1 small yellow onion, cut into quarters

4 strips bacon

Salt and freshly ground pepper

Put the quail in a nonreactive dish, add the marinade, and turn to coat. Place in the refrigerator and marinate for about 12 hours.

Remove upper grill grate of your smoker/grill and set aside.

Fill a charcoal chimney, light, and let burn until the coals are covered in a light ash.

Remove the quail from the marinade and set aside. Transfer the marinade to a small saucepan and simmer over low heat for about 15 minutes. Meanwhile, soak 4 toothpicks in a small bowl of water.

Sprinkle the herbs evenly over the quail. Place an onion quarter in the body cavity of each bird. Drain the toothpicks, wrap a bacon strip around each bird, and secure with toothpicks. Season with the salt and pepper to taste.

Place a 10-by-12-inch aluminum foil pan filled halfway with water in the center of the lower grate and distribute the charcoal evenly on two sides of the pan.

Replace the upper grill grate. Place the quail in the center of the grill above the aluminum pan; they should not be directly over any coals. Grill until the quail begin to brown, about 18 to 20 minutes, turning several times with tongs and basting often and liberally with the cooked marinade.

Move the quail directly over the coals and grill, turning several times, until the quail begin to crisp, 5 to 8 minutes longer. Remove from the grill, remove the toothpicks, and serve.

Shrimp and Sausage Gumbo

Serves **10** { As A First Course } / { As A Main Dish } Serves **5**

THIS IS ONE OF Hagood's favorite hearty dishes, perfect for a winter dinner party. Try to get the freshest local shrimp that you can find. Serve this as an appetizer in small cups or over rice as a main dish with a crisp green salad and crusty bread.

¾ cup vegetable oil

¾ cup all-purpose flour

2 yellow onions, chopped

1 green bell pepper, seeded and chopped

1 cup diced smoked sausage, such as andouille

5 bay leaves

1 teaspoon cayenne pepper

8 cups chicken stock

1 pound medium shrimp, peeled and deveined

Salt and freshly ground black pepper to taste

Tabasco, or other hot-pepper sauce

1 tablespoon filé gumbo powder

Continued ...

Jimmy Hagood readies the fire for his Big Red Rig beneath the serpentine limbs of a live oak at the McLeod Plantation in Charleston, South Carolina.

In a large, heavy stockpot, heat the oil over medium heat.

Whisk the flour into the hot oil and stir constantly for 15 to 20 minutes to make a dark brown roux.

Add the onions, bell pepper, sausage, bay leaves, and cayenne and continue cooking for 12 to 15 minutes, stirring occasionally, until the vegetables are wilted.

Add the stock slowly, stirring to blend with the roux.

Reduce the heat to very low and simmer for 1 hour, stirring occasionally, to allow the flavors to deepen. Add the shrimp and cook until opaque, about 10 minutes.

Season to taste with salt, pepper, and Tabasco. Remove and discard the bay leaves.

Ladle into bowls and serve, sprinkled with the filé gumbo powder.

Note: Filé powder is made from ground sassafras leaves and is used as a thickener and flavor enhancer in Creole cooking. It has a woodsy flavor and should only be added once the gumbo has been removed from the heat, because when heated it becomes stringy and tough.

Dee Dee's Coleslaw

Serves
12

THIS RECIPE CAME FROM Jimmy's mama, Derrill "Dee Dee" Maybank Hagood. It's a flavorful twist on a traditional side dish. The Jerusalem artichoke relish gives it an unexpected zip and texture, and helps make this slaw a perfect foil to smoky meats.

1 large green cabbage, about 1½ pounds, cored and shredded

½ cup shredded carrots

½ cup shredded purple cabbage

1 cup mayonnaise

1 cup purchased Jerusalem artichoke relish, preferably Mrs. Sassard's

Salt and freshly ground pepper

In a large bowl, combine all the ingredients and toss to mix thoroughly.

Refrigerate for at least 1 hour to allow the flavors to blend. Serve cold.

Kay Moss

Kay Moss was introduced to the art of contraption cooking at an early age by her father, Paul Kincaid, a Boy Scout troop leader in Gastonia, North Carolina.

"Cooking over an open fire was always natural to me because he was always cooking barbecues and chicken stews," says Moss, coauthor of *The Backcountry Housewife: A Study of Eighteenth-Century Foods.* "But the most important thing he taught me was that cooking is fun, and that has stayed with me a lifetime."

Moss is an expert on fireplace cookery. She annually teaches a weeklong workshop on open-hearth cooking at the John C. Campbell Folk School in Brasstown, North Carolina. She also has an amazing collection of eighteenth- and nineteenth-century iron cooking implements: Dutch ovens, skillets, rotisseries, grills, and trivets. One of her cooking rigs is an ingenious small-bird roaster—basically a large spoon with an extended handle that curves upward and is attached to the handle of the fork (see page 268). You put the bird on the fork by the fireplace, and the spoon catches the drippings.

"That's the kind of thing you learn when you start studying fireplace cooking: they were very innovative with the iron cookware they had," says Moss.

Her grandmother experienced the American kitchen's transition from wood-stove cooking to electric ranges, and Moss remembers her reaction.

"My dad bought her an electric stove, but it just stayed over in the corner," says Moss, a former schoolteacher who worked more than two decades as a historical interpreter at the Schiele Museum of Natural History in Gastonia, North Carolina. "Maybe she boiled some water on it, but she stuck with her wood fire."

Moss says one of the most important skills in hearthside cooking is "managing your fire." Her tips:

🌿 Make a fire only large enough for what you need to cook.

🌿 Create new hot coals while simultaneously cooking one dish, because you will need the coals for the next course.

Kay Moss cooks in a log cabin fireplace at the Schiele Museum in Gastonia, North Carolina.

🌿 Know which woods make the best coals. This varies locally; in the South, oak and hickory make the best coals (see page 283 for more on wood).

For someone new to fireplace cooking, she suggests starting with something relatively simple, such as making a stew in a Dutch oven, and then moving up to chicken on a string or cooking a steak. If you get hooked on fireplace cooking, she suggests you consider installing an iron crane, an old-style hearth tool that's a great help with maneuvering large pots in and out of the fireplace.

"There are also things you can cook in a fireplace without any implements at all, though," Moss points out. "You can tuck potatoes, apples, and onions in the coals, but you can also cook in the ashes." Moss even "boils" eggs in the gray ash. "You don't have to eat meat to become addicted to fireplace cookery," says Moss, who is a vegetarian.

"You can cook apple butter on an electric or gas stove," she says. "But oh my goodness, when you've had it cooked over a fireplace in a kettle…"

Carolina Snowballs

Serves
4

You won't find this recipe on Martha Stewart's menu. This is an eighteenth-century dish that, for full effect, really needs to be served by an open fireplace and/or candlelight. It can be served as a side dish, dessert, or even breakfast. The snowballs can also be boiled in a pot along with soup or stew. It's simple fare that speaks volumes about the hardships endured by Colonial-era families who found delight in this deliciously plain dish of apples and rice.

2 small apples such as Granny Smith, peeled

3 tablespoons unsalted butter

3 teaspoons sugar

2 teaspoons ground cinnamon

2 tablespoons orange marmalade and/or raisins and nuts (optional)

1 cup rice, either raw or soaked in hot water or milk for about 1 hour and drained

Snowball Finishing Sauce

½ cup (1 stick) butter, unsalted

½ cup dry white wine

Pinch of ground cinnamon

Pinch of ground nutmeg

Sugar to taste

In a saucepan, place enough water to cover the apples by 1 inch. Bring to a boil.

Core the apples, leaving about ¼ inch of the bottoms intact.

Place each apple in the center of a 12-inch square of double-layered cheesecloth.

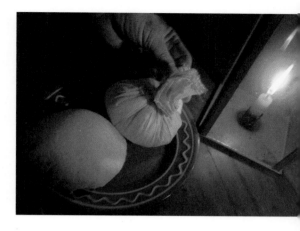

In a small bowl, stir together the butter, sugar, and cinnamon until well mixed. Divide the butter mixture between the cavities in the apples and top with the marmalade mixture, if using. Pour the rice over the apples and gently press all over the fruit.

Take up the 4 corners of the cheesecloth, pull over the top of the apples, and tie securely with kitchen string. Gently shake to distribute the rice evenly. Drop into the boiling water and cook for 1 hour, reducing the heat as needed to maintain a gentle boil.

Meanwhile, make the sauce: In a saucepan, melt the butter with the remaining ingredients and stir to combine. Set aside and keep warm.

Remove the apple bundles and gently cut away the cheesecloth with scissors. Carefully cut the apples in half with a serrated knife. Place one half on each plate and serve, drizzled with the sauce.

Stuffed Pumpkins

Serves
★ 4–6 ★

THIS IS A SEVENTEENTH-CENTURY AMERICAN DISH that is not as hard as it sounds. The pumpkins get slightly charred by the fireplace and make an incredibly rich autumnal addition to your dinner table. The trick is to cook your filling separately on the stovetop while you gently roast and rotate the pumpkins at the side of the fireplace. Adjust the coals and the position of the pumpkins as needed; if you cook them too long or too close to the heat, they will collapse. Periodically test them with your hand for firmness. The flavors of the pumpkin and either filling marry wonderfully, or use your own filling ideas.

For sweet stuffing

4 cups of a combination of peeled and cored apples and/or pears, fresh or frozen cranberries, and currants and/or chopped nuts, seasoned with spices of your choice

For savory stuffing

1½ cups each chopped leeks, mushrooms, and spinach, seasoned with fresh ground pepper and ground mace

2 small Sugar Pie or other eating pumpkins (between the size of a softball and a volleyball), tops cut off, seeds removed, tops reserved for lids when serving

If making sweet stuffing, combine the ingredients in a saucepan with water or dry white wine just to cover. Bring to a boil, then reduce the heat to medium-low. If making savory stuffing, combine the ingredients in a saucepan with just enough water or dry white wine to moisten. Bring to a simmer over medium-low heat. Simmer either stuffing until tender, about 45 minutes to 1 hour.

Meanwhile, place the pumpkins by the edge of the fireplace, on a flat stone if you have one. Roast, rotating every 5 minutes or so, until tender, about 30 minutes, depending on the heat of the fireplace.

Carefully spoon the stuffing into the pumpkins and serve, scooping stuffing and roasted pumpkin into the bowls of your guests.

Henry Gilbert

The tale of Henry Gilbert's rig is a cautionary one: DON'T LET YOUR PIG CATCH ON FIRE!

Gilbert has been around pork barbecue all of his life. His daddy, Ralph, was the best one-armed meat man in Cleveland County, North Carolina—he cured country hams, made livermush, smoked pork shoulders, and ground sausage.

In the summer of 2004, Gilbert's carpentry business partner, Pete Link, asked him to help cook a whole hog for the wedding of his eldest son, Luke. Henry considered it an honor. "Damn right," he said.

Gilbert and Link had done their share of backyard barbecuing—ribs, chicken, and smoked turkeys. Additionally, Gilbert had once worked as the camp cook for a tree-planting commune in Oregon, and since then had regularly cooked on an Oklahoma Joe smoker with an offset firebox. Neither had ever cooked a whole hog by themselves, but they both figured, *How hard could a pig be?*

So, the two porcine neophytes borrowed a pig cooker from their friend, Dobbin Lattimore. Actually, Dobbin didn't have the cooker just then—he had loaned it to a guy—but he gave them directions to get to it.

When they got to the rig, Gilbert says, they should have definitely heeded the red warning lights on their barbecuer's dashboard: rusty and wobbly rig means BIG TROUBLE AHEAD.

Nevertheless, they proceeded. They went to a meat wholesaler and bought a 125-pound pig. Pete Link still remembers the last words from the meat man: "Don't let your pig catch on fire."

They chuckled over his warning about pig pyromania, proceeded to the beer store, and then pushed onward to the outdoor wedding site. They propped up the battered rig as best they could, and set up a burn barrel to make hot coals.

Then another warning sign appeared—their "piece-of-crap burn barrel with a refrigerator grill" collapsed.

It was eighteen hours before the wedding and they had lost their only source of hot coals, but they didn't panic. They called a buddy, who brought them a new burn barrel. Crisis averted—temporarily.

Sixteen hours before the wedding, the intrepid pig duo once again were relaxing in their chairs. Henry popped a brew; Link stepped away for a moment.

Henry Gilbert (left) and Pete Link beam after rescuing their hog from culinary mayhem.

A bystander approached and inspected the cooker. "Damn, boys, what in the hell are you doing in that cooker? Smelting ore?"

"What do you mean?" they asked.

"That cooker is so hot that something like molten lava is leaking from the bottom."

Gilbert jumped to his feet and opened the lid. Flames leapt skyward. Mr. Pig was fully engulfed.

Panic ensued.

Bystanders approached, attracted by all the commotion, maybe thinking it was a fireworks show.

Gilbert fetched a 30-gallon barrel full of ice and beer and attempted to put out the fire. (Fortunately, he had the presence of mind to remove the beer first.) He singed all the hair off his forearms and some of the hair he still had on his head. "I figured it was gonna blow—I know it was over 500 degrees," he says.

He had extinguished the flames with the ice. But what about the pig?

"All I could think was, there was no way we'd ever find a whole hog at night in time for the wedding," Link says. "I was beginning to think, *alternative meats.*"

The two reconnoitered, and it turned out they had blessings to be thankful for: The fire had not engulfed the nearby tarps and wedding canopy; Laura, the bride, had not seen the disaster; the beer was saved; and the pig was scorched but salvageable.

They built a much smaller and more manageable fire, and agreed to not tell anyone about the incident. They trimmed off the outside layer of burned meat and acted like it had never happened.

And guess what? It worked—sort of. The pig was served, but its adventure was the worst-kept secret in the history of barbecue. By wedding time, everybody knew about the exploded oinker—the minister, the guy down at the convenience store, and yes, the bride. But the meat was incredible. Many say it was the best they'd ever had. And years later, Luke and Laura are still happily married.

And the burned pig? It became wrapped in the lore of the wedding celebration.

"We can all laugh about it now; the fire is one of the things everyone will always remember about the wedding," says Link. "And what can I say? The pig tasted great."

Here's a summary of what they learned that day about cooking a whole hog:

❧ Don't cook a pig in a borrowed rig with no wheels.

❧ A 125-pound dressed hog will give off more than a gallon of hot grease; have a grease drain (it can be as simple as a drilled hole in the bottom of the firebox with a metal bucket underneath to catch the drippings).

Henry Gilbert battles an out-of-control hog fire while onlookers scatter.

🌿 Without a grease drain, you can line the bottom of the cooker with sand to soak up the grease.

🌿 A somewhat burned pig can be pretty forgiving (particularly if the pig is on its back so the skin shields most of the meat from the fire).

🌿 Be sure to have a fire extinguisher nearby, in case your pig does catch fire, but try the beer-cooler water first. It tastes better than extinguisher foam.

🌿 Forget about trying to keep a pig fire secret. As long as the meat tastes good, the stories will be funny and you'll be king.

Caribbean Meat Loaf

Serves 8

THIS IS A SPICED-UP VERSION of your mom's meat loaf, brought out of her homey kitchen and thrown on the smoker. Its charred crust and unexpected smoke and spice will get your guests' attention. It's a killer combo with garlic mashed potatoes.

1 pound andouille or hot Italian sausages, removed from casings

2 pounds lean ground beef

¾ cup Anntony's Caribbean All-Purpose Sauce, or your favorite vinaigrette mixed with 1 tablespoon of hot-pepper sauce

1 onion, chopped

5 cloves garlic, minced

2 eggs, lightly beaten

2 tablespoons dry-packed sun-dried tomatoes

3 cups unseasoned dried bread crumbs

Salt and freshly ground pepper to taste

In a large bowl, stir all of the ingredients together until thoroughly blended.

Lay out a sheet of waxed paper and gently pat the meat mixture into a 12-by-15-inch rectangle.

Using the waxed paper as an aid, start from the short end and roll up the meat like a jelly roll. Peel back the paper as you roll. Place, seam side down, on a sheet of aluminum foil.

Build a fire in a smoker/grill for indirect heat. Maintain a temperature between 350°F and 375°F. Place the meat loaf on the foil in the smoker on the side opposite the coals and cook until the meat browns and begins to shrink, about 1 hour.

Serve hot, or refrigerate until chilled and slice for sandwiches or serve as pâté.

Smoked Chicken Salad with No Mayonnaise

Serves
★ 8–10 ★

THERE COULD DEFINITELY BE a more appetizing name for this recipe, but Gilbert says that's the trick with this dish: it's so good you'll forget about the mayonnaise. And Gilbert *loves* mayonnaise, especially Duke's (a staple in his mother's kitchen and in much of the South). Serve on lettuce leaves or your favorite bread.

14 chicken thighs, about 2½ pounds total weight, bone-in, skin-on

¾ cup extra-virgin olive oil

1 cup chopped cured black olives, such as kalamata

5 stalks celery, chopped

1 red onion, chopped

1 cup chopped fresh mint

1 cup chopped fresh basil

3 hard-boiled eggs, peeled and chopped

2 red bell peppers

Salt and freshly ground pepper

Build a fire in a smoker/grill for indirect heat. Maintain a temperature between 275°F and 300°F. Place the chicken in the smoker on the side opposite the coals and smoke until the meat easily falls off the bone, about 1 hour. Roast the peppers at the same time for about 30 minutes, or until the skins are blackened all over. Peel, seed, and chop the peppers.

Remove the chicken skin (don't throw it away; use it for stock or pet food). Pull the meat off the bones and chop.

In a large bowl, combine the chicken, peppers, and all the remaining ingredients. Mix thoroughly and refrigerate for at least 1 hour to allow the flavors to blend, then serve.

Note: Here's a lagniappe *("something extra")—slice a baguette, brush the slices lightly with olive oil, and grill them quickly over the coals. Slather with the chicken salad.*

Diane's Chopped Country Club

Serves
6

THIS RECIPE TAKES a little explaining. Diane Suchetka is Henry's former wife. And this recipe came from her *former* place of employment, the Kirtland Country Club, outside of Cleveland, where she worked part-time in high school and college. Now she's a reporter at the Cleveland *Plain Dealer*. This recipe was listed on the club's menu simply as a Chopped Club, which is to say, a club sandwich minus the bread and lettuce.

Henry has substituted roasted chicken for the club's usual turkey in his version. What this dish really is, is a yummy sandwich spread, which Henry smokafied on his Oklahoma Joe cooker and which Diane, a vegetarian, once gave her carnivore husband for Christmas.

Confused? Just eat it—you'll love it. Serve open-faced on grilled toast as a sandwich, or on a lettuce leaf.

12 to 14 chicken thighs, about 2½ pounds total weight, skin-on, bone-in

1 pound bacon strips

2 tomatoes, chopped

1 cup mayonnaise

Salt and freshly ground pepper

Build a fire in a smoker/grill for indirect heat. Maintain a temperature around 350°F. Place the chicken in the smoker on the side opposite from the coals and smoke for 1 hour, or until the meat easily falls off the bone. Remove the chicken skin. Pull the meat off the bones and chop.

Continued . . .

In a skillet, fry the bacon until crisp. Drain and crumble.

In a large bowl, thoroughly mix the chicken with the bacon, tomatoes, mayonnaise, and salt and pepper to taste. Chill for at least 1 hour to allow the flavors to blend, and serve.

A BEEF LOVER'S PARADISE

Parillas, or steakhouses, are as common in Buenos Aires, the capital of Argentina, as McDonald's and Wendy's are in the United States. In B.A., the most fashionable eateries boast huge hunks of meat lashed to steel crossbeams and spread-eagled over an open charcoal pit. This kind of food is definitely not for vegetarians—or anyone who doesn't crave massive amounts of protein.

We first encountered *parillas* on a trip we took to B.A. as part of a mid-career fellowship for journalists. We had no idea we were about to embark on a crash Atkins diet. Between meetings with government officials and newspaper reporters, we, along with our spouses and the rest of the fellows, sampled the best meat on the planet—paired occasionally with a simple salad of lettuce, tomato, and raw onion, but virtually no bread or pasta—and wondered why we ever thought we had eaten good steak before. The official explanation for the meat's buttery, robust taste was that the cows had been fed on the lush grasses of the pampas in the central and western parts of the country.

Even in laid-back Argentina, the art of grilling meat is taken seriously. Well-off families commonly hold an *asado*, or barbecue, on Sundays at their *estancias* (large ranches). No gas grills here—the meat is cooked over hot coals, and the only seasoning is salt. Besides the ubiquitous steak, the meat tends toward the exotic, at least to Americans: *tripa gorda* (large intestine), *ubre* (udder), and *riñones* (kidneys). We tried most of them, although the *morcillas* (blood sausages) took awhile to get used to.

Guidebooks suggest thanking the *asador*, or meat man, at restaurants in the city. That's exactly what Dan did after the first meal we ate, just a few hours after our plane landed. A weekend caterer who's gotten more than his share of compliments over the years, Dan insisted on getting his picture taken with the *asador*. He was trembling with excitement.

"Lisa," he whispered as we left the restaurant, "he let me hold *his knife*."

Kim Clanton

Among the true believers of holy barbecue, the moniker "Three-Block-High" signals a return to the past.

It's code for a poor man's grill: a rectangle of concrete blocks stacked three high. Across the top would be a hog wire stretcher to support the meat over the coals. It would either be an open pit, or a smoker/grill with a lid of tin roofing. Hot coals would be shoveled in from a side vent opening.

True Southern barbecue was not invented by backyard yuppies or tailgating frat boys. Poor folks, who could only afford the cheaper, less tender cuts of pork, developed this style of cooking. It was their way of tenderizing the meat with the two things they had in ample supply—time and firewood. The pork was cooked a long time over wood coals at a low temperature, 190° to 250°F.

This is the style of barbecue that glassblower and stonemason Kim Clanton grew up with in Greensboro, North Carolina. One of his earliest memories of barbecue is watching his dad, Mel Clanton, eat a pulled pork sandwich from Casey's Barbecue.

"He was wearing blue jeans and a T-shirt," says Kim, whose father died in 2001. "The sandwich was messy and he was eating it over the counter with a glass of buttermilk. But what I remember most was thinking about how he was smiling and what a whopper treat this barbecue was for him. Casey's was the real stuff, with vinegar and red pepper."

His dad's backyard specialty was thick steaks grilled over charcoal on their patio or beside the garage. "I didn't realize it at the time," says Kim, "but he taught me a lot. He and my sister made great salads. And he'd roast corn and potatoes on the grill and make this really strong sweet tea that I loved."

It was a desire to return to that simple aesthetic that led Kim to build a Three-Block-High in his backyard in Deerfield, Virginia. He'd had the gas grills and the smokers with the fancy offset fireboxes, but something kept nudging him back to the past, before the Food Network and international barbecue competitions. "It just had this taste, this plain smoky goodness that you just can't manufacture. There's a magic to simplicity."

Pablo Picasso said it took him a lifetime to learn to paint like a child. Kim recalls a similar comment by his brother-in-law, Hal Herring, about watching a rock-climbing documentary with an older black man.

Kim Clanton with his minimalist concrete contraption, cooking chicken in his backyard.

"The guy says to Hal, 'I've never seen anyone work harder to have fun.' And sometimes I think that is what has happened with barbecue. We're trying too hard."

Kim had a pork epiphany on his wedding day in Alabama. Before the ceremony, he drove with friends Hal and Bill Tharpe to a legendary 'cue joint, Mary's Pit in Maysville. They picked up about twenty racks of slow-smoked ribs for the wedding party.

"The smell of those ribs filled our car," he says. "It was overpowering. And we just had to get into them before going to the party. I kinda felt bad about eating them ahead of time but that smoky pork tasted soooooo good." It reminded him of the real stuff that his dad loved at Casey's.

It was this 'cue nostalgia that guided Kim on a recent fall Sunday morning. A previous Three-Block-High had been ravaged by a flooding creek and he'd gone several years cooking on store-bought cookers. On this day he began with a pickup load of about thirty concrete blocks. Some people begin with a level sand base and even fill the concrete blocks with sand for extra insulation. (Steel rebars—solid iron pipe—can be hammered into the ground through the blocks to give extra stability.) Kim just stacked the blocks in his grassy backyard, placing several of them sideways on the bottom level to provide ventilation. By 1 p.m. his fire was going and he had a half-dozen split chickens on the grill.

Kim's friend, Craig Holt, a welder and also a glassblower, had built him the grill of heavy wire that was now laying across the upper blocks. Holt also fabricated a skeleton lid of rebar, which Kim covered with griller's duct tape— heavy-duty aluminum foil.

Kim uses apple wood to fire his grill, mainly because it's plentiful in the southern Appalachians. He also tosses on a couple pieces of hickory bark if he can find some. He alternates between indirect and direct grilling as his wood goes from flame to coals.

He uses an eclectic mix of marinades and bastes—his favorite is the spicy juice from a jar of barroom pickled sausages—on his meat. He's partial to free-range chicken and Boston butts.

He cooks his chicken for about three hours, until it's a rich amber color, the wing tips are almost like beef jerky, and the chicken body is roasted perfectly—tender but just at the point where the juices no longer run freely when a knife is inserted at the drumstick joint.

The benchmark for Kim is the pit 'cue of the 1960s in North Carolina. "I'm not there yet, but this'll do," he said on a Sunday afternoon as he brought a stacked platter of still-steaming, dark red chicken to a table of family and friends, including us. His wife, Shay, served a huge home-grown garden salad with nut-brown buttered cornbread and a pitcher of sweet tea.

Kim's father would have been right at home.

Kim's Simple-Mind Barbecued Chicken

Serves **6**

KIM'S CHICKEN has a distinctive mahogany color and crisp texture. The crux of his dish is a staple of bar food throughout the South—the juice from a jar of Penrose sausages. He says his friend Johnny Marshall showed him the trick; Johnny learned it from an old black man in the 1960s.

Unless you buy a whole jar of Penrose for yourself, you need to become friendly with a barkeep and ask him or her to save it for you. It's worth the effort. Penrose has a vinegary brine that can almost be duplicated with a jar of pickled peppers spiced up with some hot sauce. Kim says the second secret to this recipe is using organic poultry, because of the superior taste and freshness of the chicken.

Advance preparations are given here, but Kim does not generally prepare in advance. "I usually prep the chicken while I'm lighting the fire. My plan is pretty much no plan, and my chicken still turns out just the way I like it."

3 whole roasting chickens, 3 to 4 pounds each, split in half

¼ cup barbecue dry rub, purchased or homemade (page 54)

¼ cup Cavender's All Purpose Greek Seasoning or other spice mix of your choice

¼ cup firmly packed brown sugar

1 teaspoon of salt

1 teaspoon of freshly ground pepper

2 cups Penrose sausage juice, or juice from jarred pickled peppers of your choice mixed with some hot-pepper sauce

1 cup barbecue sauce of your choice (Kim uses Carolina Pig Pucker)

The night before you grill, wash and pat dry the chicken. Combine the dry rub, the spice mix, brown sugar, salt, and pepper and rub all over the chicken.

Combine 1 cup of the Penrose juice and ½ cup of the barbecue sauce, and pour over the chicken. Seal in a zippered plastic bag and refrigerate overnight. Remove chicken from plastic bag and discard marinade.

Combine the remaining 1 cup Penrose juice and ½ cup barbecue sauce in a squirt bottle, to baste the chicken.

Soak a handful of wood chips for about 30 minutes.

Build a fire in a smoker/grill for indirect heat. Maintain a temperature of about 275°F. Drain the wood chips and place on the coals.

Place the chicken in the smoker and cook, basting liberally about every 30 minutes with the sauce, until an instant-read thermometer inserted in the thickest part of a thigh registers 175° to 180°F, or until the juices run clear when a leg is cut at the joint, 2½ to 3 hours.

Cook it alternately between direct and indirect heat to get the desired color and texture. "You want enough direct heat for good color and texture; just be careful not to burn it," says Kim.

Serve at once.

Kim Bass's Country-Style Steak

Serves
★ **3–4** ★

KIM BASS, KIM CLANTON'S SON, offers this, one of his favorite recipes. It comes from Arlenne Marino, a barkeep at Marino's (formerly Arch Rock Tea Room) in Staunton, Virginia. When the men are home alone, this is their favorite comfort food. Accompany with mashed potatoes; smother them with the gravy and serve Kim Bass's favorite—steamed green peas—on the side.

1 cup all-purpose flour

Salt and freshly ground pepper

1 tablespoon Sylvia's Secret Seasoning or other spice mix of your choice

2 pounds cube steak

½ cup tablespoons olive oil

2 cans (8 ounces each) condensed French onion soup (Kim uses Campbell's)

Mix the flour, salt and pepper to taste, and spice mix in a heavy-duty brown paper bag. Drop the cube steak into the bag and shake to coat thoroughly.

Heat the oil in large cast-iron skillet over medium-high heat. Add the meat and brown on both sides, 3 to 4 minutes per side.

Add the soup and one cup water to the skillet and reduce the heat to low. Let it bubble until it thickens, about 20 minutes. Add more water if needed for your desired consistency.

Serve immediately.

Shay's Mexican Corn Bread

Serves
6

KIM'S WIFE, SHAY HERRING, took the original version of this recipe from a "healthy eating" cookbook and put the southern funk to it—butter, buttermilk, and a cast-iron skillet. It's not restaurant-standard dry corn bread; it's moist and spicy. It goes well with barbecue, soup, or black beans.

1 cup yellow cornmeal, preferably stone-ground

¾ cup all-purpose flour

2 teaspoons baking powder

1 teaspoon baking soda

½ teaspoon salt

3 eggs

1 can (16 ounces) creamed corn

1 cup buttermilk

1 cup shredded cheddar cheese

1 teaspoon seeded and chopped jalapeño chile, or pinches to taste of any dried chile you like

2 tablespoons butter

Preheat the oven to 400°F.

In a large bowl, combine the cornmeal, flour, baking powder, baking soda, and salt. Set aside.

In medium bowl, lightly beat the eggs. Stir in the creamed corn, buttermilk, cheese, and chile. Stir the buttermilk mixture into the dry ingredients, just enough to combine.

Place a 9-inch cast-iron skillet in the oven. Here comes the tricky part: You want to heat the skillet enough to melt the butter, but not burn it. The skillet also needs to be hot enough so that when you pour the corn-bread mixture into the skillet, it sizzles.

Remove the skillet from the oven and add the butter. Tilt the pan to coat the bottom and sides. Pour in the batter and smooth the top.

Bake for 25 minutes, or until a toothpick inserted into the center comes out clean.

Let cool slightly and then turn the skillet upside down on a cutting board and tap the skillet lightly; the corn bread should come out cleanly.

The Noggles

Danny and Tricia Noggle skip the candelabra, linen tablecloth, and elegant china when they host a dinner party; instead, they do it up with cinder blocks, sawhorses, and a sheet of tin roofing. And it is elegant—country style.

They've been doing it that way since 1991 at their lakeside home near Shelby, North Carolina, capturing the essence of contraption cuisine: cooking on what you can scrounge up.

On the last Saturday before Thanksgiving, they host an oyster roast in their backyard for about seventy-five family members, friends, and neighbors.

"It started out as an excuse to drink and have a party outdoors before it got too cold," says Tricia Noggle, a school bookkeeper. "But then it just grew. Around here, the oysters are better after the first frost. And that's us—any excuse to throw a party."

Tricia serves side dishes of chowders, gumbo, and boiled shrimp, and Danny ices down the tub of beer, mans the fire, and roasts the oysters.

When we visited, Danny had started his hardwood fire by mid-morning in a cleared-off area about four by five feet. A U-shaped metal frame, part of an old billboard sign, made a ring around the fire pit. (He stopped using concrete blocks because the intense heat eventually crumbled them.) By late afternoon, he had a good bed of coals. He placed a heavy-gauge sheet of tin roofing over the coals, dumped a half-bushel of oysters onto the tin, and covered the oysters with a wet burlap bag. "You want the fire good and hot," he said. "The wet burlap keeps the oysters moist and helps steam them."

Danny is a low-key guy, but there was a bit of the showman in him as we watched—and heard—him dump a bucketful of oysters onto the metal with a great clatter. After about fifteen minutes, we began to smell the brine of the shellfish as they started to pop open.

Danny and a helper, both wearing thick leather gloves, slid the steaming mollusks onto a sheet of plywood set on two sawhorses. The accompaniments were simple: saltine crackers, bowls of horseradish cocktail sauce, oyster-shucking knifes, towels, and plenty of cold beer.

"If you like roasted oysters, it doesn't get any better than this," said Danny's childhood friend and "chief hepper" Henry Gilbert (see page 111 for his story). "You can't get it this steamin' hot and good in a restaurant."

Danny Noggle places handfuls of Apalachicola oysters onto a sheet of roofing material over a hardwood fire.

The Noggles don't fool around when it comes to fresh seafood. They used to summer in the Florida Panhandle and got addicted to Apalachicola oysters. After Tricia's sister Kathy moved to the South Carolina coast, the Noggles began gathering seafood during their visits to see her. On the weekend before their annual fall seafood feast, the couple drives down to the coast near Bluffton, South Carolina, close to the Georgia line. They buy locally harvested oysters, about five bushels. This year, Tricia and Kathy netted about ten pounds of creek shrimp on the May River, and caught enough blue crabs to fill an eight-gallon cooler. They bought another forty pounds of shrimp, put it all on ice, and headed home.

"It's a good bit of trouble, but it's fun because we have lots of helpers to prepare it all," says Tricia, who is assisted by her sisters, Bit and Kathy, and daughter, Nicole. "We take off from work on that Friday for kind of a pre-roast party where we fix most all of the food and drink wine. By the time Saturday night comes around, we're ready to party."

Frankly Fantastic Seafood Gumbo

Serves
32

THE NOGGLES SERVE THIS GUMBO at their annual oyster roast. Hearty and packed with seafood, it's a perfect complement to the roasted oysters, but terrific on its own, too. Serve it in heaping bowlfuls with crusty bread alongside. The name comes from Franklin County, Florida (near Apalachicola), where the Noggles used to vacation.

2 tablespoons vegetable oil

4 yellow onions, sliced

4 bell peppers (preferably a combination of red, yellow, orange, and/or green), seeded and cut into slices about ¼ inch thick

2 jars pasta sauce (26 ounces each), preferably Newman's Own All-Natural Pasta Sauce (any flavor)

3 cups water

1½ teaspoons salt

1 tablespoon Cajun spice mix

1 teaspoon freshly ground black pepper

1 teaspoon cayenne pepper

12 cups long-grain rice

1 jar oysters (1 pint) with their liquid, preferably Apalachicola

2 pounds medium shrimp, peeled and deveined

1 pound sea scallops

1 pound fresh lump crabmeat

2 pounds grouper fillets, cut into 1-inch cubes

1 pound okra, trimmed and thinly sliced crosswise

In a stockpot, heat the oil over medium heat. Add the onions and bell peppers and cook until soft. Add the pasta sauce, water, salt, spice mix, black pepper, and cayenne pepper. Simmer for 30 minutes over low heat.

Meanwhile, in a large pot, combine the rice and 6 quarts of water and bring to a boil. Reduce the heat to medium-low and cook until the water is absorbed and the rice is tender, 15 to 20 minutes.

Add seafood and okra to the gumbo and simmer for another 15 minutes, or until the seafood is cooked through and the okra is tender.

Spoon the rice into bowls and ladle the hot gumbo over it.

Tricia's Clam Chowder

Serves
32

TRICIA NOGGLE SAYS THIS RECIPE is a variation on several chowder recipes that she's picked up over the years. It's a satisfying main course, or you can serve it in small cups as an appetizer. You can make your own fish stock or buy it in cans at most seafood stores.

16 strips bacon

8 yellow onions, about 3½ pounds total weight, chopped

4 stalks celery, chopped

¼ cup all-purpose flour

1 gallon fish stock

16 medium russet potatoes, about 10 pounds total weight, peeled and diced

8 teaspoons Old Bay seasoning

2 quarts whole milk

2 quarts heavy cream

16 cans (6½ ounces each) minced clams

Freshly ground pepper

Continued ...

In a stockpot, fry the bacon over medium heat until crisp. Transfer to paper towels to drain, leaving the rendered fat in the pan.

Still over medium heat, add the onions and celery to the bacon fat, and cook until transparent, about 10 minutes.

Stir in the flour and cook for 3 minutes, stirring constantly. Add the fish stock and cook, stirring, for about 5 minutes, or until thickened.

Add the potatoes and Old Bay seasoning. Bring to a boil, reduce the heat to a simmer, and cook for 20 minutes. Add the milk, cream, clams, and pepper, and return to a simmer.

Taste and adjust the seasoning. Crumble the bacon and serve the chowder hot, topped with the bacon.

AUDREY'S APPRAISAL

Audrey Gonzalez was one of the first judges for the Memphis in May barbecue contest and shindig held every spring in Memphis, Tennessee. She recently returned to Memphis—and judging—after living for twenty years in Montevideo, Uruguay. Her take on the current state of barbecue culture:

"I grew up with my grandfather having barbecues for his superintendents at Federal Compress and Warehouse Company. I remember they'd have a jug band and African American blues music. Big John cooked by digging holes in the ground, putting crude grills over them—and tins over that. He'd drink whiskey and cook all night, and it was the best food you ever put in your mouth. He used a great lemony-vinegar tomato sauce that I've never tasted the equal of, nor have I been able to duplicate it.

"In those early days, everybody had those barrels, which had a flap with a hole inside. Now, some of the rigs have stairs. You go up the metal steps to the top and they serve you there. It's a show. It's like, who can have the biggest and the best, and the poor guy who wants to keep his barrel feels insecure.

"The fanciest one I've judged was in Covington, a suburb of Memphis. They had a big red trailer. It was so hot that day. We went in and sat at the table and it was air-conditioned, and he may have gotten a point or two for that. It was like a traveling kitchen; they had sinks and bathrooms.

"Things have gotten so fancy, it seems more about the rig than the meat. You're not gonna win because of the rig; you're gonna win because you'll have the best barbecue. If the barbecue isn't the best, I don't care what the rig's gonna do."

Jamie Westendorff

Of all the ways to become a professional barbecue cook, leave it to Jamie Westendorff to take the most original path—from the back door to the kitchen sink. Jamie is a master plumber, and once serviced many of the high-end restaurants in Charleston, South Carolina.

"I'd be in there installing pipe or unplugging a drain and I'd see what they were doing," he says with a laugh. "It didn't take this old boy long to see there was nothing magic going on back there, and they were making a whole lot more money boiling shrimp than I was unplugging drain pipes."

When we visited Jamie's catering kitchen on the way to Folly Beach and saw his array of cookers, we understood he'd met his destiny. He has a tractor-trailer storage bin that is literally stacked to the ceiling with cooking rigs. The rigs begin to tumble out when you open the doors.

His plumbing and welding handiwork is evident in his monster oyster roaster, which has so many valves and hoses, they look like octopus arms coming out from under the central tank. "I'm a plumber first, and that's a seriously good skill to have in your back pocket that most cooks don't," he says. His rig can simultaneously steam eight bushels of mollusks, which nearly fills the bed of a pickup truck. "This is oyster country, and that's how I've made my living for the last thirty-five years," he says, while we watch as his #1 man and friend, John Scott, steams a bucket of Apalachicola singles in the shell.

Westendorff says the secret of a Lowcountry oyster roast is to use the freshest oysters you can get and to have a contraption large enough to supply a steady output of heat and steam. He uses a central propane tank to fuel four large burners, which can boil four gallons of water in less than ten minutes. "With 150 to 200 oyster eaters, you cannot keep up with the demand by using conventional one-bushel steamers," he says. "The most popular time for oysters around here is late fall and winter. And that's when people want their oysters hot out of the shell. They want to see the steam a-risin'."

Westendorff is one of the principal roasters at the annual Charleston Oyster Festival, which claims to be the world's largest. Up to eighty thousand pounds of oysters are steamed there in one day.

"Jamie is right in there with everybody else, very dependable. But what really helps is to have a big rig that can handle the volume," says Cathy

Jamie Westendorff mans the steamer baskets on the massive oyster cooker he built.

Britzius of the Charleston Restaurant Association, which sponsors the fund-raising event for local charities. "Jamie brings something else to the table. In a town full of characters, Jamie stands out—he's local color personified."

A seventh-generation Charlestonian, Westendorff jokes that his ancestors were more closely associated with hangmen's nooses than the silk collars of the landed gentry. Nevertheless, he does well as owner and operator of the Charleston Outdoor Catering Company (see Sources, page 287). Some just call to hear his Lowcountry brogue accent. Westendorff cooks practically every weekend, year-round. In addition to oysters, he cooks whole hog barbecues, Frogmore stews (see page 135), fish fries, and steak dinners.

Jamie also cooks for dozens of benefits annually. He traveled to the Gulf Coast after Hurricane Katrina and carried more than a ton of sausage, shrimp, pork chops, and chicken. He and his buddies set up shop in a storm-ravaged coastal town and cooked free meals for more than a thousand storm refugees and law enforcement officials. He made similar trips to Florida after Hurricane Andrew and to St. Louis after the floods on the Mississippi. He also cooks for cancer camps and other local charities.

"That's what my folks taught me—that no matter how much money you had, if you didn't give back to your community, you weren't more than trash," he says.

When asked about what motivates him to cook for hundreds of strangers each weekend, Jamie turns from court jester to philosopher. He likens the act of cooking to *amour*.

"If you're real good at sex, you might be able to satisfy yourself, and if you're exceptional, you'd be able to satisfy your partner," he says one morning after delivering a bowl of fresh creek shrimp to an elderly friend. "But I can satisfy a thousand people a day. And when you satisfy people with a meal, it sounds just like they're satisfied with sex: 'Oh God, this is delicious. Ummmm, that is so good. I want some more of that.' Well, do you get my point? I hope you did, because that's all I've got to say on that subject."

Lowcountry Red Rice for a Crowd

Serves
★ 25-30 ★

AMERICAN RICE PRODUCTION began in the South Carolina Lowcountry in the early 1700s, and today rice is perhaps the most popular side dish in Charleston cuisine. Westendorff prefers long-grained rice, but most any type you prefer will work in this dish. This recipe is for large groups but reduce it

Continued . . .

as you like, or just plan on having tasty leftovers for the rest of the week. Westendorff says inexpensive sausage is fine here: "It's just as good, and the spicier the better."

3 tablespoons vegetable oil

2 pounds smoked sausage such as kielbasa, cut into ¼-inch slices

5 pounds Vidalia or other sweet onions, chopped

5 green bell peppers, seeded and chopped

2 quarts tomato sauce

2 quarts water

Tabasco sauce or other hot-pepper sauce

Freshly ground pepper

1 tablespoon sugar, if needed to cut acidity of tomatoes

10 cups long-grain enriched rice

3 strips bacon, cooked until crisp and crumbled

Salt (optional)

In a large stockpot, heat the oil and sausage over medium-high heat, stirring occasionally.

Add onions and bell peppers and cook until browned, about 10 to 12 minutes. Add the tomato sauce and water and bring to a boil. Stir in the Tabasco and pepper to taste, and the sugar, if needed.

Add the rice, cover, and reduce the heat to a simmer. Cook for 20 minutes, without stirring (unless you really think the rice is sticking to the bottom of the pot).

Remove from the heat and fluff the rice with a fork. Season with salt to taste, if necessary. Serve warm, with the crumbled bacon sprinkled on top.

Frogmore Stew

Serves
★ 20–25 ★

DESPITE THE NAME, there are no frogs in this dish. The name comes from a plantation near Beaufort, South Carolina. In other parts of the Southeastern coast, it goes by different names: shrimp boil, seafood boil, or, in Louisiana, simply a "boil." This one-pot dish is traditionally prepared outside and served on a picnic table covered with newspapers. The biggest challenge is timing it so all the ingredients are done at the same time. You can cook the potatoes separately or in the same pot, as long as you remove them after 20 minutes—otherwise they will turn to mush. You will need a stockpot with a strainer insert. Serve with an iced tub of cold beer and soft drinks, and plenty of napkins.

10 pounds Red Bliss or red new potatoes

½ cup salt

½ cup Old Bay seasoning

5 to 7 bay leaves

5 to 7 pounds kielbasa or your favorite sausage, cut into 2-inch chunks

2 to 3 dozen ears corn, husks and silks removed

10 to 12 pounds medium shrimp, peeled and deveined

Bring a stockpot with a strainer insert three-fourths full of water to a boil. Add the potatoes, salt, Old Bay, and bay leaves. Reduce the heat to medium and simmer until the potatoes are just tender, about 20 minutes. Lift the strainer insert to remove the potatoes and set aside.

Place the emptied strainer back in the stockpot, return the liquid to a boil, and add the sausages. Cook for 5 minutes, then add the corn. Return to a boil and cook for 5 minutes longer, then add the shrimp. Cook just until the shrimp begin to turn pink, about 3 to 4 minutes longer. Remove from the heat, drain everything, and transfer to large serving bowls, tossing with the potatoes. Serve immediately with lots of butter, cocktail sauce, and napkins.

Killer Green Beans

Serves
8

JAMIE WESTENDORFF IS FAMOUS for his red rice and beans, shrimp boils, and whole hog barbecues. But he says he's probably asked more about this recipe than all others. "It just goes well with about anything you put on the table." The trick to the dish is the smoked meat and the timing: "Yuppies cook their green beans for about 15 minutes so they are still firm and bright green—gross. Charlestonians cook them for about an hour, or until they turn dark green and some of the seeds are coming out of the beans—yummy dog." Smoked pork neck bones can be bought in many Southern grocery stores, or can be ordered from meat specialty stores (see Sources, page 284).

2 gallons water

8 ounces smoked pork neck bones, smoked bacon, or salt pork

2 pounds green beans, trimmed

2 or 3 Vidalia or other sweet onions, peeled but left whole

2 to 3 Red Bliss potatoes, about 1 pound, scrubbed but unpeeled and left whole

Salt and freshly ground pepper (remember the smoked meat is already salty)

Tabasco or other hot-pepper sauce (optional)

In a large stockpot, bring the water to a boil. Add the meat, reduce the heat to low, and simmer for about 30 minutes, or until tender.

Return the heat to a boil and add the beans and onions. Reduce to a simmer again and cook for 30 minutes. Add the potatoes and simmer for 30 more minutes, or until the potatoes are tender.

Remove the beans with a slotted spoon, and drain. Transfer to a serving bowl, toss with salt, pepper, and Tabasco (if using) to taste, and serve.

Jamie's Oysters in Thick Cream

Serves
4

WESTENDORFF LOVES OYSTERS and serves this variation of the traditional oyster stew for both his customers and his family. Be sure not to overcook the oysters, or they will toughen. Serve with a salad and crusty sourdough
bread.

½ cup (1 stick) butter

1 quart shucked oysters with their liquid

1 cup half-and-half

½ teaspoon ground mace

1 teaspoon Old Bay seasoning

4 slices bread, toasted and cut in half

3 hard-boiled eggs, peeled and sliced

In a large saucepan over medium
heat, melt the butter. Add the oysters
and their liquid and bring to a simmer.
Cook until the oysters begin to shrink
and their gills begin to shrivel, about
3 minutes.

Add the half-and-half, mace,
and Old Bay and return to a simmer.

Place a piece of toast in each of
4 large soup bowls. Cover the toast
with several slices of egg. Ladle the
oyster mixture over the toast and
eggs, and serve immediately.

CHAPTER 2

HOMEMADE RIGS &
RECIPES
OF THE
MIDWEST

F CONTRAPTION COOKING HAS AN EPICENTER, it is, aptly enough, the middle of the country—specifically, Kansas City. Where else can you find a front-end-loader-turned-grill in the same vicinity as smokers shaped into animals, or a barrel welded onto an abandoned shopping cart?

Rio has Carnival; New Orleans has Mardi Gras; Kansas City has the American Royal Invitational, where, for four days at the end of September, normally sane, sober men and women mutate into crazed barbecue fans. Folks who usually lock their doors and turn in for the night at 10 p.m. stay up for hours on end, tending their meat and sharing their life stories with total strangers. The cash prizes for the best brisket, chicken, and pulled pork are hefty, but that's not why people come—they come for the chance to show off their culinary and rig-building skills. Stroll among the straggly rows of odd-looking smokers, and you'll see the pride on the cooks' faces as visitors pepper them with questions about their ingenious equipment.

During the Roaring Twenties, African Americans migrated north and west to seek economic opportunity and escape oppressive Jim Crow laws. The culinary skills they brought with them laid the groundwork for Kansas City and the rest of America's middle section to achieve renown through barbecue. Pit masters in the Midwest had access to Kansas City's stockyards and forests of hickory, oak, and various fruitwoods for smoking all kinds of meat, while their counterparts down South stuck mostly with pork.

In the Lone Star State, Southerners as far back as the 1800s brought their tradition of cooking meat on a grate made with sticks over hot coals placed in the ground. "While the ultimate in southern barbecue was cooking a whole hog, cooking a whole steer was the ultimate in Texas barbecue," writes Robb Walsh in *Legends of Texas Barbecue*. "When Texas barbecue moved from the hole in the ground to the restaurant kitchen, the smoking process was speeded up."

Now that virtually nobody cooks underground in Texas anymore, if you want to taste barbecue that doesn't come from a commercial kitchen, your best bet is to go to one of the state's dozens of cook-offs throughout the year. At the Houston Livestock Show & Rodeo, which its organizers bill as a "colossal, Texas-sized picnic," competitors have built smokers in the shape of

Jay Vantuyl deftly turns his mahogany-hued meat in the most basic of working contraptions: the 55-gallon drum.

guns and pentagons. They're not always easy to see, though: unlike at the Royal, the rigs are hidden behind the tents as cooks' assistants set out tables, chairs, and decorations for the parties that follow the contest. It's not unusual for businesses to drop $100,000 in one weekend entertaining clients with food and liquor.

Folks in Houston will tell you anything you want to know about their rigs, rubs, and sauces. Just be prepared for tales that get pretty tall as team members get ready to turn in their meat to the judges.

"We have quite a few characters on our team," chuckles Robert Templin, whose rotisserie always draws a crowd. "They'll exaggerate a few stories."

A truism we found as we crossed the Appalachians is that the barbecue of the Midwest is more of a smorgasbord of meats—some pork, but much more chicken, sausage, beef, goat, and lamb. We realize that "everything is bigger in Texas," but there was something more than mere size characterizing the rigs we visited. Perhaps it's because the two of the country's largest annual barbecue competitions are in this region, and contraption cookers have to do more to stand out. We found rigs that place a premium on showmanship, diversity, and inventiveness. For example, Cheryl Western and her family have taken the common 55-gallon oil drum and added their own touch of whimsy—they welded it to the frame of an old shopping cart and painted a goofy face inspired by the bright colors of the Caribbean. Bill Rousseau and buddy Marty Edwards took the wings off a wrecked Cessna and placed a rotisserie in the cockpit to smoke their prizewinning ribs. And Randy Bishop and Bruce Schatte turned a used air compressor into a smoking, hand-waving Tin Man to cook Armadillo Eggs (which we out-of-towners assumed were the hatchlings of those armor-plated rats, but were delighted to discover otherwise). ★

Mark Shapiro

Mark Shapiro's rig looks like the aftermath of a yeast explosion at a pizzeria: a beer keg blown into the side of a pizza oven, dropped onto a beat-up motorcycle trailer, and welded into place. It's not bound for the trash heap, however, but the winner's circle. In 2004, it won $10,600 in prize money at the Kansas Speedway barbecue competition, and in 2005, Mark placed fourth in the pork category and twenty-seventh out of eighty-two barbecue teams at the American Royal Invitational, the premier barbecue competition in Kansas City. Mark's $500 "Ghettobago" van, his living quarters at competitions, is filled with cooking trophies and ribbons from across the Midwest.

Shapiro's prize-winning cooker may look—in Shapiro's parlance—"real wack," but the important aspect of his rig is that the sucker performs. "It's kind of my secret weapon. People are surprised it even *works*; it doesn't occur to them I win big contests with it," he says.

His "show cooker" is a canary-yellow '39 Chevy coupe—he cooks in the car's interior on an oven sporting fifty-two-inch rotating shelves.

On the surface, Shapiro is an unlikely barbecue maven. He's a motor-head in Kansas City, where he's been running the All Brand Cycle shop since the mid-'80s. He's a freak on old English bikes—Triumphs and BSAs, and don't even get him started on Indians or a Vincent Black Shadow.

The beginning of his unlikely cooking rig was a belly-up eatery. He had toyed with the idea of opening a restaurant, and thought he'd take a look at an old Blodgett pizza oven. He nixed the idea, but something about the oven caught his eye, and he bought it for $80. It took three guys to move it.

The rest he practically built for free:

♭ For a firebox, he mounted a beer keg and cut the end off it.

♭ For a fire grate, he took the metal shelf out of a refrigerator and bent it into a V.

♭ For a hinge on the firebox, he used the hardware from an old door in his shop.

🦋 For a latch, he cut a piece of angle iron from a bed frame.

🦋 For the racks in the ovens, he used shelves from a Hostess
Twinkies display rack.

"I like recycling. There ain't no sense in throwing this stuff away," he says. "In my neighborhood, old stuff doesn't last thirty seconds on the street."

Shapiro cooks because he enjoys it, but acknowledges he takes cooking competitions seriously. At the 2005 American Royal, he was the only solo cooking "team" we ran into. "My friends stay away from me because they know I wanna do things the way I wanna do things," he says.

The way he built his rig is simple, but how it works is complex: the firebox is connected to the bottom of the oven by a four-inch pipe. The heat is deflected on the bottom shelf by a layer of firebricks and a water pan.

One of the first lessons he learned about a homemade cooker is that it doesn't come with an instruction manual; you have to experiment. "Let's just say those first couple cooking trials kept the neighborhood dogs very happy," he says with a laugh.

But he says that by experimenting, he found that his cooker has four distinct cooking zones ranging in temperature and even in moisture content. To take advantage of this, he rotates his ribs, chicken, brisket, and Boston butts throughout the cooker. "What I love about this cooker is that it's so well insulated," he says. "It can cook like hell at about 200° to 250°F for as long as you want and it doesn't matter if it's raining, snowing, windy, or hot. It always cooks the damn same."

Shapiro passed on these barbecue tips and quips:

🦋 "Some people just can't cook on anything. It doesn't matter what kind of rig or what kind of money they've spent on it. If they don't under- stand the meat they're cooking and the rig they're using, it just doesn't matter. Believe me, I've tasted their meat."

🦋 "Use a strong wood like shagbark hickory for stronger cuts of meat like brisket. Use a softer fruit wood like plum for ribs. The judges don't expect it but like it."

The master at work: Mark Shapiro fine-tunes his beer keg–pizza oven cooker.

🥔 "You can oversmoke meat. I've done it. Be careful, check the color of the meat, taste it. Once you put that smoke in the meat, you can't get it out. Better to start it easy."

🥔 "My son tells me my barbecue always tastes better the next day. He's right. It needs that extra day to get that flavor in deeper."

🥔 "You don't rush barbecue. When it gets done, it gets done. Don't let nobody rush *your* meat."

Pyro's Burnt Ends

Serves
10

MARK SHAPIRO and his Pyro cooking team cook some incredible brisket and win big money at it, too. This is an all-day prep meat dish that you can cook at home, but you shouldn't attempt it unless you're putting on a shindig for some serious protein fiends. Having said that, brisket is relatively cheap and this is seriously good stuff to ease you into some championship-caliber fodder that will blow your buddies' minds and bellies. Forget the house chores; go for the 3 B's—brisket, briquettes, and beer.

1 whole beef brisket, 15 to 18 pounds

2 tablespoons seasoned meat tenderizer, such as Adolph's

1 teaspoon coarsely ground black pepper

1 teaspoon cayenne pepper

1 teaspoon onion powder

1 teaspoon garlic powder

1 cup barbecue dry rub, purchased or homemade (see page 54)

Your favorite barbecue sauce for serving (optional)

Build a fire in a smoker/grill for indirect heat. Maintain a temperature of about 225°F. Soak 1 cup of hickory and/or wild cherry wood chips.

Rub the brisket on all sides with the tenderizer, spices, and rub.

Put the brisket in the smoker/grill on the side opposite the coals and cook for about 8 to 10 hours, or until an instant-read thermometer inserted at the thin end registers 170°F. Apply some of the wood chips during the first 3 hours and half as many for the remainder.

Remove the brisket from the heat and double-wrap it in heavy-duty aluminum foil. Be careful not to lose the drippings. Set the wrapped brisket in a large roasting pan.

Let the brisket sit until cool enough to handle, 1½ to 2 hours.

Be careful to save the brisket juices as you unwrap the foil. Pour the drippings into a glass container, refrigerate, and then skim the fat off the top. You'll need it in about another hour.

Place the brisket on a large cutting board. Carve the meat against the grain into ¾- to 1-inch slices. Remove about 75 percent of the heavy fat.

Refire the grill and heat to about 325°F. Pile the charcoal in the center of the grill. Wait until the coals are covered in white ash, about 20 minutes. You will need a small table near the grill to hold the cut brisket and a large empty tray.

With a pair of tongs, place about 6 slices of the brisket on the grill. The fat will begin to drip and flame up; a little fire is good to sear the brisket steaks. Cook for about 2 to 3 minutes on each side, moving the meat to the side of the grill away from the flames as needed. Transfer the steaks to the empty pan and continue searing the remaining steaks.

When all the meat has been seared and placed in the pan, cover with foil. And now—this is a critical step—take a break, drink a beer, and call an old girlfriend.

About 15 minutes later, tell her your meat is calling and get her off the phone. In a small saucepan, reheat the drippings to a low simmer. When the meat is cool enough to handle, about 20 to 30 minutes, trim off all the fat, if you like. Mark prefers to leave a little, to keep it moist. Cut the steaks into cubes and place in a large bowl.

Now dose the meat with your favorite barbecue sauce or just the saucepan of meat drippings. You could win prizes with this meat, but go one better— serve it to your family and friends.

Pork Steak in Beef Au Jus

Serves
6

MARK SHAPIRO GUARANTEES you've never seen a meat-centric recipe like this before—pork steaks dipped in burnt end brisket drippings and grilled continuously. We know we haven't.

We also agree with Mark that you have to be one committed son-of-a-gun to even attempt this thing. Once you start, you cannot leave the grill for 30 minutes. Serve it with mashed potatoes or any vegetable dish you want, it doesn't matter—no one will remember anything but the meat.

1 teaspoon garlic powder

1 teaspoon onion powder

Salt and freshly ground pepper to taste

6 pork steaks, each about 10 ounces and ½ inch thick, with some fat, but not too fatty

2 cups brisket drippings (see page 146) or 1 can (12 ounces) beef consommé

Build a fire in a smoker/grill and bring to about 350°F.

Sprinkle the spices on the pork steaks and place the brisket drippings in a bowl near the smoker/grill.

Place the steaks directly over the hot coals. Sear them for about 2 to 3 minutes on each side.

Using tongs, dip a steak in the drippings and let it set for 1 minute, then put it back on the grill. Repeat with all the steaks, rotating them for 10 to 15 minutes, or until an instant-read thermometer inserted in the thickest part registers 170°F.

Finally, dump all the steaks back into the drippings, let stand for 10 minutes, and then serve.

Pyro's Sauce Verde
Pork Loin Chops

Serves
6

THIS IS GOOD AT A DINNER PARTY: try serving it over a bed of rice with a bowl of the salsa verde on one side and your favorite barbecue sauce on the other. Mark likes to blend both sauces.

1 tablespoon barbecue dry rub, purchased or homemade (see page 54)

1 teaspoon cayenne pepper

1 tablespoon Lawry's seasoned salt

8 pork loin chops, each about 5 ounces and ¾ to 1 inch thick

1 can (12 ounces) salsa verde, preferably Embasa

In a bowl, mix the rub and spices. Sprinkle over the pork. Place in a zippered plastic bag and refrigerate for at least 1 hour or up to overnight.

Build a fire in a smoker/grill for indirect heat. Maintain a temperature of about 350°F. Soak 1 cup of hickory and/or wild cherry wood chips. When the coals ash over, toss on a handful of the wood chips for smoke.

Place the pork on the side opposite the coals and smoke for 10 minutes. Turn the meat and smoke for 10 more minutes.

Put on gloves, remove the grill grate, and lay it aside (remember, it's hot). Use a stick to spread the coals evenly for direct heat.

Open the salsa verde and pour it into a large saucepan with a lid.

Replace the grate with the pork over the coals and grill for 3 to 4 minutes on both sides, or until slightly seared and an instant-read thermometer inserted in the thickest part of the chops registers 150°F.

Transfer the pork to the saucepan and cover it. Place it over the coals and steam for 10 minutes.

Check the internal temperature; you want the pork just done, 170°F. Serve and enjoy.

KING OF THE TEXAS BARBECUE PITS

Two decades ago, Texan David Klose built his own barbecue pit because, he explains, "I got tired of Wendy's." The smoker was so impressive that soon his friends and relatives wanted one. Pretty soon he was filling orders from governors, professional basketball players, and beauty queens. Requests came from oil drillers stationed in Russia, Europe, South America, and the North Pole.

Klose, who grew up in a housing project in Houston, today presides over a $2 million company, BBQ Pits by Klose, which employs seventeen people. He's the ultimate example of a weekend rig-builder who has made his obsession pay—in spades.

"I'm just a poor welder that got lost," Klose jokes. "I'd rather do this than have a real job."

Klose pits sell from $69 for a simple drum grill to $50,000 for a mobile catering rig. His contraptions are a common sight on the barbecue circuit, and it's easy to feel intimidated when a contestant wheels one in and ends up raking in the trophies.

But, surprisingly, Klose insists you don't need one of his cookers to turn out great brisket, ribs, chicken, or pork butt. The snazziest smoker in the world won't help a cook who doesn't know what he or she is doing.

"My pits aren't different from what other people can do," he says. "They're just a little better built and engineered to take the work out of it. A good cook could kick a hole in the ground with his boot heel and beat most people cooking."

Bill Rousseau & Marty Edwards

The weird and the wacky are on full display at the American Royal Invitational: Smokers in the shape of giant ceramic pigs. Old steam engines re-jiggered as cookers. Rigs in the shape of coffins and shotguns.

But it's the Cessna 185 that *really* grabs people. In a former life, it was a sleekly elegant blue-and-silver corporate plane before a thunderstorm flipped it over while it was tied down at an airport near Kansas City. The wings and tail of the plane were still in good shape, though.

So Bill Rousseau, a barbecuer and skydiver—he jumps out of Cessnas—hauled it home. He called up his buddy, Marty Edwards, and said, "Hey, I've got something."

"You're outta your mind," Edwards said when he saw the 1950s-era plane.

"That's beside the point," Rousseau answered. "We're gonna build a grill."

"We stuck it in my garage, then sat around for a coupla days, drinking beer and trying to think what we could do with it," Rousseau recalls. "In this case, function followed form, instead of the other way around. It was like building a ship inside a bottle."

They measured the inside of the plane and built two steel boxes. One became a firebox, which they lined with firebricks and secured inside the cargo hold using steel pipes. They slid the second box under the windshield after gutting the instrument panel and engines. Edwards snagged part of an elevator door's machinery from work and snuggled it inside the nose of the plane to make a rotisserie.

Finally, they painted "Meat-Seeking Missiles" on the side and christened their barbecue team "The Swine Flew." Team members, Rousseau says, are forbidden to take themselves too seriously.

The Cessna's been written up in magazines, local TV news reporters do their standups in front of it, and once, TWA sponsored their team. The smoker is designed to cook while the Cessna is in motion. One time, Rousseau says, they were on the way home from a contest when a guy wearing a Federal Aviation Administration cap pulled alongside the car. He gaped, then sped off.

But the plane is more than just an odd contraption, Rousseau says. Team members have taken first place in contests and gotten catering jobs after folks oohed and aahed over the meat they cooked. Rousseau and his buddies won

Bill Rousseau (left) and Marty Edwards show off glistening ribs cooked in the cockpit of a wrecked Cessna.

the Royal's Hot Wings category in 1991, the first time they entered, and they've cooked at weddings, company picnics, and skydiving conventions.

It was skydiving, in fact, that led Rousseau to the contest circuit. One night in 1990, he and three other members of his skydiving team parachuted into a high school football game carrying the ball. There was a barbecue contest across the street, and Rousseau was so intrigued that he had to check it out. The rest, as they say, is history.

Rousseau has built other rigs—one out of a steel drum, and one out of a whiskey keg—but he says the Cessna remains his favorite. Its one drawback: "Too small for a whole hog," he sighs.

Champion Hot Wings

Serves
6-8 { As An Appetizer }

BILL ROUSSEAU SWEARS that he and Marty Edwards just tossed this recipe together during their first year competing at the American Royal, in 1991. At that time, the Royal had a separate category for wings. "We were throwing things in a pot to come up with a sauce," Rousseau says. "The whole idea was to be creative and see how we'd do." Sure, guys. They did so well, they took first place. Bill makes this sauce on the grill; try it that way, too, if you like. When applying the sauce to the wings, he adds, you may want to thin it with water or beer.

8 jalapeño chiles, stems trimmed and cut into chunks

2 habanero chiles, stems trimmed and cut into chunks

1 cup white vinegar

4 cups ketchup

1½ cups Louisiana hot sauce

½ cup browning and seasoning sauce, such as Kitchen Bouquet

1 tablespoon dried minced garlic, granulated

1 tablespoon dried minced onion, granulated

1½ cups honey

5 pounds chicken wings

Build a fire in a charcoal grill.

In a food processor, combine the chiles and ½ cup of the vinegar and process until smooth.

In a double boiler over simmering water, combine the chile purée, the remaining ½ cup vinegar, the ketchup, hot sauce, seasoning sauce, garlic, and onion.

Cook, stirring occasionally, until the sauce registers 190°F on a candy thermometer.

Remove from the heat and add the honey. Stir until it melts into the sauce, about 2 minutes.

Continued . . .

During the week, the Cessna lives in Bill Rousseau's 3-car garage.

Meanwhile, open both vents on the grill halfway. Place the wings in a metal baking pan and cook until an instant-read thermometer registers 180°F, about 15 or 20 minutes. Gradually add the sauce and cover the grill. Cook until the sauce is thickened, about 5 to 10 minutes longer.

Remove and serve immediately. Leftover sauce can be stored in a tightly sealed jar in the refrigerator up to 3 months.

Sharon's Gourmet Potatoes

Serves

★ 12–15 ★

BILL ROUSSEAU LIKENS this dish to meatloaf or pot roast—comfort food like his mom used to make. Okay, a bit more complicated: This recipe is actually from Marilyn Edwards, whose son Marty is Rousseau's barbecue teammate. But it's named for Sharon Stewart, who prepares all the team's side dishes in competition while the men take care of the meat.

2 pounds thawed frozen hash browns

1 can (10¾ ounces) condensed cream of chicken soup

2 cups sour cream

2 cups shredded cheddar or American cheese

1 white onion, finely chopped

½ cup (1 stick) butter, melted

½ tablespoon freshly ground pepper

Topping

¼ cup butter, melted

*2 cups finely crushed cornflakes or
potato chips*

Build a fire in a smoker/grill for cooking at 350°F, or preheat the oven.

Combine the potatoes, soup, sour cream, cheese, onion, ½ cup melted butter, and pepper in a large bowl and stir until well mixed. Taste and adjust the seasoning. Transfer to a 9-by-13-inch metal baking pan.

To make the topping, stir together the ¼ cup melted butter and cornflakes. Spread evenly over the potato mixture.

Place in the smoker and cook (or place in the oven and bake) until bubbly and the edges are lightly browned, 30 to 45 minutes.

We Stole Mom's Green Beans

Serves
★ 12–15 ★

THIS IS A FAVORITE among Bill Rousseau's skydiving buddies. People like it, he says, because the green beans have a heartier flavor than the wimpy ones you get in restaurants with itty bits of bacon and onion. And the jalapeños give the kind of kick you don't expect green beans to have.

1 large can (1 gallon) green beans

1 large white onion, chopped

1 pound bacon strips, cooked until crisp

*1 can (10¾ ounces) condensed cream
of chicken soup*

6 large jalapeño chiles, minced

1 tablespoon freshly ground pepper

*1 pound Velveeta cheese, cut into
1-inch cubes*

Continued . . .

Bill Rousseau and Marty Edwards get a lot of grins for this colorful sign on the side of their rig.

Build a fire in a smoker/grill for cooking at 350°F, or preheat the oven.

Combine the green beans, onion, bacon, soup, jalapeños, and pepper in a bowl and mix until well blended. Transfer to two 9-by-13-inch metal baking dishes. Place in the smoker and cook (or place in the oven and bake) until the onion is tender, about 1½ hours.

Remove from the oven, sprinkle the cheese over evenly, and cover the pans with aluminum foil. Let stand until the cheese melts, about 5 minutes. Stir to mix in the cheese and serve immediately, scooping directly from the dish.

Randy Bishop & Bruce Schatte

The Tin Man looks as if it should be in a large wheat field, scaring the bejesus out of the crows, or maybe in a chic gallery in Greenwich Village, ready to be snapped up by a customer searching for high-concept Americana.

Instead, the Tin Man is a smoker that draws tourists from Asia, giggling and whispering, who beg to have their pictures taken next to it. Oh, and it turns out some fine food, too, as Randy Bishop and Bruce Schatte will be happy to tell you.

Schatte, an electrician who wires up Wal-Marts across the country, lives on a 38-acre farm in Giddings, Texas, about halfway between Austin and Houston. Most farms tend to have abandoned stuff lying around, and Schatte's was no exception. Looking at an old air compressor one day a couple of years ago, he thought, *Geez, that'd make a great smoker.*

So, Schatte cut a large rectangular door on one side for the firebox, with room inside for a top grill, a middle grill, and a lower grill. He left room between the grills and the door for wires from which to hang sausages.

Then, he gathered some leftover steel pipe from an oil field, traced his hand on a sheet of paper, and used a cutting torch to mold the hands out of sheet steel. He fastened the pipe to the middle and bottom of the compressor for arms and legs, then attached the hands. The neck is made out of more pipe, the head has two washers for eyes, and a rakish hat on top has a brim of thin plate steel. There's also a smokestack and a damper.

Schatte spent three to four weeks on the project and built it entirely from scrap. If he had wanted it custom-made, he says, it would have cost him $3,000.

Some of Schatte's expertise can be explained by the fact that he's been drawing since he was a kid. He has designed several tools and is working on getting a patent for a handcrafted fishing wire and a device that he says eliminates the need for all the wires and ropes holding bales of hay together.

Over the years, Schatte and his barbecue teammate Randy Bishop, a truck driver, have won a bunch of contests across Texas, lugging the Tin Man wherever they go. They painted it multiple colors—black, blue, orange—dressed it in overalls, and tied a big red kerchief around its neck. When we saw it, it was wearing a spray-painted outfit of an orange shirt with blue overalls.

"Everybody comes by and says, 'That's real neat,'" Schatte says. "I don't know how many families in Houston have pictures of that pit." What makes it extreme, he adds, "is the fact it looks like a person and greets everyone who walks up to it. But it's an actual working smoker, not something you put a little smoke into."

In Texas, barbecuing is as much a part of life as churchgoing, and Schatte has fond childhood memories of both. Every Sunday after church, his dad cooked chicken and sausages on a handmade metal pit that Schatte says was the size of a washing machine. Schatte himself used it for ten years before it rusted out. He followed his dad onto the contest scene, too, and has competed several times in the Houston Livestock Show and Rodeo.

Eventually, Schatte says, he'd like to make companions for the Tin Man, maybe a mom and dad so it won't feel lonely. But Schatte's work schedule is so demanding—he's had to give up competing because he's only home fifteen days a year—that the idea will have to wait. So at least for now, the Tin Man will continue puffing away on an asphalt parking lot, drawing people to its side with a wave of its arm and a loopy grin.

Bruce Schatte smoking armadillo eggs in the Tin Man cooker he built.

Armadillo Eggs

Serves
★ 75-100 ★

JALAPEÑO POPPERS, once exotic in many parts of the United States, have become so routine in Randy Bishop's corner of Texas that he wanted to try something different. He was sitting in his kitchen one day when he hit on the idea of combining his homemade pork sausage with jalapeños, cream cheese, and cracker crumbs. His so-called "armadillo eggs" have become a hit at his catering jobs.

1 box (1 pound) saltine crackers

50 jalapeño chiles, seeded and halved lengthwise

5 pounds cream cheese, at room temperature

40 pounds ground pork sausage

Build a fire in a smoker/grill and bring to 325°F.

Empty the crackers into a bowl and crush very finely.

Fill each jalapeño half with about 1 tablespoon cream cheese. Set aside.

Form the sausage into 100 small, flat patties; each should be about ¼ pound, the size of a small hamburger.

Wrap a sausage patty around each jalapeño half. Dredge each in the bowl of cracker crumbs to coat thoroughly and arrange on baking sheets.

Place on the grill and cook for 35 to 40 minutes, or until the "eggs" are golden brown. Serve immediately.

Randy's Gizzards

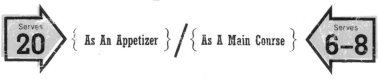

Serves
20
{ As An Appetizer } / { As A Main Course }
Serves
6-8

MANY PEOPLE don't like gizzards—they're too grisly, and chewing them takes work. But Bishop calls this dish he invented "out-of-this-world," and says he's converted several skeptics. "I've had people say, 'Oh, I could never eat that.' So, I don't tell them what they're eating. The reaction is, like, 'No way! You can't make a gizzard taste good!'" But, with this dish, he has. Gizzards are packaged for sale in large bags and can be found at most grocery stores.

5 pounds chicken gizzards

1 large red onion, halved and thinly sliced

1 green bell pepper, seeded and cut into thin strips

1 pound white button mushrooms

One bottle (16 ounces) Kraft zesty Italian dressing

½ cup Worcestershire sauce

1 cup (2 sticks) butter, at room temperature

¼ cup Cajun seasoning such as Tony Chachere's Original Cajun Seasoning

¼ cup water

Build a fire in a smoker/grill and bring to 325°F.

Put the gizzards in a 9-inch square metal baking dish. Add the onion, bell pepper, mushrooms, dressing, and Worcestershire sauce.

Place the sticks of butter on top and sprinkle with the seasoning. Pour the water over the top to allow some of the seasoning to sink to the bottom of the dish.

Cover the dish with aluminum foil and place in the smoker. Cook for 2 hours, or until the gizzards are tender, stirring every 15 to 20 minutes. Serve immediately.

Bruce's Brisket

Serves
16

MOST RECIPES for smoked meat parts require them to be wrapped in aluminum foil at some point during the cooking. This recipe calls for red butcher paper, which Bruce Schatte says is the secret to the moistness and flavor of his brisket—a cut of meat that is notoriously difficult to tenderize. (Light-colored paper doesn't work as well, he says, because it reflects heat off the meat.) "Foil seals the steam inside and boils the brisket, and it's like mush," says Bruce. "The paper breathes, and it doesn't trap all the hot steam and oil. It helps you not ruin a $25 to $30 piece of meat."

½ cup salt

¼ cup freshly ground black pepper

¼ cup cayenne pepper

¼ cup garlic powder

1 beef brisket, about 10 pounds

Build a fire in a smoker/grill for indirect heat. Maintain a temperature of 350°F.

Sprinkle the salt, black pepper, cayenne pepper, and garlic powder on both sides of the brisket. Sprinkle with just enough water to moisten the seasoning, and rub it into the meat.

Place the brisket, fat side up, in the smoker on the side opposite the coals. Cook for 1½ hours, or until the fat starts to bubble. Put on a thick pair of rubber gloves and turn the meat over. Cook for another 1½ hours, or until the meat is brown and sizzling.

Transfer the brisket to a 3-by-6-foot sheet of red butcher paper, placing it crosswise 1½ feet from the short end of the paper. Wrap the end of the paper over the brisket and fold it tightly. Roll the brisket up in the paper, continuing to pull the paper tightly over it, and finish with the fat side up.

Place the wrapped brisket back in the smoker, again fat side up (this will allow the juice from the fat to spread throughout the rest of the meat) with the thick end facing the coals. Cook for 5 more hours, allowing the temperature to gradually drop to 250°F as the fire gets lower.

Remove when the meat is so tender it gives when you poke it with a finger. Unwrap the paper, cut the brisket into ¼-inch-thick slices, and serve.

"Stick 'em up, pardner": The iron-mustachioed Tin Man in Houston.

Russell Wilson

On a Saturday morning after cooking most of the night, Russell Wilson is feeling like the Texas Star painted on his 500-gallon drum cooker—kind of faded.

"You just gotta keep going. It's daylight and the kids are roaming around, but I think I'm gonna sit down awhile, if'n you don't mind," he says as he plops into a camper's chair.

The rallying cry for this family-based barbecue team is "It Ain't Prime, But It's Close," which is what a buddy once told Russell when he asked about the quality of some beef they were cooking.

Russell and his wife, Billie, ride the barbecue circuit, traveling from their home in Krum, Texas, just north of Fort Worth. When we met them they'd been on the road for forty of the last fifty-two weekends, including the last ten weekends straight. They drive a recreational vehicle and set up a tent for their kids.

They've been doing this "right regular" for the past six years. The payoff: In 2005, they placed first in the brisket category at the Jack Daniel's Invitational.

"Traveling the circuit ain't too bad," Russell says. "The kids seem to like it. We just load up and hit the road. We get bored at home, and this way we get to see some country on the cheap. And another thing about it—we do eat *good.*"

During the week, Russell works in the heating and air conditioning business, which is "full-year work in a place called Texas." The cooking weekends are his golf and country club.

"Everybody has to have a way to relax, and this is mine," he says. "The main thing is getting away from work. I don't even bring the cell phone with me. I just hang with my family. And cook." Between the two of them—his wife is a waitress—the Wilsons put together some pretty mean dishes (check out their Texas Squash Boat on page 167).

Russell is matter-of-fact about how he learned to cook. "Mamma and Daddy was at work and Russell was hungry," he says as his children gather round, climbing on his lap and hugging his arms. "They gave me the grocery money and I had to make it last."

Russell Wilson (right) and his son, Rusty, lean on each other after a long night of cooking.

Russell's rig is impressive, if a bit road-weary. It's an all-weather, mobile cooking universe, featuring a corrugated tin roof with tiny Christmas lights woven into the ceiling between the fluorescent lights. The fine boys of the Future Farmers of America, Krum High School chapter, built it in 1983. "They did it to raise money and learn good practical skills to make it in life—you know, like welding and wiring," says Russell.

The heart of this rig is a former propane tank fitted with an offset firebox. It has a cooking surface big enough to splay out a whole hog, with enough room left over for a half-dozen whole hens. The cooker does it all—brisket, pork butt, ribs, and chicken. Russell cooks with hickory and supplements it with pecan. "Sometimes you can get too much hickory; the pecan smoke is sweet and cuts the hickory," he says.

For all his rig's glory, Russell says what he's learned from cooking barbecue is that you really don't need a huge rig to make magnificent meat. "If you cut up a chicken, rub it down, and put it in a plastic bag overnight and then put it on about any kind of grill, it would be hard to mess up," he says.

Russell Wilson's best barbecue tips:

- "Always know what your pit is doing. Is it heating up or cooling off? You can drink, sleep, talk, lie, or love, but if your meat is on the heat, you gotta know what that pit is doing."

- "Appreciate what good smoked meat is. It ain't something you can go into Wal-Mart and buy off the shelf. It's real. It don't come out of no microwave."

- "The main thing is holding your heat and getting the smoke through to your meat. You can't be guessing with barbecue, this ain't like scrambling eggs."

Texas Squash Boat

Serves
10

RUSSELL WAS NEVER a fan of spinach, until he came across this side-dish recipe. "It tastes so good, you don't even know it's good for you," he said, settling back in a chair by his RV as his kids wrestled in their tent nearby. He lit a cigarette and popped a beer. It had been a long night of cooking—it was time for breakfast.

"And besides," he added, "you need to break up all that meat with something green. It's better for your digestion tract." Sounds like pretty good dietary advice to us.

8 ounces cream cheese

Two 16-ounce packages frozen spinach

5 yellow crookneck squash, halved and seeded

¾ cup shredded Monterey Jack cheese

½ cup grated Parmesan cheese

Build a fire in a smoker/grill and bring to 300°F, or preheat an oven.

In a saucepan over low heat, combine the cream cheese and spinach and cook, stirring, for about 8 to 10 minutes, or until the cheese is melted and the spinach is softened.

Spoon the mixture into the squash boats.

Top the filling with equal amounts of the Jack and Parmesan cheeses.

Wrap each squash in aluminum foil. Place in the smoker and cook (or place in the oven and bake) until the squash is tender, about 35 minutes.

Rusty Wilson's Garlic Shrimp

Serves **4**

{ As An Appetizer }

RUSTY IS RUSSELL'S sixteen-year-old son, and a darn good cook. "I've learned from helping my dad. He cooks a lot, and sometimes I experiment with the things I like a lot—like shrimp and garlic and butter."

When asked if this dish was an appetizer or an entrée, he shrugged his shoulders, looked at his dad and said, "I don't know. If no else is around, I just eat it myself."

½ cup (1 stick) butter

1 pound large shrimp, peeled and deveined

2 tablespoons Old Bay seasoning

6 cloves garlic, minced

Salt and freshly ground pepper

In a skillet, melt the butter over medium heat. Add the shrimp, Old Bay, and garlic and cook for about 6 minutes, or until the shrimp is opaque throughout.

Remove from the heat, season with salt and pepper to taste, and serve.

Kimberly's Stuffed Pork Chops

Serves
4

KIMBERLY IS RUSSELL'S fourteen-year-old daughter. She has entered this recipe in several kids' barbecue contests and has won a first place for a Weber grill and a fourth place for a grill that she can't remember the name of.

1 pound fresh Italian sausage, removed from casings

½ cup shredded Monterey Jack cheese

4 pork chops, each about 5 ounces and 1½ inches thick

Salt and freshly ground pepper

Build a fire in a smoker/grill and bring to about 275°F.

In a large skillet over medium heat, fry the sausage until thoroughly cooked, about 6 to 8 minutes. Transfer to paper towels to drain.

In a bowl, combine the sausage and cheese and stir to mix thoroughly.

With a sharp knife, cut a 2-inch slit about 2 inches deep in the middle of one long side of each pork chop to make a pocket.

Divide the sausage mixture among the chops and secure each with a toothpick.

Place the chops directly over the hot coals and cook until the meat begins to brown, about 7 minutes per side.

Remove from the heat, season with salt and pepper to taste, remove the toothpicks, and serve.

Randy Campbell & Bob Fowler

There's probably nothing more utilitarian than a machine that moves dirt. But the one that construction worker Randy Campbell operates during the week serves multiple purposes off-hours: it roasts chicken, melts marshmallows, grills hamburgers, and grabs attention as one of the more unusual food contraptions in Kansas City, a place where outlandish-looking rigs are as common as outrageously great barbecue joints.

Campbell has been cooking since he was a kid. "My mother was a lousy cook, and she'd be the first to tell ya that. So I learned to cook real young," he says. But he learned barbecue from reading books and listening to tapes. Around 1999, he got the idea to turn the front-end loader he drove at work into a mobile food rig.

He asked permission to borrow the machine from the managers at Dasta Construction Management, the construction company for which he's worked for more than three decades. He fashioned two grates to fit at different heights within the machine's big scooper, filled the bottom of the scooper with some hickory and a bit of apple wood, lit it, and voilà—a backyard grill, only way more memorable. His success so inspired him, he says, that he considered converting a concrete mixer into a margarita blender. "But we found the acid from the tequila would pull the enzymes or something out of the bucket," he says. "So we couldn't do that."

Every September, about a week before the American Royal Invitational in Kansas City begins, Campbell pressure-washes the bright yellow machine. Then he and Bob Fowler, his childhood buddy and barbecue teammate, trundle it over to the contest grounds, set it up next to their portable camper, and string it with Christmas lights. On Friday, the night before the judging, they fire up the rig for the customers of Dasta, a small, family-owned business and the team's sponsor. Amid the small tables and plastic lawn chairs, the front-end loader stands out like a rhinoceros at a wedding.

The party's supposed to wind down by 8 p.m.—at least, that's what the invitations say—but company owner Susan Dasta has seen folks straggle out at 4 a.m., just about the time Campbell and Fowler are firing up their auxiliary rig to cook the meat for which they'll be judged. (They can't use the machine because it's strictly a grill, making it virtually impossible to cook brisket and ribs.)

This front-end loader gets a lot of attention at the American Royal Invitational, where the Barbecue Gods of the Universe grill sausages, chicken, and burgers for their supporters.

In a sea of contraptions shaped like coffins, piglets, portable toilets, and beer dispensers, Susan Dasta doesn't think it's at all strange that one of her company's machines is used, year after year, to grill food that people line up for. "I don't know that it's odd at all," she says. "By now, it seems part of the whole ambience. The whole thing is seeing how clean they get it. They get it a lot cleaner that I would imagine."

Campbell and Fowler have cooked Italian sausage, chicken wings, hamburgers, hot dogs, s'mores, and a whole chicken on a spit in the machine. "People have never seen anything like it," Fowler says. "They get a big grin on their faces and shake their heads and they can't believe it. Down here, you kinda see everything."

Dasta says the company provides "financial support, physical help, and emotional support" during the Royal. "We try to be helpful and make sure they have a lot of Bud Light," she says. Over the years, Campbell and Fowler have gotten a lot more organized. The first time they competed, a torrential rain ruined their schedule for the meat preparation. Now they sleep in a camper instead of a van, and have changed their team name from Constructive Barbecue—a nod to the company—to Barbecue Gods of the Universe. "It was intended to inspire confidence," Dasta says.

As the team's sponsor, you'd think she'd have some say in how Campbell and Fowler prepare the food. No way. "I'd much rather be the person eating it than the one cooking it," Dasta says. "They know what they're doing." That expertise extends to their super-secret seasoning. So tightly do they guard the recipe, even Dasta doesn't know how to make it.

Front-End Loader Chicken

Serves
4

BOB FOWLER, one-half of the Barbecue Gods of the Universe, says their recipes work well because they're simple, "and if you know the Gods, you know that simple is a very good thing." This dish is a variation of the Greek chicken that Fowler's mom used to make when he was a kid. Serve with salad and grilled vegetables.

1 whole roasting chicken,
2½ to 3 pounds

One bottle (16 ounces) Kraft Zesty
Italian dressing

1 cup (2 sticks) butter

Juice of 1 lemon

1 tablespoon dried oregano

Parsley sprigs for garnish

Place the chicken in a large zippered plastic bag and pour the dressing over it. Seal the bag and turn the bird to make sure the dressing gets under the skin and inside the bird. Refrigerate for 1 to 2 hours, then remove the chicken and discard the marinade.

Build a fire in a charcoal grill.

Melt the butter with the lemon juice and oregano in a saucepan over medium heat. Place the chicken on a rotisserie and tie the legs and wings with kitchen twine. Place the seasoned melted butter near the grill.

Cook directly over the hot coals, basting often and liberally with the butter, until the juices run clear when a leg is cut at the joint and an instant-read thermometer registers 170° when inserted in the thickest part of a thigh, 45 minutes to 1 hour.

Garnish with the parsley and serve.

Blues Burgers

Serves
4

THE BARBECUE GODS of the Universe just *love* the blues. Whenever they fire up the front-end loader, they make a variation of the blue cheese burgers that can be found in every grill book worth its salt. Avoid low-fat beef, Bob Fowler says, because it really dries out when it's grilled. He suggests serving these burgers with chips, baked beans, cole slaw, and beer on ice. And: "Throw some B.B. King or John Lee Hooker on the stereo, crank it up, chow down, and understand that this is how the Gods live."

Continued ...

¼ cup butter

½ pound white button mushrooms, sliced

1 yellow onion, sliced into rings

2 tablespoons barbecue dry rub, purchased or homemade (page 54)

2 ounces blue cheese, crumbled

1½ pounds ground beef or chuck

1 cup purchased barbecue sauce (Fowler uses KC Masterpiece)

4 hamburger buns or onion rolls, toasted

Build a fire in a charcoal grill.

Melt the butter in a saucepan over medium heat. Add the mushrooms and onions and sauté until soft. Transfer to a warmed platter and set aside.

Mix together the rub and blue cheese in a small bowl.

Form the ground beef into 8 patties. Top 4 of the patties with equal amounts of blue cheese mixture. Top with the remaining 4 patties and pinch to seal the edges.

Place directly over the hot coals and cook to sear and brown, about 3 minutes per side, then continue grilling to the desired doneness, 10 to 12 minutes for medium-rare, basting with the barbecue sauce during the last couple minutes of grilling time.

Remove from the heat and top with the mushrooms and onions. Serve on the toasted buns.

HAVE SMOKE, WILL TRAVEL

As a correspondent for *Time* magazine in South America in the 1970s, Charles Eisendrath developed a taste for political coups and charbroiled *carne*. He divided his time between the palaces of Salvador Allende and Juan Peron, the smoky *parilla* grills of downtown Buenos Aires, and the gaucho fire pits on the lush *estancias* of Argentina.

When he finally settled in Ann Arbor, Michigan, he missed the open grilling of fresh meat over a crackling fire. About the same time, he inherited a cherry farm in northern Michigan—and along with it, a decrepit grill.

In the early 1980s, Eisendrath began searching for a replacement grill that combined the principles of South American grilling with the magic of open fireplace cooking he'd found in Southwest France and on the slotted-surface grills of Turkey.

A Type A personality from the womb, whose hero is the inventor, gourmand, and statesman Thomas Jefferson, Eisendrath decided to build his own grill. With the help of

a welder, he created a prototype that looked like a stainless-steel surgeon's cart with a hand crank to raise and lower the cooking surface. He called it the Grillery, and its unique feature is the "juice recovery" system, a grid of V-shaped channels to catch the juice before it burns on the fire. "Anybody who knows about true grilling knows those juices are the best thing possible to baste the meat or to make gravy," Eisendrath says. Lowering and raising the cooking surface allows the flames to stay just far enough away from the meat so that it doesn't burn.

The patented Grillery appeared to rave reviews in 1984. Foodie godfather James Beard gushed in a column, "Magnificent. Brilliantly thought out and well-constructed." R.W. Apple of the *New York Times* opined: "The Grillery is unmatched. If the caveman had had one, frying and boiling would have never been invented."

"The response was so overwhelming we had to get a larger mailbox," Eisendrath says. This "Maserati of grills" comes with a price tag of between $1,200 and $1,500 and is unlikely to burn out and end up at a garage sale. A list of owners reads like a Who's Who of American journalism and entertainment, including Tom Brokaw, Morley Safer, Donald Sutherland, Faye Dunaway, and Michael J. Fox. Eisendrath also built a custom grill—for an undisclosed price—for the yacht of an Arab prince.

"My wife, Julia, and I thought maybe we'd sell maybe a hundred or so to friends," Charles says with a laugh. "All I wanted was a good grill for myself."

Jerry Hines

Jerry Hines gets right down to it: He doesn't cook for money, prizes, or to impress anyone. "I cook because it usually tastes good, it's fun, and I like cooking for my friends," he says.

On the Saturday morning we met, Hines was scratching his head while cleaning up his grill with a passel of buddies. "I reckon we had a good time last night. My liquor is all gone and most of the food," he said, while he stacked tin foil and threw beer cans in the trash. "I'm not sure what happened. I think I only had a half of a half-gallon of Jack." This earned him polite applause from a small crowd of revelers.

We asked for the secret to one of his award-winning recipes. "You don't have to buy the most expensive cheese. Spend your money on getting the best cut of meat you can," said Hines, which sounded like sage advice after the previous night's bacchanalia.

Hines is the kind of guy you can't help but like: he always wears a smile, has a hug for the pretty gals, and is willing to lend you a hand to unhook a trailer or spill his guts to a stranger about his best recipes.

He retired from the Air Force Reserves after thirty-three years and now lives in Foster, Missouri. He cooks on a one-of-a-kind 500-gallon milk tank. Mounted on a handmade trailer, it's stainless steel and gleams in the sun like a fat torpedo. Jerry burns his wood on an offset firebox at the rear of the cooker. His rig is a lot like him: nothing fancy, just a solid workhorse.

The way Hines tells it, he came upon barbecuing almost by accident. He was twenty years old before he even saw any charcoal, much less tasted any smoked meat. "I'm telling you, I'm just a plain country redneck. We didn't do no kind of grilling when I was growing up," he says.

His first grilling experience didn't turn out well. He found a five-gallon metal bucket and some grates from an old refrigerator. He built a fire, dumped some coals into the bucket, and put a grate on top. "It wasn't nothing but pitiful. I bought me a cheap steak. You can imagine how it turned out. I had a lot to learn." Then, when he was in his mid-twenties, his uncle, Emmett Hines, took him under his wing and taught him how to smoke and grill.

"No one is born knowing how to barbecue. At some point, someone just has to sit you down and show you," Jerry says. "And Uncle Emmett showed

At sunset, Jerry Hines gets a hug from one of his many assistants next to his 500-gallon milk tank smoker/grill.

me the basics–how to fire up your grill, about indirect heat, smoke, and the different cuts of meat."

Jerry began experimenting on a variety of store-bought grills—mostly gas—before crossing over to contraption cookery. His first homemade grill was a monstrosity, made from a 400-gallon home fuel oil tank with no wheels, and ugly as mud. "It took several stout men to move that sucker," he says. "It wasn't the best in the West, but I had a lot of fun with it."

Sadly, the rig was stolen from his yard. He was searching for another rig when he stumbled across a discarded bulk milk tank from a dairy farm. It turned out to be a great candidate for conversion. Because it's stainless and double-lined, the cooker holds heat longer. Once Hines gets the woodbox burning, he can nap three or four hours before having to refire it.

Hines cooks almost exclusively with hedge wood, which is plentiful in Missouri. "Hedge is a good hardwood that makes a hot fire," he says. "I'll toss in some hickory or pecan. But hedge is about perfect for this smoker."

Hines cooks on this rig about ten times a year. At Thanksgiving and Christmas, he uses it to smoke hams and turkeys for his friends and family. He can cook eight to ten at a time. He says there's no secret to his smoked turkeys, but there is an idiosyncrasy.

Most holidays, he doesn't even have time to thaw the birds, but even that has been turned into an advantage: He found that because of the low temperatures of his smoker—200° to 250°F—the frozen birds stay moist inside while crisping on the outside.

"That's it. Eight to ten hours at about 225," he says. "The only thing I use on those turkeys and hams is smoke."

Jerry's Smoked Brisket

Serves

★ **10–12** ★

THIS IS AN AMAZINGLY simple recipe that relies almost entirely on time—it takes 8 to 10 hours. "There's no two ways about it," Jerry says. "A brisket is a danged tough piece of meat and the only real way to tenderize it is by cooking it a long time."

1 beef brisket, about 10 pounds

½ cup barbecue dry rub, purchased or homemade (see page 54)

1 cup tomato-based barbecue sauce of your choice

Build a fire in a smoker/grill for indirect heat. Maintain a temperature of 200°F.

Sprinkle the dry rub all over the brisket. Place the brisket in the smoker on the side opposite the coals and cook for 4 hours.

Remove the brisket from the heat and let cool slightly, then cut the top half from the bottom half along the line of thick fat. Trim out the fat and reserve. Line a large sheet of heavy-duty aluminum foil with the fat.

Lay the larger flat piece of the brisket on top of the fat, and then place the smaller part of the brisket on top.

Wrap the meat tightly in the foil and return it to the smoker. Cook for about 3 hours and 45 minutes longer.

Remove from the heat and let rest for 20 minutes.

Remove the foil and cut the brisket against the grain into long pieces. Serve with the barbecue sauce on the side.

Jerry's Simple Sausage Delight

Serves
★ 8–10 ★

JERRY IS a self-taught cook. He came up with this dish one day when he was too lazy to go back into the grocery store for "manufactured" sausage. "I told you I was a redneck, I don't cook fancy." He got this idea from all of the deer sausage that is made there, in his part of rural Missouri. You can serve this for breakfast, as an appetizer, or just for a snack.

3 pounds ground pork

3 pounds ground beef

2 tablespoons barbecue dry rub, purchased (Jerry likes Yankee Blaster) or homemade (see page 54)

2 tablespoons Old Plantation pork sausage seasoning or other sausage seasoning of your choice, or ½ tablespoon each paprika, sage, chili powder, and garlic

Continued . . .

Build a fire in a smoker/grill for indirect heat. Maintain a temperature of 250°F. Soak a handful of wood chips in water.

In a large bowl, mix the meats and spices. Roll the meat with your hands into the shape of a thick hot dog (about 2½ inches wide and 15 inches long). Drain the wood chips and place on the hot coals.

Lay the log of meat on aluminum foil and place it in the smoker on the side opposite the coals. Cook for about 5 hours. Slice and serve.

Jerry's Potato Casserole on the Smoker

Serves

★ 8–10 ★

THIS DISH IS A BIG HIT with Jerry's buddies at the annual American Royal Invitational barbecue competition in Kansas City. It doesn't cost much, it dilutes all the meat you've been eating, and it fills you up. As Jerry says, "This is one cheesy son of a bitch."

10 to 12 russet potatoes, about 5 pounds total weight, peeled and cut into ½-inch cubes

2 yellow onions, chopped

¼ cup butter, melted

2 tablespoons dried Italian salad dressing mix

1 large green bell pepper, seeded and chopped

Salt and freshly ground pepper

½ pound Velveeta cheese, shredded

1 can (12 ounces) condensed cheddar cheese soup

½ pound mozzarella cheese, shredded

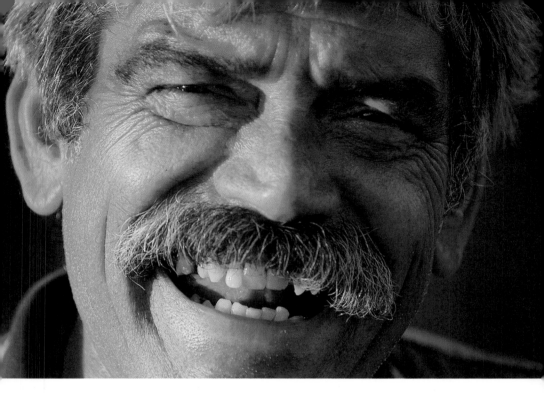

Jerry Hines, a self-described "plain country redneck," loves to smoke brisket, hams, and turkeys for his family and friends.

Build a fire in a smoker/grill for indirect heat. Maintain a temperature of 250°F.

In a large casserole dish, mix the potatoes, onions, melted butter, and Italian dressing mix. Cover tightly with a lid or aluminum foil. Place in the smoker on the side opposite the coals and cook for 1 hour and 45 minutes.

Remove from the smoker and uncover.

Sprinkle the bell pepper over the casserole. Season with salt and pepper to taste. Scatter the Velveeta on top and pour the cheddar cheese soup over the casserole. Sprinkle with the mozzarella.

Re-cover with foil, return to the smoker, and cook until the cheese begins to bubble, about 35 minutes. Serve warm.

Drew Grega

First of all, "BlinDog" is no sight-deprived canine—it's Drew Grega's *nom de 'cue* on the cooking circuit, as in "BlinDog's Outlaw Barbecue Gang." And BlinDog can see fine, at least when he's not around a glass of Jack.

One day, he got a call from one of those TV producer types. You know, "from one of those shows about fixing your screwed-up life—shave your shag-rug back, lift your butt, inflate your breasts, install skylights, and reupholster your ride."

Yeah, he got one of those calls. They wanted to build a dream barbecue rig for BlinDog: He could blue-sky anything he wanted onto a flatbed trailer.

Well, imagine *Extreme Makeover* meets *Monster Garage* with a heavy dose of "Pimp My Barbecue Rig."

Despite his grilling persona, BlinDog lives a pedestrian life in Huntsville, Alabama, where he works for an electric company and lives with his sweet wife, Becky. He was barbecuing before it got cool, back in the early '90s, when a big win was $250 and all the Coors Light his team could quaff.

The point being, BlinDog had not just ridden in on the proverbial meat wagon. But still, he was intrigued with this TV woman on the phone.

"I wasn't sure I'd ever hear from her again," he says. "I knew she was talking with other cookers."

He came up with a wish list for a dream rig: a state-of-the-art rotisserie shaped like a whiskey barrel; separate gas grill/oven; refrigerator; stereo surround sound. His wife added hot and cold running water and a DVD player. His daughters added a hammock. The TV woman called in a designer, who envisioned an Old West saloon with a copper-topped bar—he hated all the stainless steel of most commercial kitchen/smoker rigs.

BlinDog did hear from the producer again. "They were serious, and they were going to film the whole thing for a Food Network special," he says.

And so BlinDog's family found themselves in downtown Anderson, Indiana, home of Southern Yankee Bar-B-Q, a company that builds custom cooking rigs, which had agreed to build BlinDog's dream on a seven-by-eighteen-foot trailer—in under five days. And by golly, they did it, coming through with everything envisioned, plus four awnings, two decks, two stand-up bars, and a life-size statue of a dog-like human with an eye patch and a preternaturally alert snub tail that pokes out of the back of his pants. Folding brick veneer flaps hinged along the edge of the trailer make the rig look like it's permanently built wherever it's parked. Designer Lonnie Hanzon may not be a barbecue guy, but he apparently has a feel for it—the high-end copper topped bar, for example, is juxtaposed with a homey galvanized washtub sink.

But away from the klieg lights, how did the cooker smoke on the road? "Not bad," says BlinDog. "It's more of a showpiece than anything else, but it was fun being on TV. It definitely got people's attention. You couldn't walk by it and not stop."

Alas, GrillGantua and BlinDog decided to part ways (he kept his namesake statue and the Jack Daniel's whiskey barrel and hurricane lamps). The grill now resides in sunny Santa Rosa Beach, Florida, with Byron Chism, who sells butt rub (see www.buttrub.com).

And what is BlinDog smoking on these days? A custom Jedmaster. "This is more me, with the focus on the actual cooking," he says.

Yeah, we know, you never were a show dog.

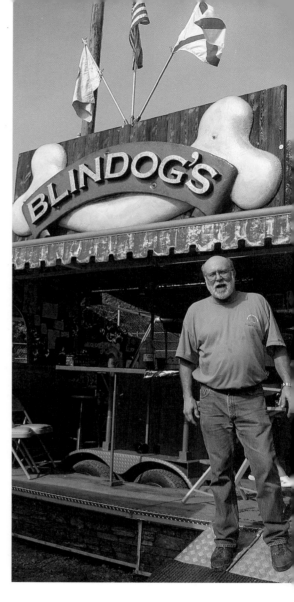

"BlinDog" Drew Grega with his "dream" barbecue rig.

Smoked Pork Loin with Raspberry Chipotle Glaze

Serves
★ **6–8** ★

BLINDOG had been experimenting with a raspberry jam glaze and was looking to add some kind of heat to balance the sweetness just when Tabasco came out with its chipotle sauce. He used it to concoct a finishing sauce with a sweet zip that complements smoky pork. For a killer rack of lamb, use the same sauce, but substitute chopped fresh rosemary for the dry rub.

1 pork loin, about 5 pounds

2 tablespoons extra-virgin olive oil

1 cup barbecue dry rub, purchased or homemade (see page 54)

1 jar (12 ounces) seedless raspberry preserves

1 bottle (5 ounces) Tabasco Chipotle Sauce

Build a fire in a smoker/grill for indirect heat. Maintain a temperature of 235°F.

Peel the white membrane from the pork loin. Coat lightly with the olive oil and sprinkle with the rub liberally on all sides.

Place the loin in the smoker on the side opposite the coals and cook until an instant-read thermometer inserted in the center registers 150°F, about 1½ to 2 hours.

Remove the loin from the smoker and tent loosely with aluminum foil. Preheat the broiler.

In a bowl, combine the preserves and about half of the Tabasco and stir to mix thoroughly. Taste and add Tabasco until you reach your heat tolerance.

Unwrap the loin and coat thoroughly with the glaze. Place under the broiler for about 3 minutes to heat and set the glaze. Remove from the oven, cut into ¾-inch slices, and serve.

BlinDog's Lamb Kabobs

Serves 8

BlinDog claims the secret to any grilled lamb dish is cooking it to medium-rare and letting it rest before serving. "I love kabobs, but I get aggravated making them with beef," he says. "I either have undercooked vegetables or burned beef. Somehow lamb-and-vegetable kabobs almost always come out right."

1 boneless leg of lamb, about 4 pounds

3 large white onions, 1 finely chopped, 2 cut into 2-inch cubes and layers separated

½ cup extra-virgin olive oil

¼ cup fresh lemon juice

¼ cup honey

6 cloves garlic, finely chopped

¼ cup chopped fresh mint

2 tablespoons chopped fresh rosemary

2 tablespoons chopped fresh oregano

5 bell peppers (preferably a combination of green, orange, red, and/or yellow), seeded and cut into 1½-inch squares

2 cups cherry tomatoes

8 ounces fresh button mushrooms

Trim all the fat from the lamb and cut into 2-inch cubes.

In a large glass bowl, combine the finely chopped onion, olive oil, lemon juice, honey, garlic, mint, rosemary, and oregano and mix well.

Add the lamb meat to the olive oil mixture and marinate in the refrigerator at least 2 hours or preferably overnight. Stir the mixture periodically.

Remove from the refrigerator and let come to room temperature.

Soak 12 wooden skewers in water for 30 minutes. Build a fire in a smoker/grill and bring it to 325°F.

Drain the skewers and alternate the lamb, onion, and pepper pieces, tomatoes, and mushrooms on them.

Continued ...

Place the skewers directly over the hot coals and grill until the lamb is medium-rare, about 4 to 5 minutes per side.

Note: For a smokier flavor, add some wet wood chips to the coals just before putting the skewers on the grill. Mesquite or cherry work wonderfully.

Grilled Asparagus with Feta

Serves
4

BLINDOG came up with this recipe while fiddling with his fire one day. He'd grilled asparagus before but was looking to jazz it up, so he added some left-over onions and feta cheese, and felt he'd hit it. The zip of the cheese and bite of the onions sets off the earthy, herbal flavor of the asparagus.

1 pound fresh asparagus

1 yellow onion, very thinly sliced

3 tablespoons extra-virgin olive oil

3 tablespoons chopped fresh thyme

Salt and freshly ground pepper

8 ounces feta cheese, crumbled

Cut about 1 inch off the end of each asparagus spear and place upright in a large jar of water for 2 to 3 hours to replenish the moisture and make the spears more tender on the grill.

Place a sheet of aluminum foil on the rack of a smoker/grill. Build a fire and bring it to 350°F.

In a large bowl, combine the asparagus, onion, olive oil, and thyme and toss to mix thoroughly.

Arrange the asparagus on the foil and cook until tender, about 8 to 10 minutes, rotating frequently to avoid scorching.

Season with salt and pepper to taste. Then either sprinkle the feta over the asparagus, wrap the foil around everything, and let the cheese get all gooey off the heat for 2 to 3 minutes, or transfer the asparagus to a large platter, sprinkle with the cheese, and serve.

BlinDog's Stuffed Mushrooms

Serves **8-10** { As An Appetizer }

LARGE AND STURDY but with lots of flavor, portobellos were made for grilling and satisfy many a meat eater craving a meal simply basted and cooked over a hot fire. BlinDog says this recipe came about because he hates "messing with those tiny-ass button mushrooms that are about impossible to stuff. These are real 'shrooms, and this is a stuffing that can stand up to their great taste."

5 large portobello mushrooms

1 tablespoon extra-virgin olive oil

3 tablespoons barbecue dry rub, purchased or homemade (see page 54)

1 pound ground beef

1 pound ground hot pork sausage

1½ cups chopped red onion

¼ cup chopped green bell pepper

2 cloves garlic, chopped

½ cup Dijon mustard

2 tablespoons prepared horseradish

½ tablespoon ground thyme

½ tablespoon red pepper flakes

Salt and freshly ground black pepper to taste

Build a fire in a smoker/grill and bring it to about 350°F.

Brush the mushrooms with the olive oil, sprinkle with the rub, and set aside.

In a large skillet over medium heat, brown the ground beef and sausage. Add the onion, bell pepper, and garlic and cook until soft.

Pour off the fat and liquid from the skillet and transfer the meat mixture to a large bowl. Add the remaining ingredients and stir to mix thoroughly.

Pile the stuffing on the underside of the mushrooms, dividing it evenly. Place on the grill and cook until the mushrooms are tender, about 5 to 6 minutes.

Remove the portobellos from the grill with a slotted spoon and serve whole or cut into quarters.

Mango Salsa Dog

Makes About 3 Cups

A DOG'S TALE: "It's sometimes amazing and amusing where a mind will wander when you're sipping alcohol around the kitchen. That's how this one came about. I just like mangoes, and I serve this on grilled fish, chicken, and pork chops. It's got a sweet/acidic bite. You can eat it on tortilla chips, or, if you're in the mood, with your hand, right out of the bowl."

2 ripe mangoes, peeled, pitted, and chopped coarsely by hand or in a food processor

½ cup minced yellow onion

1 red bell pepper, seeded and finely chopped

Juice of 1 lime

1 tablespoon sugar

1 teaspoon salt

¼ cup chopped fresh cilantro

In a large ceramic or glass bowl, mix together all the ingredients thoroughly. Let stand at room temperature for at least 30 minutes to allow the flavors to blend before serving.

Jay Vantuyl

Jay Vantuyl, a commercial artist and signmaker, swears you don't have to spend more than $40 for a good cooker that'll win a barbecue contest. The first barrel cooker he ever built, he says, cost him less than two bucks.

He got the idea for it while volunteering as a Boy Scout leader. Hoping to steer a fourteen-year-old boy away from crime, Jay asked him to help build a smoker. "We were trying to keep him out of trouble," Jay says. "But the kid got into trouble, and I got into cooking."

He's made several cookers over the years from scraps of metal and steel that people had thrown away. Complex cookers are parked in the backyard of the shop where he works, and it is clear they've seen better days. "They're basically junk, oh yeah," he says cheerfully. "I don't have any secrets about barbecue. I'll share anything I know or learned."

Unlike most smokers, Jay's trash barrel cooker uses direct rather than indirect heat. It's the simplest of methods: he builds a fire in the firebox at the bottom of the barrel, sticks the meat on a grate from an old Weber he wedged in toward the middle, and waits for the food to cook.

His fellow competitors at barbecue contests, bleary-eyed from waking up every few hours to tend their meat, are used to seeing Jay's cheerful face a couple of hours before everyone has to turn in their chicken, brisket, ribs, and pork butt. Since he cooks over direct heat—exactly the opposite of the "low and slow" method that serious barbecuers insist is the real deal—he can throw his meat on the grate, open a soda pop, and relax.

Actually, Jay's pretty relaxed about a lot of things. He generously helps other contestants who need to borrow some sauce or a rub, and can go on for hours dissecting the fine points of how to cut brisket, which he can read like a road map. Recently he has begun traveling to Mexico—where they call him *El Caracol*, "The Snail"—with his niece and her husband. He has made several barrel cookers for folks in Veracruz, and everyone swaps seasonings and techniques. *El Caracol* has become a sort of informal ambassador of Kansas City barbecue.

Jay has won barbecue contests in Wichita and Emporia, and one year he was the Massachusetts state barbecue champion. A friend of his who won the 2005 American Royal Invitational used one of Jay's trash-barrel smokers,

Jay "the Snail" Vantuyl (right) with his barbecue teammate Dale Cox.

which Jay had traded him for some tent panels. Jay's casual about this brush with fame, and you can tell that even though he cares deeply about good meat, he's not fussy about it. He refuses to rely on temperature gauges on his barrels and lives by the advice of a former pit boss at Gates & Sons Bar-BQ in Kansas City: "Any fool can tell when meat is burning!"

Folks with gizmo-loaded $20,000 contraptions used to smile indulgently at Jay's humble rig, which some people have mistaken for a trash barrel filled with garbage. Now that he's won a bunch of ribbons, though, contestants often amble over after the awards ceremony and start inspecting his cooker.

"People don't see it for what it is," Jay says. "It's too simple, too basic. People want things that are magic. But because this is so simple, it *is* magic."

Snail's Barrel Chicken Legs

Serves
6

"SO MANY PEOPLE come to a contest with expensive meat," Jay Vantuyl says. "I buy chicken on a clear-out. I buy stuff I can afford to feed people." He prefers to use legs and thighs because he thinks they have a better flavor and more moisture.

12 to 15 chicken legs, about 4 to 5 pounds total weight

⅓ cup Snail Seasoning (recipe below)

½ cup light Italian dressing

¼ cup Snail Sauce (page 192)

Build a fire in a smoker/grill and bring it to 250°F.

Remove the skin from the chicken legs. Score the legs across the grain to sever the tendons and leave more surface for the seasoning to adhere to.

Sprinkle the seasoning over the chicken and rub with the dressing.

Place directly over the hot coals and cook for 75 minutes, turning every 15 minutes. Transfer to a large zippered plastic bag with the snail sauce. Let rest for 10 minutes, then serve.

Snail Seasoning

Makes About / Enough For
1 Cup / About 5 lbs. of Meat

JAY VANTUYL'S FRIENDS and family affectionately call him "The Snail." He got his nickname when he was painting a race car and a child's collection of live snails escaped, ruining the paint job and forcing him to start over. This

Continued . . .

rub forms the base of most of the meat Jay smokes in his trash-barrel cookers. He reminds cooks to use it, or any rub, in moderation, because seasoning can always be added but never taken away.

¼ cup *seasoned meat tenderizer*

¼ cup *freshly ground pepper*

¼ cup *paprika*

¼ cup *garlic salt*

Combine all the ingredients in a small bowl. Store in a shaker bottle for up to 3 months.

Snail Sauce

Makes About

4 Cups

JAY EXPERIMENTED with various ingredients—zucchini relish, strawberry preserves—before he got the right combination down for this sauce. He says it goes well with any kind of meat.

2 cups *sugar*

1 can *tomato paste (6 ounces)*

⅓ cup *soy sauce*

½ cup *water*

¼ cup *distilled white vinegar*

2 tablespoons *garlic salt*

1 tablespoon *freshly ground black pepper*

1 teaspoon *celery salt*

¼ teaspoon *cayenne pepper*

In a saucepan, combine the sugar and tomato paste. Add the soy sauce, water, and vinegar and stir to mix well. Stir in the garlic salt, black pepper, celery salt, and cayenne.

Place over low heat and warm gently for at least 20 minutes, stirring to dissolve the sugar. Store, covered in the refrigerator, for up to 1 month.

Cheryl Western & Stoney Merrick

Of all the crazy-looking rigs out there, the ones owned by the Western and Merrick families set the standard for portable funkability (or maybe funky portability): an oil barrel spray-painted in Caribbean colors with a goofy smile and a bullet-shaped smoker bolted to an abandoned shopping cart. Both are testaments to urban recycling. And the meat that comes off them tastes amazing, too.

Every year at the American Royal, Cheryl Western and her dad, Stoney Merrick, tend the smokers in an obscure corner of the contest's parking lot. The way Stoney tells it, he's been barbecuing since he was practically knee-high, when his family moved to Kansas City from Oklahoma. Every weekend, he and his buddies—they call themselves "the Council"—get together in someone's backyard, throw a couple of ribs onto the smoker, uncap the beer, and let the stories roll.

"I fell in love with the smoke," he says. "Italian sausage, beer—you can't beat it."

Three decades ago, before he retired from the parks department in Kansas City, Stoney built a bunch of single-barrel smokers for the employee-appreciation lunches his supervisors sponsored for their workers. But the barrels eventually rusted out. The next rig he built was in 1988, when he was bed-bound with two casts on his legs after a drunk driver plowed into him. "I can't lay up here, I gotta build me a barbecue," he remembers thinking. He hauled himself to the basement, sketched out a design, and built the double-barreled rig he still cooks on today.

Stoney scouts for building materials in some pretty unlikely places. The city's shallow creeks, it turns out, contain a mother lode of overturned shopping carts. And on the streets, he's found abandoned bed rails that make perfect supports for a 55-gallon barrel. A friend of his from the Council spray-painted one old barrel green, added a red and white face, and named it "Baby Godzilla." For $300, Stoney and his buddies will build you a single-barrel smoker; a double will set you back $450.

Stoney doesn't use a rub—he says, perhaps radically, that it takes all the flavor out of the meat—and avoids honey or sugar in his sauce because he thinks it drowns out the taste of ribs and chicken. He can't stand burnt ends,

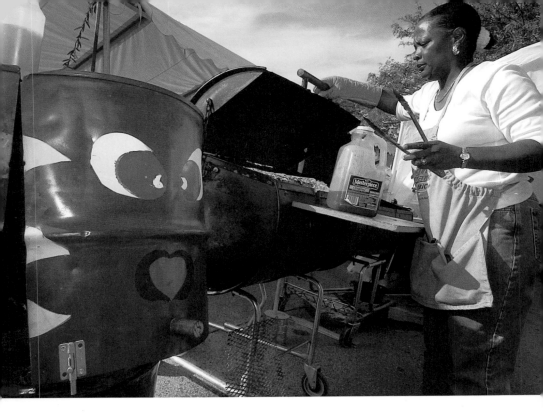

Cheryl Western cooks on conventional horizontal 55-gallon barrel smokers as well as drums mounted upright on grocery carts.

a specialty of many of Kansas City's legendary barbecue joints, and brags that his meat tastes better than what you can find at Gates & Sons Bar-BQ, one of the city's well-known haunts for down-home chicken, ribs, brisket, and pork butt.

"They have pretty good cooks, but they can't touch me on ribs," he insists. "I don't care if they've got fancy cookers and I've got a little barrel. I'll out-cook 'em."

Cheryl, meanwhile, has become the family's cooking star. She was one of a handful of competitors at the Royal one year who got to sell their own barbecue at a booth near the entrance to the competition, and she cleared $1,100 in the space of a weekend. Good cooking goes way back in her family, which is originally from New Orleans. "Everybody in my family cooks," she says. "Men, women, everyone." Her earliest memory of food is the time her grandpa taught her how to cut up chicken. She was five.

"I like to cook, I like to feed people. I got that from my grandmother," she says. "When you went to my grandmother's house, the first thing she said was, 'You hungry?' She was a little bitty woman, but she was the oldest of nine kids. I was the oldest grandchild, and I had to take over for her."

She started feeding her three siblings the easy stuff—spaghetti, hamburgers, French fries—then eventually worked her way up to grilled meats. But it wasn't until she was in her mid-thirties that she really got into barbecue. To her, food just tastes better when it's cooked outside. "Most of the time, when you cook something in the oven, it gets soggy," she says. Like her dad, Cheryl barbecues outside in the winter, even in the snow, running back and forth to check on the meat.

It took a while for her dad and his buddies to let her cook in the backyard with them. When it came to competitions, though, they let her in right away—and now, she's the one who bakes the savory bacon-wrapped cabbage slices that crowds clamor for. Of the Council, she says affectionately, "They're chauvinists. It's, 'Women can't do this, it takes a man to do this.' Now they can't do it without me."

Baked Cabbage

Serves
8

IN CHERYL WESTERN'S HANDS, this humble vegetable becomes something ethereal and ambrosia-like: buttery, rich, and slightly crisp, with a hint of smoke. She added her own touches to this recipe, which originally came from her brother. Now, before every family gathering, she is asked, "You gonna bring the cabbage? You gonna bring the cabbage?"

8 strips thick-sliced bacon

Salt, freshly ground black pepper, red pepper flakes, and brown sugar for sprinkling

1 green cabbage, about 1½ pounds, cored and sliced into 8 wedges

½ yellow onion, cut into 8 slices

½ red bell pepper, seeded and cut into 8 strips

Build a fire in a smoker/grill for indirect heat. Maintain a temperature of 375°F.

Sprinkle each strip of bacon with a pinch each of salt, black pepper, red pepper flakes, and brown sugar.

Place each bacon strip on a 6-inch square of aluminum foil, then top each piece with a wedge of cabbage. Divide the bell pepper and onion pieces among them, then seal the foil over everything.

Place in the smoker on the side opposite the coals and cook for 1 hour and 30 minutes, or until the wedges feel soft when gently squeezed. Transfer carefully to a platter, remove the foil, and serve.

Soulful Baked Beans

Serves
★ **10–12** ★

CHERYL WESTERN LOVES the baked beans served at Fiorella's Jack Stack Barbecue, a Kansas City barbecue joint, because they incorporate cut-up ribs and brisket. She tried to duplicate that soulful taste in this recipe. If you want more beans and less sauce, add another can of pork and beans.

3 cans (15 ounces each) pork and beans

⅓ cup finely chopped yellow onion

¼ cup diced red bell pepper

1 cup purchased sweet barbecue sauce (Cheryl uses KC Masterpiece)

½ cup purchased spicy barbecue sauce (Cheryl uses Gates Barbecue Sauce)

2 teaspoons prepared yellow mustard

½ cup ketchup

2 tablespoons honey

¼ cup firmly packed brown sugar

Build a fire in a smoker/grill for indirect heat. Maintain a temperature of 375°F.

Put the pork and beans in a large bowl. Add all the remaining ingredients and stir to mix well.

Pour into a 9-by-13-inch uncoated metal baking pan and cover with aluminum foil.

Bake for 1 hour and 15 minutes, or until the sauce is thickened. Serve immediately.

Waldo and Barbara Strein

Waldo and Barbara Strein have been married for eleven years. They work together, shop together, cook together. "I bet we're not separated more than an hour a week," Waldo boasts. And, every couple of weekends, they compete against each other on the barbecue circuit.

The Streins stick close to their home in Fort Worth, Texas, because, frankly, it's not like they need to race around the country to cook competitively—Texas has dozens of contests to keep them hopping. They hit eight or nine a year; the farthest they've gone is to Las Vegas.

The cooking bug bit Waldo when he was working as a contractor in his late twenties. A work buddy of his kept talking about what a great time he had entering chili cook-offs, so Waldo joined him for a contest one weekend. It turned out to be the second-biggest in Texas. "The very next weekend, I started cooking," Waldo says. "I fell in love with it."

But there's no money in chili winnings. So Waldo started lugging along his 55-gallon drum smoker to feed the competitors, and that led to him to barbecue contests. "I like the camaraderie of the people," he says. "We loan recipes back and forth, and I've loaned people ribs and briskets when they needed it. If they beat you, they beat you. There's always another weekend."

Enter Barbie Strein. She learned to make gravy and concocted her own barbecue sauce when she was twelve, but aside from that, she didn't pick up much in her mom's kitchen. "It was her kitchen, her stuff, and you couldn't touch it, but I always watched and listened and was curious and liked to experiment," she explains. Years later, when she and Waldo had divorced their first spouses and were dating each other, he started sharing his barbecue tricks. "He thought it'd be a dandy idea if I competed," she laughs. "No matter what he did, I wanted to be with him. If he said he wanted to shovel dirt, I'd have shoveled dirt."

Her first cook-off was in 1992, and, Waldo says proudly before she can, "She won three first places and a third." Chuckling, he adds, "That ruined her life." They competed against each other but cooked on the same rig until 2001, when the International Barbecue Cookers Association changed its rules to allow only one competitor per rig in its contests.

Waldo and Barbara Strein share more than smoky meat morsels; they're husband and wife.

So Waldo, who by that time was cooking on a custom-built $9,000 smoker with chrome smokestacks and an extra burner for crab boils, decided to build two new rigs for himself and Barbie—but mounted them side by side on the same trailer. (It seemed pretty pointless, he says, for each of them to have to drag their own pits to contests.)

With donated fireboxes from a friend and $1,600 in new materials, Waldo built two thirty-inch square cooking chambers with three racks each and steel tuning tubes to evenly distribute the heat from the fireboxes throughout the

"Sheila the Barbecue Slut" is the Streins' mascot on the 'cue circuit.

smoker. There aren't any hot spots in these contraptions, he says—the temperature never varies more than 3 degrees from one spot to another. And at eighteen hundred pounds, it's pretty light to haul. Barbie loves it because she can get at the meat by pulling open a door instead of lifting the handle on a heavy barrel. The racks slide out and the smoker is perfectly proportioned for her petite frame (she's just under five-foot-five).

On top of her cooker is a brunette figurine the couple fondly nicknamed "Sheila the Barbecue Slut" after Barbie rescued her from the dirt at a contest in Terrell, Texas. "She's my mascot," she says. Unexpectedly tearing up, she adds, "I've always been painfully shy, and barbecuing made me a different person. I didn't know it'd grab me the way it did. It changed my life, to be able to talk to people."

Although Waldo refuses to disclose to strangers how he makes his sauce, he and Barbie know how to prepare each other's mops and rubs and sometimes even get the other's meat ready for competition. And both say they're happy when either of them wins a contest—even if it means the other has to watch from the sidelines.

"I'm the first one to cheer when they call his number, as he is with me," Barbie says. "If we ever get mad, we'll stop cooking, because it's supposed to be fun."

Waldo's Lip Smackin' 4-Napkin Ribs

Serves
★ 3–4 ★

TO SEE IF A RIB is perfectly cooked, Waldo Strein doesn't go by the usual method of testing whether the meat pulls away from the bone. His method: "When you pick the ribs up with a pair of tongs and it kinda bends in a U shape, the meat will crack. It's gotta crack like a matchstick." He swears that you can get to the top ten in a cook-off if you follow this recipe, which calls for a St. Louis cut—trimming the tips off a slab of spareribs. The cut is larger than and nearly as tender as baby back ribs, but you get more meat.

1 rack St. Louis–cut pork ribs,
2¼ pounds to 2½ pounds

2 tablespoons barbecue seasoning
(Waldo uses Adkins Western-Style
Barbecue Seasoning)

½ cup barbecue sauce (Waldo uses KC
Masterpiece or Cattlemen's Authentic
Smoke House Barbecue Sauce)

1 cup firmly packed brown sugar

½ teaspoon freshly ground pepper

Build a fire in a smoker/grill for indirect heat. Maintain a temperature of 250°F.

Sprinkle the ribs with the barbecue seasoning, place in the smoker on the side opposite the coals, and cook for 2 hours. Remove from the smoker, brush with about half of the barbecue sauce, and return to the smoker for 15 minutes.

Remove the ribs again, sprinkle with the brown sugar and pepper, and brush again with the barbecue sauce. Wrap the ribs in 2 layers of aluminum foil, return to the smoker, and increase the heat to 300°F. Cook for 1 to 1½ hours longer, until tender. Unwrap, turn the ribs meat side down, and cut between each bone. Serve immediately.

Barbie's Competition Chicken

Serves
4

BARBIE STREIN COOKS this a lot for Sunday afternoon barbecues with friends. She's won a couple of cookoff prizes with it, too.

1 whole roasting chicken, about 4 pounds

1 bottle (16 ounces) Kraft Zesty Italian dressing

¼ cup barbecue seasoning (Barbie uses Adkins Western-Style Barbecue Seasoning)

½ cup sweet and spicy barbecue sauce (Barbie uses Kraft Thick 'n Spicy or Cattlemen's Authentic Smoke House Barbecue Sauce)

Place the chicken in a large zippered plastic bag and pour the Italian dressing over it. Seal the bag and refrigerate for 10 to 12 hours.

Build a fire in a smoker/grill for indirect heat. Maintain a temperature of 250°F.

Sprinkle the barbecue seasoning on all sides of the chicken. Place in the smoker on the side opposite the coals and cook for 1 hour.

Remove from the smoker and brush with the barbecue sauce. Return to the smoker for 15 minutes, or until the sauce has glazed and sealed to the chicken.

Remove from the smoker again and wrap in 2 layers of aluminum foil. Return to the smoker for about 1 hour longer, or until an instant-read thermometer inserted into the thickest part of a thigh registers 170°F.

Chicken Roll-ups

Serves
3-4 { As An Appetizer }

BARBIE CAME UP with these appetizers to go with a chile sauce she liked. She brings it to parties and says guests are always surprised when they bite into the chicken and find the mild cream cheese mixed with spicy peppers.

8 chicken tenders (about 5 to 6 ounces), thawed if frozen

4 ounces cold cream cheese, cut into 8 equal strips

3 jalapeño peppers, seeded and cut into 6 to 8 strips

Build a fire in a charcoal grill.

Place the chicken tenders between 2 pieces of plastic wrap and pound to ¼-inch thickness.

Place a strip of cream cheese along the length of each chicken tender. Divide the jalapeño peppers among them and roll up the strips.

Place directly over the hot coals and grill, turning the roll-ups every 3 to 4 minutes, until the chicken is opaque throughout, about 15 to 20 minutes.

TINKERBELL'S GRILL

Barbecue rigs generally come in two sizes: large and humongous. But the barrel smoker Kelly Draper built for his young daughter, Yancy, is even more petite than she is: sixteen inches across and twelve inches in diameter, with a grill about the size of a piece of typing paper. It's just large enough to cook four hamburgers or half a chicken.

"It's small enough that I can take it somewhere," says Yancy, who is eight. "I like it because my dad won't cook chicken on it, but I will."

Draper competes in barbecue competitions across Texas with his team called No Chiken, and sponsors a barbecue and chili cook-off every year in his hometown of Tahoka, located in the Texas Panhandle about thirty miles south of Lubbock. His day job is as an electrician, but his Web site advertises his skills at barbecue rig building, lawn care, tire rotation, hog trapping, bear eradication, and embroidery.

Draper and his wife, Kim, began taking Yancy with them to contests when she was still a toddler. One day when she was about five, she was watching him and his buddies mess around in the garage with some metal scraps and piped up, "When are you gonna build *me* one?" So, they did—in about four hours. "It took longer for the paint to dry than for us to build it," Draper says. "It's the smallest operating one I've ever seen."

There's no firebox—it's all direct heat—so you won't get award-winning pork shoulder or brisket off this rig. But the meat, even in small quantities, still tastes pretty good, Draper says. That's probably because Yancy uses her mom and dad's rub. While they prepare their meat for contests, she grills hamburgers and hot dogs to keep them going.

Yancy is a lot like most eight-year-olds—she can't sit still very long and prefers to run off and play with her friends rather than tending the smoker during a long cook. But she never complains when her dad gets her up at 5 a.m. to help start the fire in his smoker.

And even though she's too young to compete, she's still making a name for herself on the 'cue circuit. "She likes to show off and tell everyone what she's doing," Draper laughs. "We'll show up three hundred miles from home and she's got more friends than I do."

Kent Ingham & John Wassergord

John Wassergord's rig is proof that anything can be turned into a smoker. His ancient GE refrigerator, built in the twentieth century, has found renewed life in the twenty-first as an apparatus for smoking sturgeon, pork butt, and a host of other meats.

The way he tells it, Wassergord sort of married into the refrigerator. The Kansas City food scientist was a couple of months away from his wedding when, visiting the parents of his fiancée, Mollie Ingham, he noticed an old fridge leaning up against the side of their house. Intrigued, he asked if he could haul it away. Well, sure, they said. So he brought it home, poked a thermometer through the top, and spray-painted it black. He and Mollie's father, Kent, cleaned off the rust and rearranged the heights of the shelves.

Now, they throw pork butts, chicken, fish, or a pot of baked beans on the shelves, light the charcoal, close the door, and they've got a piece of equipment that turns out the same amazing food as a conventional oversized barrel smoker.

The refrigerator had actually been turned into a smoker in the late 1950s by Kent's dad, a surgeon named Walton Ingham. Kent thinks the refrigerator was manufactured just after World War II, and like most family stories, he can't quite remember the details of how it came to the Inghams. But he clearly remembers the smoked trout his dad cooked on it, which Walton brought back from his twice-yearly fishing trips to southern Missouri. "I don't eat fish, I don't like fish, but I loved the smoked trout," Kent says. "It's so totally different, it's unreal."

Walton Ingham was a Renaissance man, of sorts. With his nimble, inventive mind, "anything we needed, he could make," Kent says. He was a metalworker, grew apples and peaches, played five instruments, and one year made a twelve-foot-long Conestoga wagon, complete with a tarp he had sewn himself, for camping trips. He also built the family's outdoor furniture, and turned an old gas tank into the grill they used on humid summer nights.

"He loved working with his hands, whether it was on your gallbladder or on your refrigerator," Kent says. "He was a neat guy. He was my ideal adult."

Walton Ingham quit using the refrigerator for good in 1994. Just before he died in 1999, he told Julie Ingham, Kent's wife and Mollie's mom, that he approved of the young man Mollie was dating—John Wassergord.

Kent Ingham (left) and his son-in-law John Wassergord cook on a forty-plus-year-old GE refrigerator.

Kent and Julie considered selling the refrigerator after Walton's death, but couldn't bring themselves to do it. So it squatted in their yard until their son-in-law rescued it. Since then, the refrigerator has made appearances at wedding rehearsal dinners and neighborhood Christmas parties. It travels back and forth between John and Mollie's house and Kent and Julie's, since they only live a mile away from each other. "Anytime the smoker's fired up, it's a party, because the neighbors smell it," Julie laughs.

At the end of the summer barbecuing season, Kent pressure-washes the inside, but not so completely that the smoke and meat drippings disappear altogether. Then it heads for its "wintering home"—"Oh, that sounds so elegant," Julie jokes—in front of their garage. Kent has even built a brick patio for it. He figures it'll last another fifty years because of its steel construction. You could never turn a refrigerator built nowadays into a smoker, he says, because the plastic would melt and the foam insulation would destroy the meat.

John and Kent have just started entering competitions. John says he never thought much about barbecuing before the refrigerator lumbered into his life. Now, he loves it.

"This has a lot of character," he says. "People have asked, 'Are you gonna get another?' I say, 'Nah, I think I'll keep it.' It's been in the family so long."

Julie's Baked Beans

Serves
★ 12–15 ★

JULIE INGHAM has been making these beans for twenty years and calls them "a showstopper." She found the recipe somewhere and has been adding her own touches ever since. The most common response they inspire, she says, is "Are there more?"

1 pound bacon strips

One large can (7 pounds) pork and beans (about 12 cups)

2 cups firmly packed brown sugar

2½ cups purchased sweet barbecue sauce (Julie uses KC Masterpiece)

¾ cup ketchup

¾ cup molasses

2 tablespoons chili powder

2 tablespoons dry mustard

2 teaspoons liquid smoke

Build a fire in a smoker/grill for indirect heat. Maintain a temperature of 225°F.

Meanwhile cook the bacon in a skillet on the stove top over medium heat until done but not crispy. Combine the bacon with the rest of the ingredients

Continued . . .

and place in a roasting pan. Cover with aluminum foil and place in the smoker on the side opposite the coals. Cook for 4 to 6 hours, or until the beans have had a chance to absorb the taste of the meat you're cooking. Remove and serve immediately.

John's Famous Cheesy Corn

Serves
★ 6–8 ★

John Wassergord, Julie Ingham's son-in-law, is a food scientist, and put this dish together at the suggestion of one of his coworkers. "It's got fat, fat, and more fat in it," he says. "Cheese and butter—you can't really go wrong." Ingham is more succinct: "Make lots."

½ cup (1 stick) butter, melted

1 pound Velveeta cheese

1 can (15 ounces) corn

1 can (15 ounces) creamed corn

½ cup cooked ham, diced

Build a fire in a smoker/grill for indirect heat. Maintain a temperature of 225°F.

In a small saucepan, melt the butter.

Cut the cheese into cubes and place in a 1½ quart baking dish. Add the corn kernels, creamed corn, melted butter, and ham.

Cover with aluminum foil, place in the smoker on the side opposite the coals, and cook until it's hot all the way through, about 2 hours. Remove from the heat and serve immediately.

Smoky Potato Casserole

Serves
12

JULIE INGHAM GAVE a local cookbook with this recipe in it to her daughter, Mollie, when Mollie got married. The dish goes really well with ham or any kind of meat, Julie says.

½ pound bacon strips, cooked until crisp, and crumbled

1½ teaspoons salt, plus more for sprinkling

½ teaspoon garlic powder

1 cup white onion, coarsely chopped

1 cup coarsely chopped celery

1 cup shredded Swiss cheese

⅓ cup milk

⅓ cup heavy cream

48 ounces thawed frozen hash browns

Freshly ground pepper to taste

Paprika for color

6 tablespoons butter

Preheat the oven to 350°F.

Spray an 11-by-7-inch casserole dish with nonstick cooking spray.

Combine the bacon, the 1½ teaspoons salt, garlic powder, onion, celery, and cheese in a bowl. In a separate bowl, combine the milk and cream.

Spread one-third of the hash browns in the bottom of the prepared dish. Spread half of the bacon mixture on top. Layer on another one-third of the hash browns and then the rest of the bacon mixture. Finish with the last one-third of the hash browns. Sprinkle with salt and pepper to taste and dust the paprika on top.

Pour the milk mixture over the top and dot with the butter.

Bake, uncovered, for 30 minutes, or until golden brown. Cut into squares and serve warm.

Robert Templin

Wild hogs in East Texas look a lot different from their cousins elsewhere around the country—scrawny from foraging for food, instead of farm-raised and fat—and when Robert Templin started mounting them on a rotisserie he built, he liked having a little fun with the folks who dropped by his tent at the Houston Livestock Show and Rodeo.

"The first time we carried it to Houston, the guys were telling the public we were cooking a greyhound," he says with a chuckle. "They were getting us into trouble and I had to put a stop to it, or the police department would have thought we were cooking dogs."

Templin's barbecue team is part of a network of teams across the state whose members raise money for college scholarships awarded through the livestock show and rodeo, which bills itself as the largest in the world. Templin has cooked with the Nacogdoches County Go Texans team for four years. For a while the team cooked on a plain old pit smoker, but—this being Texas—the members decided they wanted something a little more attention-grabbing. So Templin, a full-time firefighter, decided to build a large, rotating spit—the kind you'd expect to see at a medieval dinner, with steins of mead and armored knights clanking around—for roasting a whole hog the next time the team headed to Houston.

"The rotisserie and pigs just go together," he explains. "I thought, heck, I could build one and we'd have one of those the next time we go down there."

Templin scouted out a couple of small rotisseries to figure out how fast they turned, and sketched a diagram. With some metal he had, he constructed two steel A-frames to hold the spit and built a large, stainless-steel pan underneath to hold the hickory logs that would fuel the fire. A friend of his gave him an electric motor to operate the gears that would rotate the spit, and Templin bought a large chain, similar to the one on a bicycle, to raise and lower it.

Templin estimates he spent about $200 on the project. Besides being pretty cheap to build, it's easily disassembled. While other folks have to buy extra-heavy tires and multiple axles to haul their rigs to contests, Templin just throws his in the back of his pickup.

Fully assembled, the rotisserie gets plenty of curiosity seekers. Templin and his teammates can't seem to resist practical jokes, and sometimes they string road kill from the top of their rig, just to watch people gasp. Renee Faulkner, the only woman on the team, tries to reassure the onlookers. "They really have a lot of fun with people who stop by," she says. "A lot of people have never seen anything like it before."

Being the only woman on a team like that may sound like it would be trying at times, but Faulkner's having a blast. The guys are very protective of her: If a stranger gets out of line, they're "right on top of it," she says. "I was real worried about the wives, but I talked to all of them before I joined and they said, 'You can take our jobs so we don't have to work so hard.' We put tablecloths on tables, and little candles there. We even decorate the Port-a-Potty with patio lights."

One big disadvantage to an outdoor rotisserie, though, and one reason you may want to think before racing out to build your own, is that the food takes forever to cook. Roasting a whole hog on a spit may sound great if you're half-drunkenly discussing the concept with your friends, but unless you have most of a day to keep throwing wood on the fire—Templin says he needs twice as much wood for a spit as for a smoker—this cooking method isn't for you.

Texan Ed Ivy prepares some "unidentified critter meat" on his friend Robert Templin's homemade rotisserie.

"I've never cooked anything off-the-wall, because it takes a lotta time," Templin says. "It's not a real effective way to cook; it's more of a fun thing."

But if you have a dedicated audience, cooking a sixty-pound hog is way more impressive on a rotisserie than hiding the pig beneath a plain old black smoker. There's something slightly hypnotic about watching the meat turn slowly, surrounded by admirers who can't wait to grab a piece of crackly-skinned meat.

"The food's right out there," Templin says. "Man and fire and meat. That's the thing—and beer, of course. It's a cool deal."

Robert Templin's Wild Hog

Serves
60

FOR THREE WEEKS in March, Houston's Reliant Park gets turned over to the Houston Livestock Show and Rodeo. In the parking lot outside the stadium, serious barbecuers compete for prizes in what's billed as "a colossal, Texas-sized picnic." It's not uncommon for businesses to drop $100,000 in food and liquor while sponsoring a team and a party inside the team's cooking tent. Templin likes to lay out his entire pig on a table and allow his guests to carve off whatever part they want.

1 whole hog, about 60 pounds, skinned

2 cups corn oil

12 ounces beer (Templin uses Miller Lite)

½ cup white vinegar

2 tablespoons Lawry's seasoned salt

1 tablespoon freshly ground pepper

1 teaspoon garlic powder

Secure the pig on a rotisserie and light a fire underneath it.

Combine the oil, beer, vinegar, seasoned salt, pepper, and garlic powder in a bowl. Baste the pig with the mixture every 15 minutes during cooking.

Cook for 7 to 10 hours, or until an instant-read thermometer inserted in the meat near the thigh registers 180°F.

THE ORIGINAL CHARCOAL GRILL

Outdoor cooking has been an American tradition for centuries, but it got a kick-start in 1952, when a guy in Illinois got tired of the wind, snow, and other extreme climate conditions that got in the way of feeding his brood of twelve.

So, George Stephen Sr. decided to build a better grill than the inferior brazier he used at his house in Mount Prospect. A welder at Weber Brothers Metal Works, where he worked assembling metal buoys for the U.S. Navy, Stephen cut a metal buoy in half and crafted a dome-shaped kettle with a rounded lid, an inside grill rack, air vents, and three legs. It worked so well that he began selling it for the  princely sum of $50 (most braziers back then sold for $7) and the company eventually changed its name to Weber-Stephen Products Co. In the late 1950s, Stephen bought out the factory's owners and became the sole proprietor.

Today, the company "pretty much owns the market" for charcoal grills, according to spokeswoman Sherry Bale. The Sputnik-like cookers are in backyards all over the U.S. and overseas, and the company's fancier rigs—they introduced a line of gas grills in 1985—are ubiquitous at barbecue contests. Bale isn't worried that barbecue worshippers will abandon their Webers for the challenge of building their own rigs: "The more people who grill, the better it is for us. Grilling has become huge in the last five years."

Weber has started a line of cookbooks, founded a "grilling school" in the Chicago suburbs, and recently opened a chain of Weber Grill restaurants, where customers can watch the chefs prepare burgers and steaks on a huge kettle grill.

As for the emotional debate over whether a charcoal grill is superior to gas, Bale is firm in her convictions: "I'm a charcoal girl." But not at home. Bale lives in downtown Chicago, and city rules forbid her from firing up her charcoal kettle grill on her balcony. She refuses to surrender it, though.

"It's like what Charlton Heston says about his gun," she says. "They'll have to pry it out of my cold, dead hands."

CHAPTER 3

HOMEMADE RIGS & RECIPES OF THE SOUTHWEST, PACIFIC NORTHWEST & WEST

COOKING RIGS HAVE A LONG HISTORY in the West, despite the fact that the region was settled much later than the rest of the country. Sketches by early explorers show intricately woven fish nets and racks used to dry buffalo meat; early cooking was done over campfires in the shadows of mountains and forests thick with Douglas firs. Lacking the numerous blacksmith shops and other suppliers used to forge contraptions, Westerners were left to devise their own.

That independence continues today in areas that remain sparsely populated even as the East Coast gets more and more crowded. If you live and die by the seasons of your crops on a remote farm in New Mexico, you're not going to shell out a bunch of cash if you need a new tractor part or cooking gadget; you'll try to fix it or improvise. And if you want to hold on to tradition—be it from your upbringing in Argentina or passed down from your Native American ancestors in Canada—you build your own rig to remind you of home.

West and Southwest food trends are ideally suited to contraption cooking, which calls for a minimum of fuss and the absence of heavy sauces and elaborate prep work. With so much fresh produce easily available, it seems wrong, somehow, to hide asparagus in cream and bake it to an olive green or to slather organically grown chicken in a gloppy red sauce.

While the rest of the country became obsessed with barbecue, Westerners built outdoor ovens and borrowed the concept of *chimineas* (outdoor clay fireplaces) from Mexico. The region's hot summers and mild winters make it possible to cook on an outdoor rig year-round, and kitchens have gradually moved outside to take advantage of the good weather.

Westerners also pioneered the idea of recycling, a concept that has gone from strange to normal in one generation. Re-using the Earth's resources carries over into rig-building. A gourmet organic restaurant in Oregon, Intaba's Kitchen, serves its food from a massive earthen oven nine feet in diameter. Builder Kiko Denzer made it from crushed firebricks and cement stucco; cooks slide pizzas into it all day and bake bread early the next morning without having to start a new fire.

Mark Doxtader turns lamb kabobs in his mobile, wood-fired bread oven.

"Humans have survived for many millennia using local materials to meet their needs," Denzer says. "How much longer can we build with steel and glass and concrete before we run out of energy and resources?" ⭐

Victor Johns Husselbee

"We don't own the land, we just pass through. What's important now is Mother Earth. She's our mother. We're all her children. It's important to thank her every day. It's all about reverence, waking up healthy, praying for people in need, and using the spirit, not just the mind."

Food festivals don't usually begin with a Native American prayer. But one September day, under a steel-gray Seattle sky, Victor Husselbee bowed his head with a group of people huddled next to a fire pit and listened as a member of an Alaskan tribe said these sonorous words.

Husselbee, a member of Canada's Taku River Tlingit First Nation, was the lead cook—actually, the only cook—at a salmon bake to benefit the United Indians of All Tribes Foundation, an organization that provides social, cultural, and economic support for local and regional tribes of the Pacific Northwest. He had said his own prayer that morning, the same one he says before all of his salmon bakes. "Salmon is sacred," he says. "If the salmon don't live, then we don't live. A lot of us have lost the old ways. We're working in this concrete jungle."

Immediately after the prayer, Husselbee got to work. He spread a ten-pound wild coho fillet on a table and mopped it with his own lemon-based sauce. Then he took two long cedar sticks joined by wire at one end—resembling a giant tuning fork—slid the salmon between them, and placed a couple of thinner sticks at 90-degree angles to the big ones. He secured the fish to the sticks with more wire, walked it over to the fire pit, and planted it firmly in the ground a couple of inches away from the hot coals. Soon there were five fillets in a semicircle, looking like snowshoes parked outside a ski lodge.

A knot of visitors gathered to watch Husselbee, who talked nonstop as he heaved fish onto the table, squeezed lemons, and twisted wire. "We've been putting on salmon bakes since the beginning of time," he says. "I learned it from my elders. It takes years to be really good. You've gotta know your salmon."

Husselbee was born in British Columbia's Taku Valley. He spent some time in a foster home, worked in a sawmill, and went to welding school, and endured the kind of in-your-face prejudice that was common back then, when restaurant signs read, "No Dogs or Indians Allowed." While in his twenties—"young and foolish," he says—he served three years in a Washington State prison for grand

The Seattle skyline was the backdrop for the salmon bake Victor Husselbee organized to benefit the United Indians of All Tribes Foundation.

larceny. It was there that he met Bernie Whitebear, a prominent advocate for the rights of urban Native Americans, who had come to the prison to speak.

The meeting changed Husselbee's life, and he began reading philosophy and playing chess behind bars. When he got out, he made his way to Seattle, where Whitebear had staged an invasion of Fort Lawton, a U.S. Army base that the government had declared was surplus property. Whitebear says Native Americans deserved a part of the land that originally was theirs, and eventually the U.S. government agreed to set aside twenty acres for a cultural center. Whitebear ran the center for nearly thirty years, and Husselbee apprenticed himself to him.

He got Whitebear to teach him how to put on salmon bakes, and the men cooked for visitors from South America, Spain, and England, as well as for U.S. senators and mayors. "I've done every kind of reception you can think of—dinner theaters, fund-raisers, campaigns," Husselbee says. "Every one's got its own special spirit. It's like I'm on stage, the spirit has to be right."

A series of strokes slowed Husselbee down for a while. As the festival near Lake Union wore on, he barely stopped to eat. His son was supposed to have helped, but he never showed up. So it was Husselbee alone who worked as fast as he could to get the salmon ready so others could feed the crowd. After a couple of hours, his left side—the one where he'd had the strokes—started to burn as though someone was holding a torch to it. But he remained upbeat, constantly checking the skin side of the fish before flipping it around so the flesh would cook to a light caramel color. In less than an hour, the salmon was ready to serve.

As the crowd thinned, Husselbee rejected offers to help clean up. He carried his empty cooler and the pail that had held the basting sauce back to his trailer, where he keeps a history book of the Tlingit people and a photo of a salmon bake he once did in the woods. The day had gone well.

"Every salmon bake I do, I get butterflies," he says. "To a lot of people, it's another day. To me, this is a ceremony."

Victor's Salmon Baste

Makes **7 Cups** { Enough To Baste
10 Salmon Fillets of 8-12 lbs. Each }

VICTOR HUSSELBEE has used this baste for the hundreds of large-scale salmon bakes he's done over the years. He says it's a good, basic recipe to feed the public, but when he's cooking for family he might alter it a bit by adding some sugar or honey. He says the best time to eat his salmon is right after it comes off the coals, and his favorite compliment is "when they come and smile and say it's the best salmon they've ever had."

Juice of 10 lemons

2 pounds (8 sticks) butter

¼ cup dried parsley

½ cup garlic powder

Build a fire in a fire pit.

Combine the lemon juice, butter, and parsley in a large cast-iron pot. Place on the edge of a pile of hot coals.

Warm until the butter melts but the mixture is just short of boiling, about 10 minutes.

Remove from the coals and stir in the garlic powder. Use a pastry brush to baste salmon or other fish with the warm butter sauce before grilling or baking.

Mark Doxtader

With his easygoing smile, meaty hands, and tall, burly frame, Mark Doxtader looks like the village breadmaker in a sixteenth-century Bavarian burg as he twirls a ball of dough around his knuckles, flattens it, and brushes it with oil.

After that, it's up to his imagination how to finish it. Maybe he'll dribble poppy seeds along the sides for a savory flatbread, or arrange nectarines on top and sprinkle rosemary and ricotta cheese between the cracks. Or he'll pinch off pieces of the dough and braid it around a lamb sausage in a dressed-up version of a pig-in-a-blanket.

Then he slides the dough into a mobile bread oven he made himself. Every Saturday and Wednesday he hauls it to the Portland Farmers' Market and turns out dozens of pita sandwiches and fruit cobblers for his customers, who wait patiently in line, sometimes in a cold drizzle. (In Oregon, folks are polite even if they have to wait hours for something.)

Doxtader was raised in Colorado and worked as a photographer in Los Angeles for a few years until, tired of the city's frenetic pace, he set off for a back-packing trip in Europe and the Middle East. He lived on inexpensive street food in Cairo and fell in love with the diced tomato-and-onion salads his girlfriend's Israeli relatives introduced him to.

When he got back to the States, he and his girlfriend, Dina Temkin, got married and settled in Oregon. They bought a farm on a patch of land just outside the city and grew more than fifty types of fruits and vegetables on two acres. Doxtader started a catering business and signed up for a spot at the farmers' market, which has more than two hundred vendors and a three-year waiting list for the Wednesday market.

It was a market-sponsored artisan baking event called Summerloaf that propelled Doxtader into building his mobile oven, which weighs 4,500 pounds and cost about $4,000 to construct.

With the help of a fellow baker, who said he wanted to build an oven to show off at Summerloaf, Doxtader and some friends poured a four-inch slab of concrete for the base. Using a wood frame as a guide, they lined the hearth, vault, and roof with erosion-resistant firebricks. Finally, they covered the top with three inches of concrete, giving the oven more insulation than it needed— meaning it takes longer to heat up than other ovens like it. More often than

Mark Doxtader with one of the sandwiches he prepared for customers at the Portland Farmer's Market.

Pita bread bakes inside Mark Doxtader's mobile bread oven.

not, pizzas and pitas come out with quarter-sized black spots, but Doxtader isn't perturbed. "Part of our style is a little bit of rustic and a little bit of burnt," he says.

Getting the oven to market takes careful maneuvering down the highway to avoid potholes. The first year Doxtader took it to Summerloaf, he was so worried about chunks of it falling off that he lugged along extra bags of bricks and mortar. Now, he doesn't seem concerned about a couple of hairline cracks, even as he acknowledges the oven has long outlived its design life.

Also that first year, he offered an elaborate menu—hazelnut sticky buns, apple bread puddings, goat cheese bread puddings, cinnamon rolls with fresh berries, upside-down cakes—before realizing he needed to trim back or he'd collapse. Now he sticks to dough-based items that can be prepared the night before. If he can't get the fresh vegetables, herbs, and spices that he needs during the week, he'll buy them from his fellow vendors when he arrives at the market at 6 a.m.

Doxtader heats his oven around 11 p.m. Friday night with oak or maple logs, then seals it up for a long, slow burn. He cooks pitas, cobblers, and pizzas in shifts to take advantage of slowly dropping temperatures throughout the day; foods that need more heat get cooked first.

Camping as a kid is probably what led him to a love of cooking outdoors, Doxtader says. His wife calls the type of cooking he does "medieval."

"There's a certain level of complexity of the food that's brought down," he says. "The kind of food we do is simple, down-to-earth, no sauce reductions. It's just kind of raw."

Compact and elegant, the oven sits on a trailer with heavy-duty axles strong enough to haul a couple of horses—and instantly transforms his corner of the sidewalk into a blacktop bakery.

Customers pepper him with questions throughout the day about how the oven works. One rainy morning at the farmers' market, the woman who supplies the lamb sausages for his sandwiches dashed over, grabbed one straight out of the oven, and paused just long enough to say, "Mark's an artisan with them." Then she hurried back to her tent.

"People are surprised to see a brick oven at the market," Doxtader says. "A lot of folks have memories of having Iranian or Persian ovens in their houses or villages. There's some sort of community in having fire and coals and warmth."

Pocket Pita Bread

Makes 16–20 Pitas

IN ADDITION TO BEING a fixture at the Saturday farmers' market in Portland, which runs from April until December, Mark Doxtader also brings his mobile bread oven to a Wednesday farmers' market next to the Portland Art Museum, a few blocks away. He gets so much business at lunchtime that he needed to make something that takes less time than pizza. So he thought about pita bread, which he could make into sandwiches ahead of time for customers to carry back to the office.

2 teaspoons active dry yeast

4 cups warm water (105° to 115°F)

7 cups unbleached all-purpose flour

3 cups whole-wheat flour

¼ cup extra-virgin olive oil

2 tablespoons kosher salt

In a large bowl, dissolve the yeast in the warm water and let stand until foamy. Add 4 cups of the all-purpose flour and mix until smooth. Gradually add the whole-wheat flour, olive oil, and salt and continue to mix until smooth. Add just enough of the remaining 3 cups all-purpose flour so that the mixture forms a stiff ball, but can still be easily kneaded. Knead just until the dough is smooth, adding more flour as needed to keep it from sticking to your hands.

Put the dough in a clean, large, oiled bowl and turn to coat. Let the dough rest for 15 minutes, then fold it in half 3 times in the bowl. Refrigerate overnight.

Turn the dough out onto a lightly floured work surface and cut into ½-cup pieces. Roll each piece into a tight ball.

Place the balls on a floured baking sheet and cover with a clean kitchen towel. Let rise for about 20 minutes, or until the balls become soft.

Mark Doxtader pats his pita bread a final time before placing it in the oven.

Build a fire in a wood-fired bread oven and bring to 650°F.

Roll out the dough into rounds no more than ¼ inch thick. Put on a floured baker's paddle, then transfer to the hearth of the oven.

Bake in small batches until the disks just begin to brown, about 2 to 3 minutes. Remove from the heat and keep covered with cloth until ready to eat.

Grilled Ground Lamb Kabobs

Serves
5

MARK DOXTADER FEEDS these to his kids—Ivy, age seven, and Linden, age four—as an alternative to hamburgers. They both like the idea of eating meat on a stick. And the kabobs also fit easily into a pita pocket; try making your own pitas with the recipe on page 226.

1 pound ground lamb

1 yellow onion, minced

1½ tablespoons kosher salt

Freshly ground pepper to taste

Tahini sauce for serving (facing page)

Warmed pita pockets for serving (optional)

Soak wooden skewers in water for 1 hour, then drain. In a large bowl, combine all the ingredients and mix well. Form slightly less than ½ cupfuls of the mixture into ovals and thread onto the skewers.

Build a fire in wood-fired bread oven and bring to 650°F. Spread the glowing coals out on the hearth and set up a preheated grill and rack directly over the coals. Place the kabobs on the grill and cook, turning once, until medium-rare, 5 to 7 minutes. Remove from the grill and serve with the tahini sauce, or tuck into pita pockets with the sauce if you like.

Tahini Sauce

2 Cups / 5-6 Sandwiches
Makes / Enough For

THIS GARLICKY RECIPE is from Mark Doxtader's mother-in-law, Dvora Temkin, who was born in Persia and eventually moved to Israel. It's a staple of Middle Eastern cooking. Doxtader ate a lot of pita bread sandwiches slathered with this sauce when he backpacked through the Middle East in the 1990s.

¾ cup tahini paste

8 cloves garlic, coarsely chopped

¾ cup water, plus more as needed

¼ cup fresh lemon juice

½ tablespoon kosher salt

¼ cup extra-virgin olive oil

Combine the tahini paste, garlic, and water in a food processor and process until smooth.

Add the lemon juice and salt and pulse to blend. With the machine running, gradually add the olive oil. You may need to add more water to bring the mixture to the desired consistency. It should thin enough to pour, about the consistency of salad dressing.

Refrigerate until ready to use. The sauce will thicken a bit. Bring to room temperature before serving.

Ronnie Franzoy

It's easy to get lost on the way to Jennifer and Jason Franzoy's house outside of Hatch, New Mexico. It's mostly dirt roads, about as far from a supermarket or department store as you can get. When we finally arrived for a backyard barbecue one October weekend at the end of the annual chile harvest, the first thing we saw was a garage as big as an airplane hangar. Outside, fluorescent lights illuminated three round disks plunked atop three portable burners. The scent of frying steak and chile peppers bit cleanly into the warm night air.

A handful of guys in jeans and cowboy boots were watching the progress of the food while Jennifer bustled around the garage, placing a vase of flowers on the buffet table and shooing away the fruit flies. The young men drank beer; the older ones, hard liquor. Every once in a while, someone stirred the tequila-soaked meat with a spatula and a fork. The contraptions looked like woks, but this wasn't fragile Asian fusion food they were cooking; it was plain, hearty fare for folks who farm year-round and work hard at it.

"Back in the 1970s, a friend of mine, he loved cooking, and one day he says, 'Ya know those woks everyone cooks food in? Well, I made one out of a disk blade,'" says Ronnie Franzoy, Jason's dad, who made the *discos* his son and daughter-in-law were using. "I went to his house and he was cooking on it. He made me one and I made others some."

Large tractors have disk blades on them to rotate the soil and prepare the ground for planting smooth rows of onions, chiles, and cotton. Occasionally a big rock will dent a disk, making it useless for farm work. So, Ronnie and other farmers will remove it from the tractor, scrub the dirt off it with a wire brush and seal up the small hole in the center with a piece of scrap metal. Then, to make the handles, they take two horseshoes and attach them at opposite sides of the disc, using a welding torch. They place the *disco* on a portable burner and fry up skirt steak, vegetables, and anything else they think of.

A *disco* isn't really like a wok because the sides aren't deep enough to maintain different temperature zones, making it impractical to stir-fry. It's more like a giant frying pan, the ultimate example of a farm's built-in recycling program. Cooking on a *disco* is a great way to show off your culinary skills: Smokers are big and clumsy and easy to hide behind, but a rainbow-hued assortment of bell peppers sizzling on a waist-high, open rig is sure to attract attention.

"Disco" parties are common on New Mexico farms after the chile harvest.

Ronnie follows the same drill that experienced cooks use when washing their cast-iron pots: they don't. Wash them much, that is—Ronnie dumps salt on his *disco* and wipes it down with a paper towel. "It's good to wash with soap once in a while, but not often because you lose the seasoning," he explains. He insists that repeated use seals the seasoning in the *disco* and infuses the food with more flavor. During the fall, he says, he cooks on it every two weeks or so.

The Franzoy family has sunk deep roots in this soil. Ronnie's grandfather, Joseph Carlio Franzoi, came to the Hatch Valley in 1913 from Italy by way of New York and Arizona. "Back then, the Valley was just river and trees," Ronnie says. "He bought land cheap and started to clear it for farmland." Joseph

A minimum of prep work is needed to turn out delicious food on the *disco*.

started an export business, J.C. Franzoy & Sons, and, according to Ronnie, was the first farmer in the area to ship chiles out of New Mexico. He had ten children, who eventually gave him seventy grand- and great-grandchildren. The Franzoys are so numerous now that, in an area with sixteen hundred people, at least six hundred are related to Ronnie.

Ronnie's uncle, Albert Franzoy, passed down the rig-building tradition to his nephew. When Ronnie was young, he and his uncle went deer hunting, and relied for warmth on an old oil barrel that Albert had converted into a portable heater. The campers would stick it in the middle of their tent, with a smokestack running out of a hole in the tent's top, and play cards around it. Nowadays it's the guest of honor at barbecues, with a metal plate allowing a cook to heat up tortillas or a pot of coffee, and make pancakes.

But the *discos* are clearly the big draw. After the chile harvest, it's common for laborers to throw *disco* parties, where the beer flows liberally and there's more than enough meat to go around.

"It's a great invention because food tastes better than in a wok," Ronnie says. "You can cook better on it and get the crowds. Everyone smells the food, and it has a beautiful flavor."

Franzoy's Fiery Fritters

Serves **10** { As A Side Dish }

JENNIFER FRANZOY, Ronnie's daughter-in-law, grew up two blocks from Martha Stewart's house in Westport, Connecticut. "When she came out here, she fell in love with chiles," says her husband, Jason Franzoy. For the past couple of years Jennifer has helped organize the Hatch Chile Festival, which draws twenty thousand visitors to this corner of New Mexico. When we called her for suggestions about what rigs to include in this book, she suggested *discos*, and invited us to a *disco* party one October weekend, where she served this dish that seems tailor-made for the rig.

40 mild chile peppers, preferably sandías

2 cups all-purpose flour

2 teaspoons salt

1 teaspoon pepper

2 teaspoons garlic powder

16 ounces beer (Jennifer uses Keystone Light)

½ cup canola or olive oil

Ranch dressing for serving

Preheat a broiler.

Place the chiles in the broiler and roast until the skin on the peppers becomes wrinkled and there are black spots, about 3 to 4 minutes. Turn the peppers over and repeat. Remove from the oven and place on damp paper towels to cool. Remove the skins and seeds and cut into 1-inch pieces.

Combine 1½ cups of the flour, the salt, pepper, and garlic powder in a bowl and add the beer. Whisk together until the mixture is smooth; it should be about the consistency of pancake batter.

Put the remaining ½ cup flour in a bowl, add the chile pieces, and toss to coat. Submerge the floured chile pieces in the bowl of batter.

Continued . . .

In a *disco* or large skillet, heat the oil over medium heat until a drop of water sizzles in it. Using a slotted spoon, lift some of the chile pieces from the batter and add to the skillet, being careful not to crowd the pan (cook in batches if necessary). Cook until golden brown on both sides, about 1 to 2 minutes per side. Transfer to paper towels to drain. Repeat with remaining chiles.

Serve immediately, with the ranch dressing on the side.

AN HOG BARBECUED, OR BROIL'D WHOLE, FROM VAUX-HALL, SURREY

Take an Hog of five or six Months old, kill it, and take out the Inwards, so that the Hog is clear of the Harslet; then turn the Hog upon its Back, and from three Inches below the place where it was stuck, to kill it, cut the Belly in a strait Line down to the Bottom, near the joining of the Gammons; but not so far, but that the whole Body of the Hog may hold any Liquor we would put into it.

Then stretch out the Ribs, and open the Belly, as wide as may be; then strew into it what Pepper and Salt you please.

After this, take a large Grid-Iron, with two or three Ribs in it, and set it upon a stand of Iron, about three Foot and a half high, and upon that, lay your Hog, open'd as above, with the Belly-side downwards, and with a good clear Fire of Charcoal under it. Broil that side till it is enough, flouring the Back at the same time often. Memorandum, This should be done in a Yard, or Garden, with a Covering like a Tent over it.

When the Belly-part of the Hog is enough, and turn'd upwards, and well fix'd to be steady upon the Grid-Iron, or Barbacue, pour into the Belly of the Hog, three or four Quarts of Water, and half as much White-Wine, and as much Salt as you will, with some Sage cut small; adding the Peels of six or eight Lemons, and an Ounce of fresh Cloves whole.

Then let it broil till it is enough, which will be, from the beginning to the end, about seven or eight Hours; and when you serve it, pour out the Sauce, and lay it in a Dish, with the Back upwards. Memorandum, The Skin must not be cut before you lay it on the Gridiron, to keep in the Gravey; neither should any of the Skin be cut, when you have any Pork roasted for the same Reason.

—from *The Country Housewife and Lady's Director*
by Richard Bradley, first published in 1727

Heidi Moore

Even in a city where bumper stickers read "Keep Portland Weird" and skate-boarding is a legally acceptable way to commute, Heidi Moore stands out.

She's banished anything made with plastic from her house, tossed out all her synthetic clothing in favor of natural fibers, and renounced electricity by unplugging her computer and unscrewing the light bulb in her refrigerator. So it's not a huge stretch to imagine that the slender, long-haired woman who grew up listening to the howls of wolves in Alaska, lived with French anar-chists, and volunteered with Mother Teresa would decide, for her master's thesis, to build a cob oven in the center of the Rose City.

For an entire summer, Heidi and her classmates at Portland State University spent the warm weekends stomping on a pile of clay and sand, trying to break up the clay and press the grains of sand into it so the mixture would be firm enough to shape into a dome that makes up the heart of the oven. They left a rounded hole for a door. After the first layer was done, they built a second—this time, with straw added in to shore up the foundation—then covered the whole thing with plaster. Last came the wooden door and a wood eco-roof above the oven to keep it dry during Oregon's rainy winters.

Now that they're finished, it looks like an upside-down egg perched on four gnarled tree legs, much like something Bilbo Baggins might have built.

Cob, which comes from an English word meaning "lump," is a mixture of clay, sand, and straw. The material has been used for centuries to build homes and ovens from Africa to the United Kingdom. Since the walls of a cob oven are so thick, they retain heat for hours longer than a conventional oven, allowing cooks to start a fire in the morning and cook a week's worth of meals in a couple of hours, perhaps starting with pizza and ending with rice pudding. Kiko Denzer, a cob oven expert who lives near the Oregon Coast, suggests using thin strips of wood to start the fire at the front of the oven, then allowing it to burn toward the back.

Moore's oven sits on a sidewalk on PSU's downtown Portland campus, a stone's throw from the city's Saturday afternoon farmers' market. It's a hulking example of sustainability—reusing the Earth's resources as much as possible to avoid despoiling it further—which has particular resonance in Oregon, where

Heidi Moore savors the aromas rising from a homemade cob oven during a christening ceremony on the campus of Portland State University.

VW buses from the 1960s still tool around and people recycle religiously. PSU offers a master's degree in conflict resolution, with a focus on the environment.

With the help of fellow students, in 2005 Moore and a classmate, Ryan Matson, applied for and won a grant to pay for building the oven, then tussled with school officials over where and how soon it could be built. At one point the stress was eating away at her so much that a friend of hers, Anna Mays, dropped in from San Diego to make sure Moore was eating and paying rent. Moore, who was thirty-six at the time, was living on student loans and food stamps.

"It's been transformational," Mays says of the final success of the project. "The community loves this. It's got magic, it's got energy, it brought people together. I'm so proud to be part of this. People have given their guts and soul to this."

The plan is for the oven to be an extension of PSU's student-run cafeteria, Food For Thought, which serves organic food and avoids using paper plates and plastic cutlery. "It's really gorgeous," says Jason Wallace, who gave up several hours of study time to help build it. "It's natural and can decompose a lot easier than cement."

The idea of sustainability drives Moore's life. One night as she and her friend Casey were sitting on the couch in Wallace's house, they got into an argument about whether or not to fly to Greece for a vacation. Casey was all for it, but Moore chided him: After walking and biking everywhere in Portland, why would he want to blow all of his efforts at sustainability on a plane trip requiring hundreds of gallons of fuel?

Ulysses Martinez, a friend of Moore's and a fellow student, says building the oven was "kind of like making a statement. We've been evolving so quickly and things have been changing so fast that the younger generation is starting to lose track of the indigenous in a place that's all concrete."

"Before, that corner [of the campus] was drab," he says. "Starting the project brought a feng shui–ness to it."

Rice Pud

Serves
4

WHEN BUILDING HER COB OVEN, Moore turned to *Build Your Own Earth Oven*, a step-by-step reference guide written by sculptor, gardener, author, and Oregonian Kiko Denzer. Denzer helped Moore in the beginning stages of her project. This recipe for rice pudding is one that Denzer's wife, Hannah, makes often in their cob oven and serves for breakfast, dessert, or as a snack with tea. It's very unlike typical American rice pudding, Denzer says, "which tends to be sweeter, overpowered with cinnamon, and more noticeably just 'rice with milk.'" This, he says, is more like a "toothy custard."

¼ cup plus 1½ teaspoon polished short-grain rice

Scant ¼ cup white sugar

2½ cups whole milk

1 teaspoon butter

¼ cup raisins (optional)

Pinch of ground nutmeg

Build a fire in a cob oven or preheat a conventional oven to 275°F.

Combine the rice, sugar, and milk in a saucepan and bring to a boil, stirring to prevent it from foaming up and overflowing.

Pour into a 1-quart baking dish and add the butter, the raisins if you like, and a pinch of nutmeg. Place the dish in a roasting pan and add water to come 1 inch up the sides of the dish.

Bake for 2 to 5 hours in the cob oven, or until the rice is very soft but still a bit chewy and the pudding has a nice, dark brown crust. In a conventional oven, it will take at least 3 hours. Serve warm.

Roasted 'Snips 'n' Taters

Serves 4

THIS IS A TRADITIONAL COMBINATION of winter root vegetables. "It's a really lovely solstice celebration," says Kiko Denzer, "as the central ingredients are the roots that come from down deep in the dark soil, that both sustain our bodies through the winter and survive long storage through the garden's dormant season." This side dish, he says, is wonderful with roasted poultry, steak, or soup—or eggs, if your chickens are still laying.

4 medium parsnips, peeled and cut into 1-inch cubes

4 russet potatoes, peeled and cut into 1-inch cubes

2 carrots, peeled and cut into 1-inch chunks

2 heads garlic, separated into cloves and peeled

4 sprigs rosemary

2 sprigs sage

2 sprigs thyme

Salt and freshly ground pepper

3 tablespoons extra-virgin olive oil

Build a fire in a cob oven or preheat a conventional oven to 350°F.

Fill a 10-by-13-inch roasting pan with the parsnips, potatoes, and carrots. Sprinkle the garlic and herbs on top. Drizzle with the olive oil, season with salt and pepper to taste, and stir the mixture until all the vegetables are coated with the oil.

Place the dish in a larger roasting pan and add water to come 1 inch up the sides of the pan.

Roast in the cob oven for 5 to 10 minutes, or until the vegetables are tender. In a conventional oven, roast for 30 to 45 minutes.

David & Yolanda Stegman

On a remote spit of land in the San Juan Islands, David and Yolanda Stegman have carved out a tiny piece of Argentina, Yolanda's homeland.

The living room of their airy house has a table with bottles of Quilmes, the national beer of Argentina; fancy cups designed to hold a bitter tea called *yerba mate*; a copy of an Argentine passport; and a box of *alfajores*, thin and crispy cookies filled with *dulce de leche*.

It can get lonely in this corner of Washington state, so every once in a while the Stegmans will throw an Argentinian-style barbecue for their friends, neighbors, and their partners in their horse-importing business, Claudia Ots and Daniel Aristimuño, who are also from Argentina. A Stegman barbecue typically involves a whole lamb, side dishes, and lots of Malbec wine.

"In Argentina, to make a barbecue is just a fact to get a meeting with my friends, no?" Yolanda trills in her high, light voice. "I like the flavor of the meat mixed with the smoke. It's the best thing for me."

Preparations begin several days before with the butchering of a twenty-pound lamb. Dave Stegman removes the head and discards the heart and kidneys if they're still attached to the animal's body. He takes construction wire and fastens the lamb to an iron rod he welded with rings at the bottom to help adjust the height, then slides the rod onto another one planted on the sandy patch of ground near the back of his house that serves as the family's permanent fire pit. For the next six hours, the lamb will roast vertically about three feet away from the large alder wood fire.

Lamb (*cordero* in Spanish) is often served at weddings and *quinceañeras*, parties held to celebrate a girl's fifteenth birthday. Argentina is heavily Catholic, Yolanda explains, and couples tend to have more children than Americans do. So it's not uncommon for two hundred guests to turn out for a reception-hall wedding with several lambs served out back. Argentinians avoid indoor cooking during the hot summer months, which run from December to February in the Southern Hemisphere. "You don't want to fill your house with that heat, so you usually do lunch and dinner outside," Dave says. "But even in the winter, you sit outside."

"Argentinians are very social," he adds. "If you go two or three days without anyone coming to visit you and staying for supper, you must be in trouble. Everybody must be mad at you."

David Stegman (left) and Daniel Aristimuño make final adjustments to a lamb as they prepare to roast it Argentinian-style.

A different version of Stegman's rig can be seen in *parillas*, or steak-houses, throughout Buenos Aires. The city itself has a relaxed European ambience; afternoon siestas are common and people often don't eat dinner until 9 or 10 at night. In a country that embraces leisurely meals, roasting meat over an open fire is about the slowest method of cooking there is.

For the Stegmans' barbecue to be ready by dinnertime, Dave Stegman must stake the lamb in front of the fire by 1 p.m. Traditionally, the men fuss over the meat while the women set up, clean up, and take care of accompaniments such as empañadas, cheeses, and small, sweet pickles.

There are no thermometers or kitchen alarm clocks to tell Stegman when the lamb is ready. He looks to see how brown the meat is on the side closest to the fire. When it reaches a pleasing caramel color, he turns it around and roasts the other side.

Daniel Aristimuño learned the craft of grilling meat in Argentina from a relative, whom he describes as "a very special maker of barbecue. Every cooker has a different way to make the barbecue. There is not one rule, really."

That extends to eating the lamb when it's finished. Some people like it directly from the *asador*, the barbecuer, who carves up the pieces while the lamb remains on the rod and hands the meat to his guests. Others prefer sitting at a long picnic table and waiting until the meat is brought to them on plates, along with bread and a simple salad of lettuce, tomato, and onion. Other meats such as *chorizo* (spicy sausage), *morcilla* (blood sausage), *chinchulines* (chitterlings), or *mojellas* (sweetbreads) are also served.

"The diet starts Monday," jokes Yolanda, as the smell of roasted meat drifted upward past the pine trees. "Of course, I'm not saying which Monday."

Claudia Ots says the Stegmans' style of cooking the lamb goes back centuries, to when cattle roamed freely on the pampas, Argentina's large and flat grasslands. The gauchos of the plains developed it because they were far from town and needed to scrounge up what they could for cooking equipment.

Even though the method looks impressive—and the tender, succulent meat gets raves from his guests—Dave Stegman actually prefers cooking on the firepit he built nearby.

"In Argentina, you make a grill and you expect it to last twenty-five years," he says. "It's more forgiving."

Chimichurri Sauce

Makes 3½ Cups

ARGENTINIANS USE this sauce as an accompaniment to barbecue, much like Americans provide bottles of ketchup at family picnics.

3 cups distilled white vinegar

1 tablespoon salt

1 tablespoon chopped fresh parsley

3 cloves garlic, thinly sliced

1 tablespoon chili powder

1 tablespoon chopped fresh oregano

1 tablespoon chopped fresh basil

⅓ cup water

Mix all the ingredients in a small bowl and let stand at room temperature for 2 hours. Store, covered in the refrigerator, for up to 4 months.

Claudia Ots feeds her four-year-old daughter, Camilla, after Claudia's husband, Daniel Aristimuño, carved and served the meat.

THE PIG COFFIN

A cooking rig that's been floating around southern climes for decades recently got a boost from La Caja China, a Cuban-American company in Miami.

A *caja* looks like a plywood coffin on wheels, and it can cook a seventy-pound pig in less than four hours, compared to ten to twelve hours on a smoker/grill. But forget about its speed—what this rig does is produce pig candy. The reflected heat produces a crisp outer skin without steaming the meat.

It's a charcoal-heated box lined with metal that's part pressure cooker and part convection oven. It's large enough to cook sixteen chickens or six turkeys. The meat is suspended off the bottom of the cooker so that the heat can circulate around it. The charcoal is placed on the top of the metal lid and the meat cooks from above, quite unlike traditional barbecue rigs because the meat never comes in contact with smoke or fire.

A *New York Times* food piece in January 2004 helped put La Caja China on the culinary map. No one seems to really know where or how the name "La Caja" originated, other than that it became popular for roasting *lechón* (suckling pig) in Cuba. Somehow, at a smoky point in culinary history, the name "China" got attached.

Down in Louisiana, contraptions like this are called "the Cajun microwave," and many are handmade.

Outside of Lafayette one winter weekend, we sampled a roasted pig out of what was essentially a box made of plywood and pine and lined with stainless steel. The lid had a lip like one on a Dutch oven. The glowing coals came from a campfire on a distant island.

When we first approached it aboard a flat-bottom *bateau*, we thought it was some sort of funeral pyre or voodoo sacrifice. The whole thing was hung from the limbs of a cypress tree by four lengths of logging chain.

The skin of the pig was mahogany and the moist meat had a tropical taste. The Cajuns, like the Cubans, use a magical elixir common to the Caribbean called *mojo criollo*. It's a marinade of sour orange juice, garlic, oregano, salt, and cumin.

Clay Bush

Working only from a crudely scribbled blueprint, Clay Bush built a rig with enough add-ons to sell it—if he wanted to—for $10,000, easy.

"It's expensive, but worth it," he says proudly, pointing out the gas burners behind the smoker, the attached weed burner to start the fire, and the steel plate over the firebox that he uses to warm tortillas. "The times I've used it, it's worked out excellent. It's very user-friendly."

Bush got the idea to build it when he and a buddy walked into a hunting and fishing store during a football game and noticed a similar-sized rig. His friend urged him to buy it, but Bush figured he could construct a better one on his own, with thicker steel and superior craftsmanship.

He sketched an outline from memory, bought an old well casing, and added a couple of his own inventions: a tortilla plate, which he welded to the side of his firebox, and frames for his cooler and propane tank, so that when he heads out of town he doesn't have to worry about either of them sliding onto the highway. The whole thing cost about $2,500 and took eight months to build.

Bush, a freight broker and landlord, is used to building things. When he and his wife were a struggling young married couple, he built their furniture to save money. He picked up his welding skills growing up on a farm. The experience paid off: from the chromium tire hubs to his stainless steel storage box, Bush's rig more closely resembles a spotless NASA lunar rover than your typical black, greasy backyard barbecue cooker. No space is wasted—even the lid to his storage box doubles as a prep table.

"Wherever you pull this," he says, "people are gonna crowd around it and have a good time."

The rig made its debut at a tailgate party at a football game between New Mexico State and the University of Texas at El Paso. The aroma of Bush's brisket, pork butt, and sausage attracted a group of college students who looked hungry. "I said, 'Ya need to eat something,'" says Bush, a tall, easy-going guy whose sandy blond hair is just beginning to gray. "All those kids probably had three plates apiece. I'm very giving, and it made me feel good. You know university students—they're poor starving kids."

During the week, Bush parks his smoker at the top of his driveway in Las Cruces, New Mexico, 350 yards from the Rio Grande. To get to his house, you

Clay Bush prepares chicken for his smoker/grill before a Friday night cookout with his neighbors.

drive through a maze of highway billboards advertising foot massage therapists and spa treatments, then end up in a small suburban development surrounded by Mondale pines, the only ones left from what was once a well-known Christmas tree farm. At night, when Bush looks up, he can see the Big Dipper.

Bush was raised in a small Texas town, can tell you anything you want to know about onions, and, like most folks who live in Las Cruces, regularly salts his sentences with a Spanish phrase or two. He loves spicy foods—"something that explodes on the tongue"—and doctors his meat with a mixture of red chile powder and a roux. His mom loves his baby-back ribs. As for his kids, he says, "as long as they can have French fries and a Coke, they're happy."

When he's not cooking on the smoker, Bush hangs out in the kitchen he built with extra-tall counters to accommodate his six-foot-six-inch frame. "Everything's centered around the kitchen," Bush says. "I like to experiment a lot, but my wife gets mad at me because nothing ever tastes the same."

On a soft October night, we joined Bush and a couple of buddies at his house, where he cranked up the country music in his garage and peeled a half-dozen jalapeños while keeping his cell phone cupped to his ear to take calls from work. Around sunset, clouds of smoke rose from the cooker, and the chickens, brushed with chile sauce, were beginning to turn a deep orange. After the darkness settled in, Bush grabbed a flashlight and propped it up on a shelf as he checked the chicken a final time before preparing to dish it out on paper plates. He had also prepared turkey sausage and beans. As the guests ran out of napkins, he passed around a big roll of paper towels.

Bush is pretty genial, but he has no patience with people who drop by and expect to get served the second they arrive. Smoking ribs, chicken, and pork butts takes time, he says: "One time, I tried to cook a hog fast and I had people around me saying, 'I'm hungry!' Well, I felt like saying, 'You want something to eat? Go to McDonald's.' I just had to tell myself to walk away.'"

Borracho Beans

Serves
★ 4–6 ★

BORRACHO MEANS "DRUNK" in Spanish. Variations of this stewlike dish made with beer are common in restaurants around Las Cruces. Clay Bush likes Tecate, a Mexican beer, but you can use any kind. Serve with warm tortillas or cornbread.

2½ cups dried pinto beans, picked over and rinsed

1 tablespoon olive oil

1 ham hock (optional)

¾ cup chopped yellow onion

4 plum tomatoes, diced

2 jalapeño peppers, chopped

½ cup chopped fresh cilantro

12 ounces beer

The night before you want to serve the beans, place them in a heavy-bottomed pot, cover them with water, and add the olive oil and ham hock, if using. Simmer over low heat for 8 hours, or overnight in a crockpot on a low setting. About 1 hour before you're ready to serve, add the onions, tomatoes, jalapeños, and cilantro to the pot with the beans. Pour in the beer and stir to mix well.

Bring to a boil, then reduce the heat and simmer, uncovered, for 30 to 40 minutes, stirring occasionally. Ladle into bowls and serve.

Sam Goff

Forget the crudely welded-together oil drums and uneven grill doors on most contraptions. Sam Goff's rig looks like a toy locomotive as it chugs down the interstate, smoke curling from the chimney and ribs smoking inside. Which makes sense, since Goff's day job is running the purchasing department at Pacific & Western Railroad in Corvallis, Oregon.

At Goff's cooking gigs, folks pepper him with questions as they scoop up plates of his chicken and ribs. Did he design his rig himself? "You betcha," he answers. How'd he figure out how to build it? "Trial and error," he says. Would he ever quit his job someday to churn out cookers assembly-line-style, full-time? Nah, he replies—that'd take the fun out of building them.

Food is in Goff's blood. As a kid, he salivated over stories about his Depression-era grandparents from Oklahoma, dirt poor but expert at frying up potatoes and venison steaks. His Aunt Violet taught him to make a mean chicken gravy with biscuits.

In his own house, he handles the cooking, while his wife, Kori, washes the dishes. Life was uneventful until a couple of years ago, when Goff's long-standing interest in building his own cooker bloomed into an obsession.

He dragged home two abandoned eight-foot steel cylinders he found at the rail yard and let them rust out on the front lawn—driving his wife crazy—until he figured out how to convert them into a smoker by wading through blueprints he found on the Internet. He mounted the cylinders side-by-side on a boat trailer, attached an ancient firebox that a store was giving away for free, then drilled a space from the firebox to the cylinders to allow the heat to waft around the meat low and slow.

Each cylinder has its own chimney. The doors have giant counterweights to hold them upright while smoking, and valves allow the grease to drain. About three times a year, Goff uses a steam cleaner to remove all the gunk. Then he re-seasons the rig by brushing a mixture of bacon grease, vegetable oil, and peanut oil over the grill shelves.

When Goff began building his cooker, he and Kori were living paycheck to paycheck, diapering babies, and scraping to pay the mortgage. Now, he runs his own catering company on the side, and business is great. A big college sports fan, Goff is often asked to cook for the golf teams at the

Sam Goff mans his fire while preparing a moveable feast.

University of Oregon and Oregon State. His toddler-age daughter and son sometimes join him.

"He loves being the center of attention," says Kori, who has managed to stay whip-thin even after eating platefuls of her husband's barbecue. "He's the baby in his family, the youngest of four, and that has a lot to do with it."

Goff lugs his cooker all over the Willamette Valley in western Oregon. The area's idyllic summers—rain-free and pleasantly warm—are perfect for outdoor feasts, and Goff's ribs and chicken have become staples at golf tournaments and company picnics.

At Pacific and Western's annual outing one afternoon, Goff patted his homemade rub of garlic, onion powder, and paprika on more than one hundred chicken thighs. "Got probably a little bit of overkill here," he said, checking the packed racks of chicken before closing the door of his rig and wiping his sweat-drenched forehead. "But the person who ordered this requested it."

Goff uses oak for fuel, partly because he likes its mild flavor and partly because he gets it free at the railyard. He says he'd love to experiment with pecan, but it's expensive and hard to get. The oak is practically odorless, so instead of the smoky flavor of hickory, Goff concentrates the meat's flavors with his sauce, which has just a hint of a kick to it.

He insists he's just an amateur, even though he's been feeding people for years. He had yet to record a spectacular accident until the day of his company picnic, when the firebox flamed up and ruined two racks of ribs. Luckily, he had brought extra meat.

Goff has only recently begun to enter competitions. Although he gets raves for his chicken, pork, and salmon, he hasn't been able to crack the top ten in contests yet. But when asked if a commercial grill with all the bells and whistles would boost his chances for serious cash, Goff shakes his head.

"I'd like to have a fancy one, sure, but then that takes away from the character," he says. "This pit, I know its characteristics. I know what to do with it; I know where I've got hot spots. I like the challenge."

Sam's Sweet Smoky Barbecue Sauce

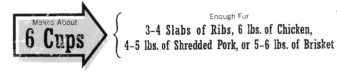

Makes About

6 Cups

Enough For
3-4 Slabs of Ribs, 6 lbs. of Chicken,
4-5 lbs. of Shredded Pork, or 5-6 lbs. of Brisket

SAM GOFF'S GRANDMOTHER, Betty Stewart, taught him the philosophy of the "some of" method of cooking—whenever anyone asked her what or how much to put in a recipe, she'd say, "some of this, some of that." Sam used a similar approach when concocting this sauce. "I don't do a lot of things scientifically," he says. "This just comes from playing around."

3 cups ketchup

½ cup honey mustard

¼ cup apple cider vinegar

¼ cup firmly packed brown sugar

½ teaspoon kosher salt

½ teaspoon garlic powder

½ teaspoon onion powder

½ teaspoon freshly ground black pepper

¼ teaspoon chipotle chile powder

In a saucepan, combine all the ingredients and mix well. Bring to a boil on the stovetop over medium-high heat. Transfer to a baking dish and cook, uncovered, in a smoker with your meat for as long as the meat is inside, or a maximum of 6 hours. Store, covered in the refrigerator, for up to 4 months.

Island Pulled Pork

Serves
★ 15–20 ★

SAM GOFF DEVELOPED the sauce in this recipe for a neighborhood party with a luau theme. Reduced-sodium soy sauce may be substituted to reduce the saltiness.

1 pork shoulder, about 8 pounds, cooked and shredded

2 cups apple cider vinegar

1½ cups soy sauce

1½ cups firmly packed brown sugar

1 cup honey

¼ cup apple juice

1½ teaspoons ground ginger

Build a fire in a smoker for indirect heat. Maintain a temperature of 250°F. Place the shredded pork in a large roasting pan.

Combine the remaining ingredients in a large saucepan and bring to a boil on the stove top over medium heat. Reduce the heat and simmer for 30 minutes.

Pour the sauce over the shredded pork. Cover the pan with aluminum foil. Place in the smoker on the side opposite the coals and cook for 1½ to 2 hours.

Remove the foil, stir, and serve.

Sam took pictures of other cookers and consulted barbecue groups in other states for guidance as he built his rig.

John McJunkin

Guests arriving at John McJunkin's pig roast in the heart of Napa Valley quickly figured out this wasn't going to be your typical backyard barbecue.

Tables scattered around the lawn were covered in stylish lime-green linens. A valet was on hand to relieve visitors of their cars. Guests sipped wine and sampled stuffed figs under a tall persimmon tree.

Meanwhile, at the back of the vineyard, McJunkin and his friend, Dave McLaren, were laboring over a humble, unlovely contraption constructed of cinderblocks.

"The rig itself is fairly ugly," McJunkin says. "But it makes a beautiful pig."

It takes a special occasion for McJunkin, a food and wine photographer for area wineries, to assemble his roaster and slow-cook a 105-pound pig—skin and all. This particular party, celebrating the end of Northern California's annual grape harvest, was for growers and other players in the wine industry. It featured a pig cooked Cuban-style, with sauces from the Carolinas on the side.

For years, McJunkin helped a buddy of his in Mendocino put on an in-ground pig roast, where the pig is steamed instead of roasted. (Actually, his friend did most of the work; all McJunkin remembers is gathering driftwood for the fire.) The first time McJunkin decided to cook his own hog, he couldn't track down his friend for advice. The invitations had already been sent, and he was committed.

So, he decided to build an aboveground contraption to roast the pig instead of steam it. He prefers roasted pig anyway, because of its earthier flavor. And there's no chance of it getting soggy.

"Soft, mushy things don't go well with me, never have," he says. "Crispy skin is like the world's best pork potato chip."

For this roast, McJunkin and McLaren built a remarkably simple but effective device with about $60 in supplies from their local hardware store. It consists of an elevated roasting pit, which they constructed with forty-eight cinderblocks stacked four rows high. They lined it with aluminum foil to trap the heat and loaded it with two fifty-pound bags of charcoal for the daylong roast. Three pans were placed underneath the pig to catch the drippings.

McJunkin is an experienced griller. He once took a cooking course in Thailand and, every Father's Day, he and his friends participate in a local cook-off and fundraiser, Valley Men Who Cook, with the proceeds going to the

John McJunkin shows off his properly trussed whole hog for roasting at his annual end-of-the-harvest barbecue.

John McJunkin (left) and Dave McLaren demonstrate the fine art of turning a whole hog over the fire without dropping the centerpiece of their annual Napa Valley Pig Pickin'.

charity of the winner's choice. One year, his team's winning entry was a pile of oysters, some of them barbecued.

To prepare his hog for roasting, McJunkin split the animal's spine, then marinated the whole hog in his special "mojo" sauce overnight. When it was ready, he covered it in aluminum foil and sandwiched it between two flats of galvanized rebar shaped into an intricate cage. Then he covered the foil with small rocks from his yard to keep the wind from lifting it.

McJunkin and McLaren mixed two sauces to pour onto the pork after they pulled it. One was vinegar-based; the other had a sweet-and-sour kick.

During the roast, McLaren exuded confidence. A consultant by trade, he considers himself a vegetarian, but makes an exception for whole-hog roasts.

"The thought of killing is rather abhorrent to him," McJunkin says. "Whereas I consider myself the superior predator. I'm at the top of the food chain."

For all the effort that McJunkin and McLaren put into turning the pig and constantly checking to see if the skin was crispy, most guests showed little interest in the hog until it was nearly done. But eventually, a handful of people wandered over to the cinderblocks.

This may be wine country, where it's easy to get blasé about food fads that come and go, but the crowd soon abandoned their sophisticated hors d'oeuvres to grab a taste of the pig's crackling skin.

McLaren, McJunkin, and McJunkin's dad, Bill, slowly drew away the foil. They lugged it over to the cutting table, and McJunkin quickly started pulling pork. Knives flew and the sauce poured as guests reached out to grab the meat. A woman in a suede jacket asked for a fat-laden ear; McJunkin gave it to her, along with the nose, too.

It was a fitting end to a wine season that always involves tough work—from pruning the vines in February to hovering over the plants during cold snaps in April, making sure they don't freeze, and harvesting the grapes in September. Whole-hog roasts are common throughout the Napa Valley, McJunkin says, as a way for vintners to thank their workers.

"Everyone feels pretty elated and relieved when the crop comes in," he says. "It's a time for celebration."

Mojo Sauce

Makes About
5 Cups / An 80 lb. Hog
Enough For
Serves
45-50

THIS SAUCE, pronounced "moho," is a basic Cuban-style marinade that McJunkin likes to use on pork, although it also goes with fish and poultry. Cilantro is "kind of a John addition, because I like the flavor," he says. "I'm a big fan of Thai food, and cilantro is the ultimate crossover ingredient." Sour oranges grow in Florida and the Caribbean and can be found in specialty stores such as Dean & DeLuca. If you can't find them, substitute a mixture of 2 cups orange juice, 1 cup lemon juice, and 1 cup lime juice.

1 quart sour-orange juice

85 cloves garlic (about 5 heads), chopped

1 cup fresh cilantro leaves

1 teaspoon salt

1 teaspoon freshly ground pepper

Working in batches, combine all the ingredients in a food processor and process to a coarse purée, about 30 seconds. Store, covered tightly in the refrigerator, for up to 1 week.

Carolina Barbecue Sauce

Makes About
2 Cups / An 80 lb. Hog
Enough For
Serves
45-50

FOR PULLED PORK, McJunkin prefers the mustardy taste of Eastern Carolina barbecue sauce to the tomato-based versions so beloved in the East and Midwest. He thinks the Carolina sauce makes the pork taste cleaner.

"I like the way the vinegar offsets the garlic," he says. "You don't have a sweet, sticky mess—you actually taste good pork."

1 cup white vinegar

1 cup cider vinegar

2 tablespoons brown sugar

2 tablespoons prepared yellow mustard

1 teaspoon salt

1 teaspoon cayenne pepper

Tabasco or other hot-pepper sauce to taste

Stir together the ingredients in a nonreactive bowl and refrigerate overnight to allow the flavors to blend before serving. Store, covered tightly in the refrigerator, for up to 1 week.

SMOKIN' IN THE SAN JUANS

Imagine owning an oven that's only used at Christmas, or a fireplace that's lit no more than once a year. That's the story of two salmon smokers, shaped like tall, skinny houses, that live on the grounds of the American Legion, where the Lions meet each week, in Washington state's San Juan Islands. Club members fire them up for one day only: the Saturday closest to the Fourth of July. That's the day of the organization's annual salmon-bake fundraiser, which raises money for college scholarships.

Billie Wilson, a veteran of World War II, operated a resort on Orcas Island until he retired in 1963. A longtime Lions Club member, he built the smokers and arranged to have them moved to the club grounds after he closed the resort. Until his death in 1983, he supervised every salmon bake. Now, former club president Dick Boberg, still spry at eighty-one, constructs new shelves for the smokers from fir boards and metal netting he finds at the hardware store.

The salmon bakes take three to four days of prep work, which is why the mostly elderly Lions don't do them more than once a year. "Apparently we're doing something right, because people keep coming back," Boberg says. "I imagine it's because it's a beautiful setting and we put out a good product."

What goes into the product, however, remains a secret. On his deathbed, Wilson gave the recipe for the salmon marinade to a fellow club member with these instructions: anyone who wanted it could get it—but only after making a donation of $25 to the Lions Club. The members have honored that request ever since.

Willie & Heather Villegas

If the Villegas clan had a coat of arms, its central emblem would be a wrinkled red chile pepper.

Willie Villegas and his wife, Heather, are the fourth generation of chile farmers to work the thin, loamy soil of New Mexico's Hatch Valley. In the kitchen of their house is a plaque that says in Spanish, "Food without chiles is no food at all."

"I like chiles for breakfast, chiles for lunch, chiles with chiles," says Willie, a stocky guy with a cheerful, open face. "It's been in my life, all my life."

A chile roaster Willie designed and built sits in the driveway of the old farmhouse he and Heather bought a few years ago. It looks like the giant baskets that lottery officials used to rotate a few times before pulling out a winning ticket. But the bounty that's harvested from this 55-gallon rig is a sackful of slippery-skinned peppers, smelling like roasted wet earth.

At night the roaster is a fireworks show, with the whoosh of the barrel sounding like the crackling of thousands of corn kernels. Sparks from the propane-fueled fire spiral upward above the trees. In less than two minutes, the scorched peppers are ready to be dumped into a bucket of cold water and the skin rubbed off—a task that must be done with gloves, since capsaicin, the heat-producing chemical in chiles, can burn the skin.

Willie's great-grandfather, Guillermo, migrated from Mexico to Anthony, New Mexico—a town halfway between Las Cruces and El Paso—to grow cotton and chiles. Guillermo's son settled in Hatch in the 1950s, trading chiles for jewelry made by the Zunis, one of several Native American tribes living in what is now New Mexico and Arizona. He claimed to be the first in the valley to build a mechanical chile roaster, in the late 1970s.

Willie's parents, Willie Sr. and Esther, continue to farm the same plot of land as Willie Sr.'s father. But they also run B&E Burritos, a local restaurant. The chiles that Willie grows end up in B&E's enchiladas, salsas, and tacos. One of his favorite snacks is a tortilla wrapped around cheddar cheese and a freshly roasted chile pepper.

"We can't see ourselves doing anything else," Heather says. "It's in our blood, this is where we want to be, this is where we want our children to be. We wouldn't be happier anywhere else."

Willie Villegas fire-roasts a bushel of freshly picked chiles on a propane-fueled roaster he made on his family ranch.

He and Heather live just outside downtown Hatch, which is a shrine to the chile pepper. Strings of them, called *ristras*, dangle from the roofs of gas stations and bodegas, and almost everyone has a chile roaster outside their store. Get too close when the rigs are rotating, though, and the acrid smell can sting your eyes and make you cough.

There are dozens of varieties of chiles grown here, but the most popular— and the one Willie and Heather grow—is the long, curved, green *sandía* pepper. Most people favor the *sandía* because it's mild compared to jalapeños and habaneros. Folks in the valley supposedly are so sensitive to the chiles' subtle flavors that just by tasting a chile pod, they can tell whether it was grown north or south of Interstate 40.

Sparks from the chile roaster provide a homemade fireworks show.

Every Labor Day weekend, a festival celebrating chiles brings thousands to this town of 1,673 people on the banks of the Rio Grande. Willie says that he and his dad were the first to roast chiles at the festival in the mid-1980s, when cooking chiles mostly involved heating them over charcoal (extremely time-consuming) or frying them in oil (which ran the risk of turning the chiles soggy and inedible).

As the festival's popularity spread beyond the valley—and the lines of customers hoisting 40-pound sacks of chiles for roasting grew—Willie started tinkering with his rig, trying to get the cooking time down from four minutes. He tried altering the size of the basket and getting it to turn faster. He tested different type of burners for a more powerful flame.

About five years ago, after more than a dozen experiments, Willie hit on the perfect combination of rotating speed and firepower. He installed an electric motor, built four iron burners, and used a customized nozzle to force a potent blend of air and liquid propane into the burners. The resulting blue flame is as hot as the cutting torches welders use to rip through metal. The burners are set at 45-degree angles instead of directly under the basket, so they don't set the chiles on fire.

Now, Willie says proudly, he and his dad can roast a sack of chiles in under a minute. "We walk around and see how different people are roasting, and I don't think they run under two minutes," he says, sounding like a golfer who's finally broken par. "We have one of the best ones."

Jalapeño Salsa

WILLIE VILLEGAS'S PARENTS serve this at their restaurant, B&E Burritos, a local landmark in Hatch, New Mexico. His mom, Esther, invented it. Willie's wife, Heather, says he makes her carry a container of this salsa whenever they go out to eat. "Willie makes me stash it in my purse," Heather says. "His excuse is they can never make any salsa close to ours."

20 jalapeño peppers, roasted and peeled (see Note)

1 can (10 ounces) diced tomatoes

Garlic powder

Salt

Tortilla chips for serving

In a blender or food processor, process the peppers to a coarse pureé. Add the tomatoes and garlic powder and salt to taste and process to combine. Serve with tortilla chips.

Note: To roast peppers, place in a preheated chile roaster, on a hot grill, or under a preheated broiler and cook, turning as needed, until the skins are charred and blistered on all sides. Transfer to a bowl or a paper bag. Cover the bowl or close the bag and let the peppers steam for about 10 minutes. Peel away the skins.

Grandma's
Homemade Flour Tortillas

Makes
12–15 Tortillas

HEATHER REMEMBERS going to her great-grandmother Rose's house when she was a child to eat these tortillas, which were made on an old wood stove. The kids could hear the elderly woman kneading and pounding the dough into flat circles. They waited patiently until Rose was finished, then fought over who got the first one. "We'd sit there and eat off the *placa* (griddle) until we couldn't eat any more," Heather says.

4 cups all-purpose flour

2 teaspoons salt

½ cup vegetable shortening, at room temperature

1¼ cups warm water

Sift the flour and salt together in a bowl. Using a pastry blender, 2 knives, or your fingers, cut in the shortening until the mixture is uniformly crumbly. Add the water and mix until the dough comes together.

Turn the dough out onto a lightly floured work surface and knead for 65 to 70 strokes.

Divide the dough into 12 to 15 equal-sized pieces and form each piece into a ball. Cover them with a clean kitchen towel for 15 to 20 minutes.

Roll out each ball into a round about 8 to 10 inches in diameter. Place, one at a time, on an ungreased griddle over low heat.

Cook until lightly browned, about 2 to 3 minutes per side. Serve warm.

DOG-POWERED ROTISSERIE

Only in Jolly Old England would you find a dog bred to turn a rotisserie set in front of a fireplace. The juxtaposition of a slobbering mongrel on a treadmill and a spit of roasting meat in a restaurant sounds like a skit out of Monty Python.

But Professor Edmund Russell of the University of Virginia says it's no hoax. He has researched and written about the rare breed of dog.

"The dogs doing the work were called Turnspits, and were bred for the job. The breed died out with mechanization," says Russell, who presented "Working Like a Dog: Harnessing Canine Energy in Nineteenth-Century Britain" at a meeting of the American Society for Environmental History in Houston in 2005.

"I don't know what it is about this story, but everyone seems to love it and wants to know more," Russell says. "It's kind of sad. I guess the reason the breed died out was they weren't romantic, like the sheep-herding dogs or the higher status of a show dog."

Turnspit dogs were short-legged and long-bodied, sort of like a botched science experiment mixing a dachshund with a schnauzer. Although the breed is extinct, there's a stuffed one at the Abergavenny Museum in Wales.

The dogs were used in pairs and would alternate on a four-foot-wide tread wheel mounted high on a wall near the fireplace. A series of pulleys and belts would rotate the meat in front of the fireplace. In one illustration, a large ham was strung in front of the dog. A five-pound roast would take about three hours on the dog-powered spit.

That's a dog tale if we've ever heard one. Those Brits ... and we thought only Americans were crazy for a rotisseried roast.

A Grab-Bag of Gizmos

IN OUR TRAVELS, we were intrigued by a category of special—or extra-special—tools that some outdoor cooks use to make their lives easier. Call them gizmos. For example, to make a true Louisiana jambalaya, sure, you need a huge cast-iron washpot with a burner—but the gizmo that brings it all together is a four-foot-long stainless-steel spoon/scraper with a curved end, so you can scrape the rice from the bottom of the pot and keep it from burning.

Check out this grab-bag of gizmos. Most are homemade, but some have been made into commercial products, and others are sure to follow (probably not the Baconator, though; see page 269). Remember when all you really needed to make a beer can chicken was a beer can (and a chicken)? Well now you can also buy a fancy stand to hold the can. Make 'em or seek 'em out, but for now, here are some ideas:

Beer-Keg Chicken Cooker

This one is so simple, you'll marvel that you didn't come up with it yourself. It comes from Bubba Farris, who saw it at a USC tailgate party. First of all, find a standard beer keg (sometimes beer distributors have damaged ones you can buy, or you can just eat the deposit fee after your next keg party). Take the keg and cut out the bottom—we used a drill-attachment cutter. Inside the keg there is a

stainless-steel rod; take that out, wash it in hot, soapy water, and set it aside. Find yourself a clear spot and make a big X on the ground with two 4-foot-sections of heavy-duty aluminum foil. In the center of the X, drive the steel rod into the earth with a hammer so that about 10 inches remain above ground. Take 2 fryer hens, and rub them with your favorite dry rub and/or inject them with a marinade. Place the chickens, legs down, on the rod. Cover the chicken with the keg. Fill a charcoal chimney from a 20-pound bag of charcoal and light. When the coals have turned gray, spread around the keg and on top, then spread the remaining unlit coals from the bag on top of the hot ones. And here's the beauty of this gizmo: leave it alone for the next 3 hours—you don't have to baste or turn the chickens or put on any more charcoal. Then, with some heavy gloves—and a slight magician's flourish before your astonished guests—you remove the keg and reveal 2 perfectly browned and crisp chickens ready to eat.

Burn Barrel/Hot Coal Maker

Every serious smoker could use one of these. They're easy to make, and in cold weather they provide a great place for guests to gather and warm their hands. Find a 55-gallon barrel. Cut out the top (or remove the band with a screwdriver), and then cut out an 8-by-12-inch rectangle near the bottom to shovel out hot coals. This is the fun part: Buy four 5-foot lengths of ¾-inch rebar and cut them into 26-inch lengths with a bolt cutter. Drill ¾-inch diameter holes about every 6 inches around the circumference of the barrel about 15 inches from the base. Hammer the rebar pieces through opposing pairs of holes to make a crosshatch grid in the bottom, just above the shovel hole. Drop cut firewood into the barrel from the top and light it. As the wood burns down, occasionally shake the barrel and shovel out hot coals for your smoker.

Oyster-Shucking Table

You can make this in less than 2 hours and it will last you a lifetime. Buy the thickest sheet of exterior-grade plywood you can find. Build or buy 2 sawhorses, place the plywood on the sawhorses, and start shucking. The deluxe version of this gizmo is to cut a hole in the center of the plywood to fit a trash barrel for throwing away the oyster shells. The *ultra*-deluxe version has a tray to hold hot sauce, crackers, hand towels, and oyster knives on a raised platform over the trash-barrel hole.

Fork/Spoon Quail Roaster

This one-of-a-kind tool is a work of art. Historian Kay Moss (see page 106) has this in her collection of iron fireplace cookers. It is simply a large spoon with an elongated handle that's bent into a fork centered above the bowl of the spoon. You place a bacon-wrapped quail on the fork and set it beside an open fireplace. The spoon catches the drippings and you just rotate the combo roaster/utensil to evenly cook the bird. The colonial blacksmith responsible for this gizmo deserves a design award for functional aestheticism.

Iron Wash-Pot Cooking Tools

If you can find a large iron wash pot, your cooking repertoire will be greatly expanded—but you'll need a couple of gizmos to make it all work. These can

all be built, or you can go online and buy them from suppliers such as www.jambalayapots.com. Get a 4-foot stainless-steel spoon/scraper—yeah, it's more fun to use a cypress boat paddle to stir your stew, but nothing beats a long-handled steel spoon for scraping the bottom of the barrel to keep your stew from burning and sticking (plus the health department much prefers stainless steel over a boat paddle). You'll also need a heavy-duty burner stand to support the heavy pot and house the gas burner; a metal lid with a wooden handle; and a dedicated table to hold your lid and spoon while you're cooking—don't lay them down on the ground.

Jalapeño Pepper Popper Stand

You see these out west in Texas and New Mexico. It's a remarkably simple and fun gizmo used to hold jalapeño chiles upright for smoking in a smoker/grill.

The tops are sliced off and the chiles stuffed with cream cheese or Monterey Jack cheese; this clever stand keeps the cheese from leaking out. Take 2 plates of metal about 12 inches square. Drill holes in the 4 corners and add bolts and nuts to separate the plates by about 2 inches. Drill about a dozen holes 1 to 1¼ inches  in diameter in the top plate. Put some heatproof handles on it and you're done. The coolest one we've seen was cut in the shape of the state of Texas.

Firebricks, Concrete Blocks & Tire Rims

These are the Lego blocks of contraption cookers, and you should have a pile of them among your contraption accessories. Tire rims can be welded as a base for a halogen light stand for night cooking, or for a burner base for large pots. Firebricks and blocks can be used to raise a grill over a too-hot fire. They'll also  keep the lid tight on your jambalaya pot, and you can jam them under the wheels on your trailer cooker to keep it from rolling down the hill.

Baconator

Every summer, lawyer Peter McKee hosts a backyard barbecue and cook-off at his house in Seattle. One year his teenage daughter, Elizabeth, announced she intended to enter bacon, cooked on a grill, in the contest. She and her dad sketched a design, talked to a welder, and came up with a roof-like device of stainless steel they called the "baconator." On contest day, Elizabeth draped a couple pieces of bacon on the baconator and placed it over an ancient Weber she had christened the "You Go, Grill." She installed two cans underneath the grill to catch the grease drippings, but as they filled they caught fire. Peter quickly doused the flames. The bacon actually ended up being edi-

ble, with a pleasantly smoky taste. But the baconator is now in retirement. "It's sort of the Edsel of barbecue equipment," he says. "Honored, but not necessarily the finest product."

Hand-Forged Grilling Tools

Graceful yet practical, these iron grill tools aren't the run-of-the-mill implements you can buy at a big-box store. Mike Schmidt crafted them one Christmas for his sister and brother-in-law, Sue and Brent Teasley, who barbecue competitively. Mike is a chemical engineer by day and a blacksmith at a historic village in Chesterfield, Missouri, dur-

ing his off hours. He buys his own steel and coal, so he can make anything he wants while visitors to the village ply him with questions. For the shovel, poker, and rake that he gave Sue and Brent, Mike used ½-inch square mild carbon steel, heated it to 1,500°F, and cut it. He fashioned the top of each tool into a pineapple, a popular nineteenth-century design symbolizing hospitality. "It's part of the whole barbecue ethos," he says. "I can't imagine putting the effort into food preparation that they do, and I wanted the tools they got to reflect the same kind of effort."

Safety Tips, or, How to Smoke Your Butt Without Burning Your Ass

GARDEN HOSE, garden hose, garden hose.

You do not want to burn yourself, scorch your lawn, or—the worst crime for a backyard griller—set your neighborhood on fire. Here are some tips to ensure you will return to grill another day:

1 Get some big leather gloves. We prefer welder's gloves, which also protect your forearms (plus they look really cool, compared to floral-design oven mitts). For that matter, we prefer leather aprons because we have had more than one cotton apron catch fire, which, while it momentarily entertains your guests, you do not want to make a habit of.

2 Do not grill barefoot. We know this sounds silly, but if you have ever stepped on a hot coal while carrying a platter of meat, you will heed this warning. You can wear flip-flops if you must, but you probably won't after you've dropped some lava-colored coals on the top of your bare foot.

3 We're not going to say *never* mix alcohol and fire, but we will say we know drunken cooks who have lost control of their fire, their meat, and their dinner party because of excess. Everything in moderation until the guests are served; then you can hit the moonshine mason jar.

4 Be careful whenever you're cooking with propane on a homemade rig, particularly with an enclosed smoker. If the flame goes out, the fumes can build up and blow. We saw a pig cooker blow a door off like a grenade when the fumes built up and a spark hit. When using a propane fish cooker or deep-fryer, set the tanks and hoses well away from the burners. (We were once at a child's birthday party where a coiled hose got too close to a burner. The rubber coating was bubbling when someone saw it and turned the gas off. Yikes.)

5 If you don't have a garden hose at hand, you need a fire extinguisher and a five-gallon bucket of water. We're not kidding—you're dealing with fire, and the best antidote is water. Most barbecue competitions now require cookers to carry their own extinguishers and first-aid kits. We've seen hot coals ignite a dry lawn, and a garden hose could have extinguished it in five seconds. Firefighters are nice folks but you don't want to have them working at your backyard wienie roast.

A brew-seasoned chef stirs chicken stew in an iron washpot over a tire-rim burner.

Grill Glossary

NO ONE WILL EVER solve the riddle that has puzzled mankind since a slab of protein first met fire: "Is 'barbecue' a noun or a verb?"

Leaving aside the semantics of contraption cuisine, here's an easy-reference digest of the principal types, tools, techniques, and other phenomena of barbecue.

Barbecuing

The basic barbecue is some variation of a barrel smoker/grill, used with wood chips, chunks, and/or logs, sometimes combined with charcoal. The meat is generally put to the side of the coals or burner, and the cooker is closed, which cooks the meat more slowly by indirect heat and allows the flavors of the wood or charcoal smoke to penetrate further. Also called smoking, true aficionados often refer to this method as "low and slow" because it takes so dang long. Tougher meats such as brisket can take up to eighteen hours to cook, so this method requires a lot of patience. Unlike with direct heat, where you sear meat at a high temperature, with indirect heat, excessive turning of the meat is largely discouraged. When cooking a pork shoulder or ham in a smoker, you don't turn the meat at all because keeping the fat cap on the top allows the rendered fat to drip down and keep the meat moist. Additionally, in an enclosed smoker, the heat is more diffused and circulates around the food naturally.

Both grilling and barbecuing may use combinations of direct and indirect heat for some meats, which doubtless contributes to the smoke that often clouds the difference between the two terms.

See also Grilling.

Bastes & Glazes

Basting is the process of brushing the surface of the meat with a liquid while it is cooking, either to keep the meat moist or to add sweetness or another layer of flavor, or both. In barbecue, bastes (also called mops) are generally thin mixes of vinegar, beer, and wine or fruit juices such as apple or pineapple. Bastes are applied by brush, mop, or spray bottle. Some competitive barbecuers work their bastes to give the meat an attractive sheen as well.

Usually thinner than barbecue sauces and used to add a glossy coating in addition to flavor, glazes are sometimes applied after the meat is removed from the heat. This is because most contain sugar and will caramelize and burn easily, even in indirect heat. Some cooks employ techniques with glazes to get around this difficulty; for example, pork ribs may be removed from the heat after cooking for some hours and dosed liberally with a thick sauce or glaze, then wrapped tightly in aluminum foil and returned to the smoker/grill for the remaining hour or two of cooking. The meat is then removed from the foil and grilled quickly over direct heat for a few minutes to set the glaze.

See also Rubs & Sauces.

Brushes & Mops

Generally speaking, the bigger the better when it comes to brushes or mops for outdoor grilling and smoking. For smaller cuts of meat, brushes are good for painting on sauces and glazes at the end of the cooking process. For larger cuts of meats, the mop, a special cotton tool that is indeed moplike, is faster and more efficient, particularly with thinner vinegar-based bastes (the bastes themselves are also often called mops). For a whole hog, some cookers use new and clean cotton floor mops. A professor we met at North Carolina State University uses a doubled-up clean cotton athletic sock tied to the end of a broomstick. In the Greek Peloponnesus, we saw a Pascal lamb being basted with a handkerchief-sized piece of lamb membrane tied to the end of an olive branch. The organic mop gradually shrank until, after 3 to 4 hours, just a nubbin remained and the lamb was ready to eat.

Charcoal

Purists argue about the differences between briquettes and lump. We prefer the aesthetic factor of lump, which generally burns faster. Avoid the extra expense and elitism of "gourmet lump." For dependability and cost, it's hard to beat a high grade of briquettes like Kingsford. If you have a ready supply of hardwood, making your own charcoal is much cheaper, but it's labor intensive and requires almost constant monitoring and periodic shoveling of the hot coals to the smoker (see the charcoal maker in the gizmo section on page 267). Most barbecuers use charcoal briquettes for heat and wood chunks or chips for smoke, although some, like competition-cooker Bill Eason of Marshville, North Carolina, use nothing but charcoal: "As the fat is rendered out of the meat, it drips onto the hot coals where it creates its own smoke, which is all it really needs."

See also Starting a Fire; Wood.

Charcoal Grill

This is the base of the backyard barbecuer's equipment pyramid. After WWII, this was the Holy Grill to which all patio daddy-Os bowed in worship. The so-called kettle grill is probably the most perfectly designed and economical cooker for the typical backyard barbecuer. It can do it all—direct heat for steaks, burgers and hot dogs; indirect for brisket and pork roasts; rotisserie grilling for chickens; and smoking for sausage and fish. The domed lid allows for indirect grilling and smoking; adjustable air vent holes above and below the grill allow the cook to better regulate the heat and flame.

Chimney Fire Starter

Throw out your liquid petroleum charcoal starter. You don't need it, and enclosed smokers will sometimes keep the chemical smell in your cooker. These simple rigs cost about $15, and all you need is a match and a single sheet of newspaper. Your charcoal will be glowing like lava in fifteen minutes.

Dampers

These vents with sliding covers control the amount of air flowing through your smoker, allowing you to slow your fire down or speed it up. Generally speaking, the more oxygen that a fire gets, the hotter and faster it will burn. A campfire, for instance, has an unlimited oxygen supply and burns hot and quickly; a wood-stove fire is tightly controlled with dampers so that the fire can be made to burn efficiently for long hours, even holding through the night. When you start a fire in a smoker/grill, the dampers should be open; as you achieve your desired temperature, adjust the dampers so the fire has just enough oxygen to maintain the heat you want. Top dampers (the ones above the meat) can also be adjusted to direct the smoke. For instance, if your firebox is on the left side of your smoker, you can close the top dampers on the left side and open the top dampers on the right side to draw the smoke across the meat. You can also close the top dampers completely for a greater intensity of smoke.

Drip Pan

An extremely utilitarian tool for the extreme barbecuer. It's primarily used in indirect cooking, placed under the meat to deflect the heat, as well as to catch the drippings to prevent flare-ups and to self-baste the meat as the water and/or drippings steam. Many barbecuers place a small pan with various mixtures of beer, water, whole onions, and/or garlic in a large cooker to keep the meat moist. You can use a stainless-steel pan, but they're hard to clean; aluminum pie pans are handiest.

Drum/Barrel Smokers

Fifty-five gallon industrial drums are practically premade smoker/grills—or at least they can be, with minimal work. Drums, preferably food-grade, can be found at salvage/junk yards and recycled metal centers. Whatever the source, it's a good idea to thoroughly scrub out, then burn a fire in the barrels before attempting to cook in them. Some can be used as upright smokers by simply dropping in a small hibachi of already-hot coals and then placing meat on a grill suspended over the fire source (see the story of Jay Vantuyl's prize-winning drums on page 189). The drums are more typically—and more conveniently—cut in half horizontally; the halves are then hinged and the barrel is fitted with a wire mesh grill and mounted on a stand (see Cheryl Western's barrels on page 193). To convert a barrel to a cooker, you will need some basic metal cutting tools and/or access to a welder/sheet metal expert to fabricate it for you. There are also conversion kits available.

See Sources, page 284.

Gas Grill

You can't beat these for convenience—turn on the gas and hit the ignition switch and you're ready to grill in thirty seconds. Gas grills have come a long way since the one-burner rigs of the 1960s, which were pretty much limited to the direct-heat style of cooking steaks, burgers, and hot dogs. Today's gas grills offer much more variety, with two- and three-burner rigs that allow you to cut off one burner and place the meat there for indirect heat barbecue for brisket and pork roasts. To introduce smoke, wet some wood chips, drain them, then roll them up in aluminum foil, poke holes in the packet, and lay it directly on the gas burners. When finished, remove the foil packet and discard; no ashes to clean up. Be warned, though: barbecue purists scoff at gas grills, claiming they don't impart the "real" barbecue flavors that wood coals provide.

Grill Scrapers and Cleaners

It's good to have greased and seasoned grill grates, but no one wants to eat off a dirty grill. Barbecue guru Steven Raichlen's mantra is: "Keep your grill clean, hot, and greased." And he's right. Periodically, it's a good idea to remove your grill grate and spray it with one of those oven cleaner abrasives. Scrub it hard on both sides (particularly the underside, where all the drippings will hang and harden). Be sure to thoroughly rinse the grill after using a cleaner. For day-to-day cleaning, use a good stiff wire brush; we've found it's easiest to clean after the food has been removed but while the grill is still hot. In a pinch, you can also crumple up a ball of aluminum foil and vigorously scrape it back and forth on the grill. Once it's clean, take a paper towel or cloth soaked in cooking oil and rub down the grill grate. In Tsitalia, Greece, we once watched restaurateur George Sarris take a large lemon off a nearby tree, cut it in half, and rub the inside with kosher salt to act as an abrasive. He cleaned the grill with the lemon scrubber and then tossed the spent lemon into the coals for an additional dose of lemon smoke. "In America, you clean grills with an aerosol can of chemicals," Sarris said. "In Greece, we do it the natural way and it tastes better—and what is best for the environment?"

Grilling

Cooking the meat directly above hot coals, a burner, or a fire. This method of direct-heat cooking sears the meat quickly, leaving impressive-looking char marks, and imparts a pleasant, smoky taste. Use this method when you've got a craving for great steaks or chicken cooked outside fairly quickly under a hot night sky, with cold beer or a full-bodied wine as accompaniments. Folks unfamiliar with contraption cuisine often confuse grilling, which can be done over a charcoal or gas grill, with barbecuing. They are not the same.

See also Barbecuing.

Olive Oil

This is a versatile oil of varying grades. Generally speaking, it is better to fry in the less-expensive olive oils called "pure" grade and save the extra-virgin olive oil for vinaigrettes, drizzling over pasta, and dipping artisan breads. Barbecuing raconteur Carl Wharton achieves the golden color on his roasted whole hogs by rubbing the skin down with pure olive oil.

Pit Barbecue

Before modern, portable smoker/grills, there was pit style—both above-ground brick pits and in-ground pits. These are basic, high-volume cookers that require much labor to build, stoke, and maintain a constant supply of hot coals. Most pits have domes to better capture the smoke and heat. It's hot and smoky, working a pit. In a Mexican *barbacoa*, they use in-ground pits differently, actually wrapping their meat in banana leaves or heavy aluminum foil before burying it in the pit to hold the moisture and protect it from the smoke. In some parts of the country—Texas and parts of the South—pit barbecue on a large scale still exists. At Sweatman's Barbecue in South Carolina, they cook more than a half-dozen hogs over hardwood coals in huge concrete-block pits inside a screened smokehouse; they crank hand-winches to raise and lower sheets of aluminum siding to hold in the smoke and heat.

Propane

Bottled in its ubiquitous little white tanks, this fuel has revolutionized back-yard grilling in the last half of the twentieth century. You can't beat it for convenience and instant heat. Be careful about using a homemade propane cooker with an enclosed smoker; if the burner goes out, you can have a dangerous build-up of gas. Purists believe charcoal or wood imparts a better taste to smoked meats. We agree.

Refrigerator Smokers

Admittedly, these converted fridge cookers may seem dubious at a glance, but some of the best smoked meats we've ever tasted have come out of refrigerator smokers like the one on the Two Men and a Fridge barbecue team, which uses a General Electric refrigerator from the 1950s (see page 205). The trick is getting an old enough model that has metal insides instead of plastic, which would melt under heat. When you find a metal one of the proper vintage, fit it with a simple, electric hot plate and a pan to smoke wood chips, and drill a hole in the top to create a draft for the smoke; you can wrap the shelves with aluminum foil and stack your meat there. Junkyards, appliance stores, and appliance repair shops are good places to begin your search.

Rotisseries

These cooking tools use metal rods as spits to slowly rotate the meat over direct heat (wood fire or coals) in order to cook it evenly. Rotisseries are essentially self-basting because most of the juices stay on the meat and distribute across it while the rotisserie is being turned. Almost any meat that will stay on a stick can be cooked on a rotisserie, but it produces particularly good results with whole chickens and turkeys, lamb (whole or a leg), and pork or beef roasts. Rotisseries can be freestanding (often custom- or homemade) to cook a whole lamb (see Carroll Robinson's entry on page 73), or they can be bought as an accessory for gas and charcoal grills. One of the most fun things about a rotisserie is inviting your guests early so they can stand around it and salivate.

Rubs & Sauces

Wet? Dry? Or wet *and* dry? Besides the smoke, barbecue meat flavoring comes from three main sources: bastes, rubs (also called dry rubs, which typically include salt, pepper, garlic and onion powder, and an assortment of herbs; "wet rubs" add a little oil or liquid to form a paste), and barbecue sauces, which range from the vinegar-based versions found throughout the Carolinas to the tomato-based recipes famous throughout the Midwest. Rubs are applied before the meat is smoked. Sauces are generally slathered on after the meat is removed from the heat, or used as a dip, although sometimes a sauce may be applied during the final few minutes in the smoker. Just remember to apply rubs and sauces sparingly. The idea is to bring out your meat's true flavor, not to overpower your guests.

See also Bastes & Glazes.

Smoke

Many barbecue aficionados believe the adage, "If the meat's got no smoke, then it ain't no barbecue." Before the advent of refrigeration, smoke (along with salt) was used to preserve meats. More recently, smoke has found new life, beyond its practical powers, in the art of adding flavor. Smoke as a flavoring agent is sublime; it can carry a delicate scent from basil branches or the rich, heavy taste of green shagbark hickory. Geography has played a role in matching smoke with meats. In the Pacific Northwest, abundantly available alder fueled many a fire, and was found to accentuate the subtleties of salmon. In the Southeast, beef and pork are the popular choices for smoking with the common local hickory, as they hold up best to its strong flavor.

Note: There is such a thing as too much smoke, which can actually make meat taste bitter. Start by adding a handful of wet hickory chips to the hot coals, but then cut the intensity by switching to milder fruitwood like apple, peach, or cherry.

See the chart on page 283 for more information on pairing wood and meat. See also Charcoal; Wood.

Starting a Fire

The best and cheapest way to start a charcoal fire is with a chimney—all it takes is a match and a single sheet of newspaper. For a wood fire, start with crumpled newspaper by a tepee of twigs and small dry kindling, and gradually build up with split hardwood. Of course with a gas grill, all you need to do is hit the ignition button, but it's always handy to have one of those long-handled butane lighters. Never use gasoline to start a fire; you'll be lucky if all you burn off is your eyebrows from the backdraft.

See also Charcoal; Chimney Fire Starter.

Thermometers

Unfortunately, the built-in thermometers on many smoker/grills are next to worthless. Invest in a good one from a solid manufacturer such as Taylor Instruments ($15 to $30) that can be mounted on the lid of the grill. You can also supplement that with an oven gauge, which sits directly on the grill grate. If you find yourself without a thermometer or just plain don't like them, use the old-fashioned method: For a low fire, you should be able to hold your hand near the grill surface for about 5 seconds; for a medium fire, 3 to 4 seconds; and for a really hot fire, only about 1 second.

When it comes to testing the internal temperature of meat to see if it is done, there is no substitute for a good-quality instant-read thermometer. Readily available, inexpensive, and not much bigger than a ballpoint pen, these are accurate and easy to use, clean up, and store. Insert the thermometer into the thickest part of the meat. Some cooks prefer electronic probes, which are connected by a thin steel cable to a remote sensor. Candy thermometers are useful for measuring hot liquids.

Tongs & Spatulas

Keep a set of tongs handy to turn your meat, because the last thing you want to do is ruin a perfectly crisp skin by stabbing a leg or a wing repeatedly as you try to flip it. Repeated cutting causes all that lovely juice to escape, robbing the meat of the moisture it needs to seal in the flavor. And you'll need spatulas to turn burgers and fish. Make sure yours are made of metal; you don't want the heat to melt the plastic if, say, you accidentally leave your spatula in your cooker while you're sitting down to dinner.

Wood

To make your meal truly memorable, you'll need wood in two forms: charcoal (for heat) and chips, chunks, or logs (for smoke). Use charcoal to start the fire and to provide a long-lasting source of heat (although some cooks prefer wood alone). Use hardwoods, such as oak or hickory, or fruitwoods, such as apple and cherry, to infuse the meat with a heavenly aroma. Since cooking times are affected by so many variables (an extreme drop in temperature outside your cooker, for instance, can lead to a corresponding drop of as much as 50 degrees inside of it), it's impossible to say how much wood you should use to get a desired temperature. Just make sure to have a big sack of charcoal handy along with dry or wet smoking wood and add charcoal for more heat and wood for more smoke. And one more tip: use aged wood, which has less moisture than young, green wood. Green wood can create an acrid-smelling smoke, and you don't want that taste to contaminate your meat.

See also Charcoal; Smoke; Starting a Fire.

Wood Glossary

THERE'S NO SMELL quite like that of wood smoke curling through the neighborhood on a languid summer day. It conjures up images of picnic tables covered in red-and-white-checked oilcloth, fresh slices of watermelon, and mom and dad sweating it out at the grill. To create your own memories, you'll need one crucial ingredient: wood.

We've heard of folks who are so obsessive about infusing their meat with just the right flavor of smoke that they soak their wood chips in Beaujolais. That strikes us as a waste of good wine. There are, however, types of wood that are the optimal complements to certain foods, so we've provided some simple guidelines for pairing wood with meat and fish. But don't get anxious if you can't find exactly what you're looking for. The most confident backyard cooks we know make do with whatever wood is available—hickory in the Carolinas, for example, or mesquite in Texas.

Be careful about the amount of wood you use; the aroma of smoke should never be so overpowering that it obscures the taste of the food. And avoid woods with resin, such as pine or cedar (unless the cedar comes in a plank that has been presoaked in fresh, cold water for at least 6 hours); the sap will ruin your cooker and your food.

WOOD	FLAVOR	USE IT WITH...
alder	mild and sweet	fish, especially salmon
apple and cherry	mild and fruity	poultry, pork
cedar (planked)	sharp	fish
corncobs (dried)	mild and sweet	poultry
grapevine	fruity and full-bodied	lamb
hickory	pungent	chicken, pork
maple	mild and sweet	ham, poultry
mesquite	strong, slightly bitter	beef, pork
oak	slightly acidic	brisket, duck, pork
pecan	mellow and nutty	chicken, pork, wild fowl

Sources

ONLINE AND MAIL-ORDER SOURCES for food products and information on cookers featured in this book:

Sauces, Rubs, and Seasoning

ANNTONY'S CARIBBEAN
Sauces, rubs, and dry jerk.
(704) 342-0749
www.anntonys.com
info@anntonys.com

BLACKJACK
Mustard, vinegar, and tomato-based championship sauces.
(843) 762-9200
www.foodforthesouthernsoul.com/Sauces/sauces.htm

CALIDO CHILI FOR TRADERS
A great source of salsas and spices.
(888) 243-1821
www.calido-indiana.com/home/

CAROLINA PIG PUCKER BARBECUE SAUCE
Available at Outdoor Feasts.
1089 Cedar Spring Road, York, South Carolina 29745
(803) 684-2278

CATTLEMEN'S
Three sauces: classic, golden honey, and authentic smokehouse.
See the Web site, www.cattlemens.net, for recipes and customer testimonials.
(800) 841-1256

TONY CHACHERE'S ORIGINAL SEASONINGS
Our favorite all-around seasoning that doubles in seafood boils and dry-rub ribs.
www.tonychachere.com

CHAR BROIL & GRILL SEASONINGS
Order through the Spice Barn:
www.spicebarn.com/char_broil_&_grill_seasoning.htm

CIMARRON DOC'S BAR-B-Q AND CHILI CO.
Killer barbecue rib rub.
www.cimarrondoc.com/rib_rub_seasoning.html

KC MASTERPIECE
Lots of experts use this as a base for sauces, then doctor it up with vegetables and spices. Available in groceries and mass retailers such as Target and Wal-Mart. See the Web site for a list of products and tips on grilling and marinades.
www.kcmasterpiece.com

OLD PLANTATION
Sausage seasonings.
www.aclegg.com/indexeng.htm

PENROSE SAUSAGES
For that incredible sausage juice (their sausages aren't bad, either).
www.conagrafoods.com/brands/penrose/index.jsp

PENZEYS SPICES
If there's a spice this place doesn't have, you probably don't need it.
(800) 741-7787
www.penzeys.com/cgi-bin/penzeys/shophome.html

MRS. SASSARD'S JERUSALEM ARTICHOKE RELISH
Available through the Lee Brothers Boiled Peanut Catalog.
www.boiledpeanuts.com/relishproducts.html

THE SLABS
Rubs and sauces. We like their Kyle Style sauce.
www.theslabs.com/store/

SYLVIA'S
Sauce and spices.
(800) 263-4825
www.sylviassoulfood.com/SecretSeasoning.html

Meats

EDDY PACKING COMPANY
Smoked pork neckbones.
Yoakum, Texas
(800) 292-2361
www.eddypacking.com/Retail.htm

POLYFACE FARMS
Operated by Joel Salatin of Swoope, Virginia. Cooker Kim Clanton's favorite source of organic meats.
(540) 885-3590
e-mail: husbandman@ntelos.net

Cookers

THE GRILLERY
Charles Eisendrath's specialty cooker business.
www.grillery.com

LA CAJA CHINA COOKERS
The Cuban wood-and-metal pig cooker that produces "meat candy."
www.lacajachina.com

THE VOGELZANG CORP.

55-gallon barrel conversion kits to get you started on a barrel smoker/grill.

Holland, Michigan

(616) 396-1911

www.vogelzang.com/barrel_stoves.htm

Catering

TIDEWATER FOODS AND CATERING

Jimmy Hagood's full-time gig.

Charleston, South Carolina

(843) 762-9200

www.FoodForTheSouthernSoul.com

T. R. MCGRATH

Catering in Newport, Rhode Island.

(401) 847-7743

www.riclambake.com/clients.html

McGrath recommends Mt. Hope Farm in Bristol, Rhode Island, for outdoor weddings and anniversaries; it was the site for our photo shoot for the book's clambake.

(401) 254-1745

www.mounthopefarm.com

PIG OUT BARBECUE CATERING

Sam Goff is a caterer in Oregon's Willamette Valley.

(541) 905-6456

CHARLESTON OUTDOOR CATERING CO.

Jamie Westendorff's full-time gig.

Charleston, South Carolina

(843) 769-6889

e-mail: chasfreak@aol.com

Bibliography

BOSKER, GIDEON, Karen Brooks, and Leland and Crystal Payton. *Patio Daddy-O.* San Francisco: Chronicle Books, 1996.

BROWNE, RICK, and Jack Bettridge. *The Barbecue America Cookbook.* Guilford, CT: The Lyons Press, 2002.

HERBST, SHARON TYLER. *The New Food Lover's Companion.* New York: Barron's Educational Series, 2001.

CALTA, MARIALISA, Jimmy Kennedy, and Maya Kennedy. *River Run Cookbook: Southern Comfort from Vermont.* New York: HarperCollins, 2001.

JAMISON, BILL, and Cheryl Alters. *The Border Cookbook.* Boston: Harvard Common Press, 1995.

KARMEL, ELIZABETH. *Taming the Flame.* Hoboken: John Wiley & Sons, 2005.

LUKINS, SHEILA, and Julee Rosso. *The New Basics Cookbook.* New York: Workman, 1989.

RAICHLEN, STEVEN. *BBQ USA: 425 Fiery Recipes from All Across America.* New York: Workman, 2003.

SHEWCHUK, RON. *Barbecue Secrets.* Vancouver, B.C.: Whitecap, 2004.

WALSH, ROBB. *Legends of Texas Barbecue Cookbook.* San Francisco: Chronicle Books, 2002.

WILLINGHAM, JOHN. *John Willingham's World Champion Bar-B-Q.* New York: William Morrow, 1996.

Contact Us

NOW THAT YOU'VE FINISHED THIS BOOK, we hope you're just itching to build your own rig, complete with fold-out seats, a wet bar, coffee stand, crab steamer, or whatever tickles your imagination. We say, "Go for it!" When you're done, e-mail or write us with a photo. We're hungry to do a sequel and we need your help, particularly with contraptions outside the United States.

We also figure that at least some of you think your rigs are way more extreme than anything we've found so far. So prove it! Invite us out for a visit; we love hitting the road in search of serious funk.

Here's how to reach us:

Web: www.extremebarbecuethebook.com

DAN HUNTLEY
1089 Cedar Spring Road
York, SC 29745
e-mail: danthepigman@mac.com

LISA GRACE LEDNICER
3012 NE 24th Avenue
Portland, OR 97212
e-mail: lisathepiggal@yahoo.com

LAYNE BAILEY
1879 Steeple Chase Drive
Rock Hill, SC 29732
e-mail: shooter@laynebailey.com

Bon appétit, y'all...

Index

A

Alder, 283
American Royal Invitational, 140, 143, 144, 151, 170, 171, 193
Anne's Grilled Chicken Sauce, 72
Apples
Carolina Snowballs, 108–9
Puerto Appleito, 65–66
Stuffed Pumpkins, 110
Applesauce
Brown Bears in the Orchard, 83
Apple wood, 283
Aprons, 271
Argentinian-style barbecue, 118, 240–42
Aristimuño, Daniel, 241, 242
Armadillo Eggs, 160
Asparagus, Grilled, with Feta, 186
Award-Winning Pork Loin, 93–94

B

Baby Godzilla, 193
Bacon
Diane's Chopped Country Club, 117–18
Grilled Bacon-Wrapped Quail, 102–3
Hobo Jungle Breakfast, 88
Julie's Baked Beans, 207–8
Smoky Potato Casserole, 209
We Stole Mom's Green Beans, 155–56
Baconator, 269–70
Baked Cabbage, 196
Bale, Sherry, 213
Barbacoa, 38–40
Barbecue Gods of the Universe, 171, 172, 173
Barbecuing
definition of, 273
history of, 18
Barbie's Competition Chicken, 202
Barrel smokers, 276
Barstow, Betsy, 18, 43–48
Basic Brine, 94–95
Bass, Kim, 124

Bastes
definition of, 273
Victor's Salmon Baste, 221
BBQ Pits by Klose, 150
Bean-Hole Beans, 45–47
Bean-Hole Supper Coleslaw, 48
Beans
Bean-Hole Beans, 45–47
Borracho Beans, 248
Julie's Baked Beans, 207–8
Killer Green Beans, 136
Shug's Black-Eyed Pea Salad, 28
Soulful Baked Beans, 197
We Stole Mom's Green Beans, 155–56
Beard, Daniel Carter, 84
Beef
BlinDog's Stuffed Mushrooms, 187
Bobcat Blues Burgers, 173–74
Bruce's Brisket, 162–63
Caribbean Meat Loaf, 115
Jerry's Simple Sausage Delight, 179–80
Jerry's Smoked Brisket, 178–79
Kim Bass's Country-Style Steak, 124
Pork Steak in Beef Au Jus, 148
Pyro's Burnt Ends, 146–47
Tarzan Steak, 89
Beer-keg chicken cooker, 266–67
Big Red Rig, 98, 99, 104
Bishop, Randy, 142, 157–63
Black-Eyed Pea Salad, Shug's, 28
Blakeman, Peter, 92–93
BlinDog's Lamb Kabobs, 185–86
BlinDog's Stuffed Mushrooms, 187
Blueberry Muffins, Box Oven, 82
Blues Burgers, 173–74
Boberg, Dick, 259
Borracho Beans, 248
Box Oven Blueberry Muffins, 82
Box ovens, 80–81
Bread
Pocket Pita Bread, 226–27
Shay's Mexican Corn Bread, 125
Brine, Basic, 94–95
Britzius, Cathy, 131–32

Table of Equivalents

THE EXACT EQUIVALENTS in the following tables have been rounded for convenience.

Liquid/Dry Measures

U.S.	METRIC
¼ teaspoon	1.25 milliliters
½ teaspoon	2.5 milliliters
1 teaspoon	5 milliliters
1 tablespoon (3 teaspoons)	15 milliliters
1 fluid ounce (2 tablespoons)	30 milliliters
¼ cup	60 milliliters
⅓ cup	80 milliliters
½ cup	120 milliliters
1 cup	240 milliliters
1 pint (2 cups)	480 milliliters
1 quart (4 cups, 32 ounces)	960 milliliters
1 gallon (4 quarts)	3.84 liters
1 ounce (by weight)	28 grams
1 pound	448 grams
2.2 pounds	1 kilogram

Length

U.S.	METRIC
⅛ inch	3 millimeters
¼ inch	6 millimeters
½ inch	12 millimeters
1 inch	2.5 centimeters

Oven Temperature

FAHRENHEIT	CELSIUS	GAS
250	120	½
275	140	1
300	150	2
325	160	3
350	180	4
375	190	5
400	200	6
425	220	7
450	230	8
475	240	9
500	260	10